BOUND BY STEEL & STONE

TIMBERLINE BOOKS

Stephen J. Leonard and Thomas J. Noel, Editors

BOUND BY STEEL & STONE

The Colorado-Kansas Railway and the Frontier
of Enterprise in Colorado, 1890–1960

J. BRADFORD BOWERS

UNIVERSITY PRESS OF COLORADO
Louisville

Published by University Press of Colorado
245 Century Circle, Suite 202
Louisville, Colorado 80027

All rights reserved
First paperback edition 2022
Manufactured in the United States of America

 The University Press of Colorado is a proud member of
the Association of University Presses.

The University Press of Colorado is a cooperative publishing enterprise supported, in part, by
Adams State University, Colorado State University, Fort Lewis College, Metropolitan State University
of Denver, Regis University, University of Alaska Fairbanks, University of Colorado, University
of Denver, University of Northern Colorado, University of Wyoming, Utah State University, and
Western Colorado University.

∞ This paper meets the requirements of the ANSI/NISO Z39.48–1992 (Permanence of Paper)

ISBN: 978-1-64642-127-5 (hardcover)
ISBN: 978-1-64642-128-2 (ebook)
ISBN: 978-1-64642-349-1 (paperback)
https://doi.org/10.5876/9781646421282

Library of Congress Cataloging-in-Publication Data

Names: Bowers, J. Bradford, 1966– author.
Title: Bound by steel and stone : the Colorado-Kansas Railway and the frontier of enterprise in
    Colorado, 1890–1960 / J. Bradford Bowers.
Other titles: Timberline books.
Description: Louisville : University Press of Colorado, [2021] | Series: Timberline series | Includes
    bibliographical references and index.
Identifiers: LCCN 2020033055 (print) | LCCN 2020033056 (ebook) | ISBN 9781646421275 (hardcover)
    | ISBN 9781646423491 (paperback) | ISBN 9781646421282 (ebook)
Subjects: LCSH: MacDaniel, Irma, 1893–1971. | Colorado-Kansas Railway. | Railroads—Colorado—
    Pueblo—History. | Railroads—Management. | Pueblo (Colo.)—History—20th century. | Stone
    City (Colo.)—History—20th century.
Classification: LCC HE2771.C6 B68 2021 (print) | LCC HE2771.C6 (ebook) | DDC
    385.09788/5509041—dc23
LC record available at https://lccn.loc.gov/2020033055
LC ebook record available at https://lccn.loc.gov/2020033056

Material from "Prairie Dreams and Apple Schemes" by J. Bradford Bowers was previously
published in *The Pueblo Lore* (September 2003) and is reprinted with permission from the Pueblo
County Historical Society.

Front-cover photograph courtesy of Pueblo City-County Library District.

For Irma

Contents

Figures

Foreword

STEPHEN LEONARD

Robert Athearn in his *The Denver and Rio Grande Railroad* quotes pioneer railroad builder John Evans: "Colorado without railroads, is comparatively worthless." Evans obviously reflected a European-American point of view. Ancestral Puebloans at Mesa Verde prospered for centuries without railroads, as did the Utes and other Indigenous peoples whose world the iron horse trampled.

Yet, given his acquisitive, competitive, expansive world, Evans had a point. If Colorado were to prosper, to grow rapidly, to ship tons of coal, potatoes, steel, and sugar beets, railroads were vital. If the state were to knit together its far-flung cities and towns, railroads were crucial. Entrepreneurs such as Evans, organizer of the Denver Pacific, and William Jackson Palmer of the Denver and Rio Grande, spent much of their lives building, financing, constructing, and reorganizing railroads. Thanks to them and thousands of others, trackage in Colorado peaked at 5,814 miles in 1914.

Some of the lines such as the Union Pacific and the BNSF (Burlington Northern Santa Fe) still play an important part in the state's economy. A few

DOI: 10.5876/9781646421282.c000a

chug along as tourist attractions. Many others are mere embers of memory kept glowing by enthusiastic buffs and railroad historians.

The Colorado-Kansas Railway, later called Colorado Railroad Inc., has, until now, ranked high among the state's most forgotten railroads. With twenty-five miles of track and with one engine and a few cars, it quietly died in 1957 at age forty-five. But, as J. Bradford Bowers points out, its story is less a tale of failure than of struggle and survival. Originally touted as an electrified line that would stretch from Cañon City, Colorado, to Garden City, Kansas, it was part of a grand scheme to bring electricity, water, and improved transportation to a vast area. Bankrupt after laying only 1.5 miles of track, it turned its back on Kansas and decided to connect Pueblo with Stone City, twenty-two miles northwest of Pueblo, where quarries produced Turkey Creek sandstone and where clay was mined. Stone City, like the railroad, is now gone—its buildings razed; its citizens evicted, after it was incorporated into Fort Carson's vast military reservation in 1966.

Originally dependent for its revenues on hauling stone and clay, the shortline road also carried passengers—3,449 of them in 1914, 2 in 1925. That precipitous decline, triggered by bus competition, was one of many challenges facing the anemic road. It was so poor that when its one steam engine, bought secondhand for $7,000, died in the early 1920s, it decided to lease, rather than buy, its second engine. Not until 1940 did it again own an engine. Yet it survived, largely thanks, after 1940, to Irma MacDaniel, one of the few women in the United States to head a railroad. She kept the rickety railroad functioning until it finally, slowly clickety-clacked its way to oblivion.

Bowers details how the shortline survived rocky relations with its home city, the Pueblo Flood of 1922, the closing of Stone City's quarries in the early 1930s, the Great Depression, dodgy equipment, and sloppily laid tracks that impeded its speed and sapped its meager bank account. He also chronicles the rise and fall of Stone City, which, like the little railroad that served it, has been almost totally forgotten.

As a case study of grit, determination, occasional luck, and the tenacity of Irma MacDaniel, *Bound by Steel and Stone* is a welcome addition to the University Press of Colorado's Timberline Series, which aims to publish or republish significant books on Colorado and the West.

Acknowledgments

There are so many people to thank for this book that it is hard to know where to begin. I feel I must be as complete as I can, because without these folks my book would not exist, at least not in its current form. I'm the guy that sits through the credits at the end of the film to watch the names scroll past so I can give them their due recognition; I would be remiss if I didn't do the same here. I will start with the organizations that have been so much help to me. First, thanks to the late Kenton Forrest, to Bob LeMassena, to Stephanie Gilmore, and to all the folks at the Robert W. Richardson Library at the Colorado Railroad Museum in Golden, Colorado. They have been most generous with their time in helping excavate the records of the Colorado-Kansas Railway. Noreen Riffe, Maria Tucker-Sanchez, Aaron Ramirez, and all of the staff in Special Collections at the Robert Hoag Rawlings Public Library with the Pueblo City-County Library District contributed much time and generosity to my research. My friends at the Pueblo County Historical Society helped immensely, notably, the late George Williams, Mary Wallace, Ione Miller, Arla Aschermann, Pat Crum, Eleanor Fry, and John Korber, along with Harold "Bud"

Moore, of Pueblo. David Pfeiffer with the National Archives at College Park, Maryland, helped to fill in the gaps, as did Ann Waidelich at the Wisconsin Historical Society in Madison; and Miss Edna L. Jones, with the Washington County Historical Society in Washington, Iowa. Olga Montgomery, with the Finney County Historical Society in Garden City, Kansas, was kind enough to answer my query regarding Geo. H. Paul. Additional thanks go to the Denver Public Library, Chelsea Stone, Jori Johnson, Katie Bush, and all of the wonderful staff at the Stephen H. Hart Research Library at History Colorado in Denver, the Local History Center at the Cañon City Public Library, in Cañon City, Colorado, and the Colorado State Archives. The staff at the Custer County Courthouse were most helpful when it came to finding information about John J. Burns' Custer City town-building venture. I finally hit paydirt in my long-fruitless search for a photograph of Irma MacDaniel, thanks to the staff at the Centennial High School Museum. Victoria Miller and Chris Schreck, at the Steelworks Center of the West in Pueblo, are custodians of the archives of Colorado Fuel & Iron and cheerleaders of this project. Their assistance in digitizing the county's Stone City plat map was a nice way to cap off the research. Over the course of three years, I practically became a resident at the Pueblo County Courthouse, where Scott Wright and the rest of the staff made me feel right at home as I poured through their hundreds of record books. It was comforting to do research for this book in a building constructed out of Turkey Creek stone; my traditional ritual upon climbing the steps to enter the building is to lovingly pat the stone columns in honor of the quarrymen and stonecutters from Stone City and Pueblo.

For their time and efforts in aiding my research, I would like to thank Beau Schriever for his invaluable assistance with the archaeology of Fort Carson, Colorado; Cathy Hawthorne and the First Presbyterian Church of Pueblo, Colorado; the late Connie Sumara and late Charles F. "Chick" Simpson of the Chicago Freight Car Leasing Company, in Rosemont, Illinois, as well as Christopher Brown at Sasser Family Holdings; and, most gratefully, for letting me traipse around the old Stone City site, thanks to Randy Korgel, Mike Flowers, and Brian Goss from the Directorate, Environmental Compliance and Management at Fort Carson. Robert W. Richardson, the savior of much of Colorado's railroad history, was generous enough to share his memories with me, as well. Thanks also to Dennis John for allowing me to visit the former Colorado Railroad, Inc.'s engine house. My appreciation goes out to Allan C. Lewis and the late Albert Knicklebine for the use of their photographs. I owe an immense debt to Kent Stephens and Brian S. Osborne for their prior work on the history of this railroad and for giving me enough information to whet my appetite to continue the story of Stone City and the Colorado-Kansas Railway. I want to recognize former Stone City residents Jerry Waller, Jake Hobson, Ruth Ann Venezio, and most especially, the "Stone City Ladies," Wanda McConnell, Lee Oldham, Shirley Baker, and Norma Fuller, with whom I had a delightful afternoon of tea and conversation about the old days in Stone City.

My late grandmother, Iris Tucker, wrote down her family history, wherein I discovered while researching this book that I was not the first in my family to move to Pueblo. My great-grandfather, a lifelong contractor, moved his family to Pueblo and then Stone City in 1912 and helped construct the Geo. H. Paul Orchard Company's large barn at their headquarters, only three-quarters of a mile from where I unknowingly settled for a few years in Pueblo West. Words cannot express how I felt when I discovered this amazing and happy coincidence. Thank you, Grandma Iris, for keeping this record. My mother, Shirley, and my father and stepmom, John and Linda, have been very supportive of my academic career, and I thank them profusely for their love, kindness, and support. To my wife, Cree, who has suffered most of all through this process, I owe a big thank you. I love you.

My colleagues and friends at Pueblo Community College—including Michael Engle, Donna Fitzsimmons, Charles Bonfadini, Rosemary Breckenfelder, Rich Keilholtz, Renee Gust, and my dean, Dr. Jeffrey Alexander—have been extremely supportive and encouraging as I finished the rewrites and edits on this book to prepare it for publication. I must also give a very big shout-out to my friends Kathy, Les, Bryan, and Alyson Schickling in Westcliffe for introducing me to the history of Custer County, with which I was mostly unfamiliar.

Finally, I want to thank two good friends with whom I share a love of railroading: Larry Green and Charles Powell. Thanks, Larry, fellow railroad historian, for helping with my research, answering a thousand questions, and generally being supportive of my work. And Charlie, thanks for showing me a dusty, abandoned railroad grade stretching across the windswept prairies of Pueblo West, and prompting me to ask, "What was this railroad, where did it run to, and what did it do?" Without you, there would be no book.

BOUND BY STEEL & STONE

Introduction

It was a pleasant, late spring day in southern Colorado, not too warm and not too cool, with plenty of sunshine to create a festive mood. Perfect for a train ride and a picnic. The crowd gathered at the depot was in festive spirits, aided, no doubt, by the lively tunes springing from the instruments of the city's beloved Santa Fe Trail Band. Embossed and engraved invitations had been sent out for the trip, and it seemed as if half the city of Pueblo turned out for the celebration. Indeed, all of the city officials and most of the county officials were aboard. Countless citizens from the community assembled around the depot as well-wishers.

"All aboard!" ordered the conductor, and promptly at 10 a.m., with two short whistles from clean and shining Colorado-Kansas Railway Locomotive No. 1, the four-car train rolled away from the depot and headed along the river levee, out of Pueblo. The little train chugged through the prairie north-west of town, past the lands of the Geo. H. Paul Orchard Company. It would

DOI: 10.5876/9781646421282.c000b

not be long before these nearly 17,000 acres were teaming with apple and cherry trees, waiting to feed thousands of hungry Coloradans and provide a good living to hundreds of families in Pueblo County.

Nearly twenty miles into the trip, the train paused at Turkey Creek so that the passengers could stretch their legs. Looking two miles northeast, through a cut in the hills, they could admire the verdant, grass-covered face of the Teller Dam, holding back enough water to eventually turn the thirsty land they had just traversed into a veritable Garden of Eden. Another shout of "All Aboard!" and the train began the climb up the grade into the foothills. Crossing over a long, wooden trestle over Booth Gulch, then passing a large stone sawmill still under construction, the train squealed to a stop beside a small, tidy, white depot. The conductor shouted, "Stone City!" but that was plainly evident from the sign on the depot. This was it, their destination for the afternoon. Several men stood around the depot platform to greet the train, accompanied by a plump young lady wearing blue and white shoes "just like the city girls wear."

As the passengers stepped off the train, it was a toss-up as to what they noted first. Some saw the valley, surrounded on three sides by rugged hog-backs and dominated by Booth Mountain. Over one of the hills appeared a young girl, carrying a pail of milk. Others first saw the fledgling community, so new that many structures were just canvas tents, and the few wooden buildings had yet to be painted. Even the railroad was still a work in progress, for just 200 yards away, a track gang was busy ballasting track on a spur. This was not to be a party day for them.

Some of the men from the train headed off on a two-mile hike to examine the quarries that gave Stone City its name, though they were back in time for the one o'clock luncheon. And what a feast it was! Barbecued beef, tender and sliced, placed between soft buns, six sheep, chicken, ham and gravy, olives, pickles, radishes, breads, cakes, coffee. . . . Though there were nearly 300 folks gathered for the big feast, no one would go hungry this day. Otto Kinkel and his crew were to be commended for the delicious bounty.

The railroad's officials gave gratuitous speeches, overflowing with superlatives about what the railroad, the stone quarries, and the clay mines would mean for Pueblo, Colorado, and the nation. These were followed by equally flowery praises from Pueblo's business community and punctuated by delightful music, once again from the Santa Fe Trail Band. It seemed as if every man had a cigar in hand or mouth.

FIGURE 0.1. *Visitors to the clay mines at Stone City upon its grand-opening celebration, June 12, 1912. Photo by John W. Floyd. Courtesy of Pueblo County Historical Society.*

Although the crowd was expected to travel to see the famous quarries, the size of the meal prompted many to relax and eventually fall asleep. Around three o'clock a storm moved in over the town, and the crowd sought refuge from the rain. At 3:45 p.m., the little train commenced its return journey to Pueblo, the passengers dozing in their seats or quietly recapping their stories of the festivities with each other so they could remember the details, which they would share with family and friends in the coming days. The train pulled back into Pueblo at 5 p.m., the passengers dispersed to their lives. Undoubtedly many were confident in the knowledge that the economic futures of the railroad, the quarries and clay mines, and especially Pueblo itself, were most assuredly bright.[1]

———•—

The Colorado-Kansas Railway, later known as the Colorado Railroad, Inc., was an anomaly, a quaint, colorful shortline railroad that by all accounting, should never have been built. That it managed to survive in one form or another for nearly fifty years is a testament to the men, and one woman, who envisioned, owned, and operated the rail line. Everything was against the line from the beginning: competition from other railroads, a limited revenue base, and even more limited capital financing. Technology was leaving the company behind even as the railroad was being constructed. Yet, this weather-beaten line doggedly managed to carry on business, struggling through the years, continually trying to find new sources of revenue, none of which kept it out of the red ink.

Conceived as a grandiose scheme that would have left a unique stamp on western railroading, the line that would have connected Colorado and Kansas by electric interurban wires only managed to build twenty-five miles of track in its history, a mere pittance of what might have been. The scheme, backed by a company that manufactured electrical motors used for pumping wells, involved building power plants along the Arkansas River at regular intervals to supply electricity to power these pumps, which would in turn irrigate the arid soil away from the river. Excess power would also be used to electrify the homes of valley residents. In order to provide cheap fuel for the power plants, a railroad would be built from the coal mines near Cañon City, Colorado, following the river all the way to Garden City, Kansas. The railroad itself would be electrified, using power from the plants, making it one of the longest electrified railroads in America.

Financial difficulties forced the first bankruptcy for the railroad after only a mile and a half of track had been laid, and the plan to electrify and irrigate

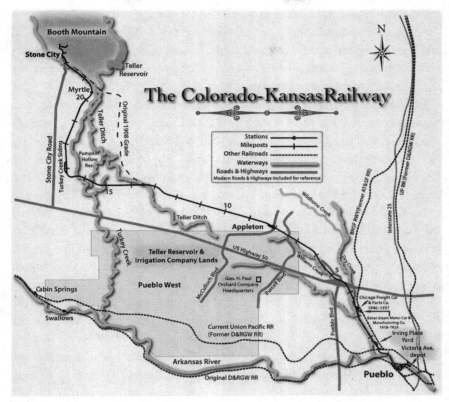

FIGURE 0.2. *Map of the Colorado-Kansas Railway, 1912–1957. Drawn by the author.*

the Arkansas River Valley collapsed. The railroad as finally constructed was originally designed to be merely a branch line from the electrified main line, but after the larger scheme failed, the railroad's backers carried on with what construction they could afford. Without the power plants, the railroad reverted to traditional steam-powered locomotives.

The Colorado-Kansas Railway pushed northwest from Pueblo, Colorado, to Stone City, a distance of twenty-two miles, during the years 1910 to 1912. It crossed the high plains occupied by cattle ranches and a failed attempt at a major agricultural development. Stone City, a company town also belonging to the railroad owners, was the primary objective because of the fine sandstone quarries being developed there. The stone was quarried and worked into decorative fascia stone for use in building construction, and many public buildings and private residences around Colorado and the rest of the nation used this stone. Stone went out of favor for buildings when concrete and steel became popular, and so the quarries closed in 1930. The mines for clay and other minerals used in the steelmaking process continued operating throughout the railroad's history.

Perhaps the most fascinating aspect of the railroad was the evolution of its management in later years. From 1940 until abandonment in 1957, management of the railroad was left up to Irma MacDaniel, the railroad's secretary. In a male-dominated industry, Irma stood out as a corporate executive, and her life both with the railroad and away from it reflects her competence and ambition as a businesswoman at a time when women were still struggling to make inroads into management in any field. Her management helped to keep the railroad afloat for over a decade after the owners were ready to call it quits.

A new source of revenue appeared in 1946, when the Chicago Freight Car & Parts Company opened a shop in Pueblo to turn surplus World War II troop sleeper cars into refrigerated cars to carry western fruits to market. Reorganized as the Colorado Railroad, Inc., the company took over the switching operations for Chicago Freight Car, and this remained the bulk of its business until the end. In 1957, the railroad joined the multitudinous abandoned workings of men, though faint traces remain of this shortline railroad and the town it served, traces that hint at the intriguing history disappearing beneath the dusty prairie soil.

Shortline railroads provided important connections in America's economy, but they were seldom stable connections. In the case of the Colorado-Kansas Railway, the owners reinvented the railroad several times, seeking out new business opportunities when they could, providing raw materials and services to larger rail lines and companies. While the railroad may seem, on the face of it, to be a failure, it did operate for nearly half a century. In his book, *Railroaded: The Transcontinentals and the Making of Modern America*, historian Richard White suggests railroads "created modernity as much by their failure as their success."[2] He notes the transcontinental railroads were not just business failures, but also political and social failures. Bankruptcy and receivership were no strangers to these lines, but most railroads suffered the same fates, especially in times of economic turmoil. The Colorado-Kansas Railway was no exception. And while the corporate lobby as created by the large corporate railroads added to the public's perception of political corruption in the Gilded Age and beyond, it did not dissuade further railroad construction.[3] To the contrary, railroad construction continued apace, with over 90,000 miles of track laid between 1890 and 1916, the peak year for trackage, at 254,037 miles.[4] As White points out, transcontinental railroads were subsidized by federal and state governments granting land to sell for construction monies.[5] Regional railroads enjoyed little of this benefit. Whether steam or electric, these smaller roads were supported locally, through local investors buying stocks in them or local landowners donating or willingly selling their lands for a right-of-way for the proposed railroad.[6] To attract railroad competition, communities across the West desiring cheaper shipping rates would attract other railroads through the siren call of floating bonds and offering subsidies.[7] These antimonopolistic desires of the smaller cities and towns benefited shortlines such as the Colorado-Kansas, as they offered competition against real or imagined railroad monopolies. That antimonopolism was often key to a shortline being built in the first place.

White's social failure argument is that the transcontinental railroads encouraged settlement of the West but that these same settlers overproduced in agriculture and mining, and their resulting surpluses led to depressed markets, crushed livelihoods, environmental damage, and social problems across the region. These problems were widespread, he contends, because the railroads overbuilt, saturating the landscape with miles of iron and steel that were unneeded; more and more settlers were brought west to produce business for the transcontinental lines and, ultimately, profits.[8] This outcome is quite obvious to the casual observer when looking at historic railroad maps. Multiple railroads, usually considered part of a transcontinental system, were built through the Midwest into the western states, resulting in many cities being served by five or more railroads.

Shortlines belie this argument, though. They often went to places the larger railroads had no interest in going, who saw no profit in building into the hinterlands. Branch lines of larger railroads and independent shortlines were needed, however, to supply agricultural, mineral, and timber resources to the main lines; a web of rails began to stretch into the hinterlands of the West. Settlers followed, to be sure, often brought west by real estate promoters or lured by the promise of jobs in these newly opened landscapes. But the areas served by shortlines and branches were often limited in their economic success, if they succeeded at all, their landscapes remaining relatively undeveloped. They contributed resources to the national market, but much of their extractions supported local markets first. They did also support jobs in their service territory. Even if those jobs were few in number, they still provided that economic benefit in regions where there might be little benefit otherwise. Building a railroad or other industry in the landscapes of the American West was a gamble, no matter how much enthusiasm and capital were expended. Whether it was misinterpreting the potential of the landscape, underestimating the weather, failing to apply the appropriate science or technology to overcome the limitations that landscape placed upon settlers and developers, or simply the vagaries of the marketplace, there were many ways to fail in the entrepreneurial West. Admittedly, extractive businesses and environmental damage go hand in hand, but this has been true throughout history, regardless if a railroad is involved or not. And as for social problems? The shortlines kept people from being isolated, connecting them to the national network of transportation and communication, giving them access to the national marketplace for consumer goods, and strengthening social ties across small communities and the larger cities to which they were bound.

Typifying many small businesses, the Colorado-Kansas Railway was marginal when compared to larger railroads, or larger businesses of any type. It is this very marginality, however, that is crucial to the understanding of American economic history, for there are probably hundreds of marginal businesses for every large corporation across the country. Marginality forced the railroad to be flexible, to adapt. These unique aspects of the railroad—its marginality, its flexibility, its management, and its connections to the larger economic world—make it a worthy subject of study. This is a saga of adaptation, a call to change or perish and to stay solvent in an increasingly competitive economic environment. The railroad's flexibility in management and adaptability to economic situations enabled it to remain viable components of the economy, despite its marginality.

Shortlines provided—indeed, they still provide—a vital service link in the larger scale of the American railroad scene. They bridged the gap between business opportunities, such as extractive industries, and the national railroad system. In many cases, they created and developed that business themselves. They are the forgotten link in American railroad and economic history. This knowledge of shortlines is important, not just for the sake of the past, but for the present, and future as well, and for a very good reason: shortlines in America are on the rise again. This growth is not due to additional construction of railroads, but to the Staggers Rail Act of 1980, which deregulated the railroad industry, undoing what years of regulation under the Interstate Commerce Commission (ICC) had done. Freed of their regulatory burdens, railroads could respond better to the changes in the marketplace.[9] Consolidation of the larger railroads achieved a rapid pace during the merger mania of the 1980s. Class I railroads aggressively sold off unprofitable lines or duplicate mileage, and the resulting spin-offs have created new and expanding shortline railroads that still fight to earn a profit by serving local customers.[10] Many times, local shippers took over these routes and operated them as regional railroads. Often, local and state governments offer subsidies to keep these vital connections alive in a highly competitive marketplace.[11]

The Interstate Commerce Commission has always classified railroads according to their annual revenues. Class I was, and still is, the top tier. During the lifetime of the Colorado-Kansas Railway, those Class I railroads earned a minimum of $1 million a year. The ICC raised this figure many times in the last half of the twentieth century to reflect inflation. Today, this number is $505 million per year.[12] The Colorado-Kansas Railway was a Class III, which meant it earned $100,000 or less per year.[13] In the class restructuring of 1956, Class III was eliminated altogether.[14]

Between deregulation and the rising definition figure, the number of Class I railroads dropped precipitously. In 1957, there were 110 Class I railroads to 626 shortlines.[15] By 1987, those numbers had declined to 16 Class I roads and 484 shortlines.[16] Compare that to 2021, when there were just seven Class I railroads and approximately 630 local and regional shortlines in the United States.[17] Clearly, the numbers of shortlines have reversed their decline, and actually grown ever so slowly, but the ratio to the Class I railroads has changed dramatically. The railroad is still as vital an economic engine to the United States as it was 150 years ago.[18]

One aspect that all railroads faced was the increasing competition with automobiles and trucks, and this was especially true for the Colorado-Kansas Railway. Throughout the last half of its life, much of the shipment of fireclay and other extracted resources moved via truck. Passenger service between Pueblo and Stone City also tapered off prior to 1921 with the addition of bus service.

An important facet of railroad success is their economic-development efforts to find or create new markets for their services. The Colorado-Kansas was built entirely around this idea, serving the clay mines and stone quarries that were jointly owned by the railroad's investors. When this business began to die off, they actively pursued other business, mainly offering switching services, to remain a viable company.

The early history of the Colorado-Kansas Railway, before the laying of rails ever began, is the story of a four-year financial and political debacle that was finally resolved in the courts. The railroad's backers started out with the notion of building a 300-plus mile electric interurban line from Cañon City, Colorado, to Garden City, Kansas, following the Arkansas River, and ultimately, the already-built Atchison, Topeka & Santa Fe Railway. The late nineteenth and early twentieth centuries were the heyday for electric interurban construction, and they were seen as the next step in the evolution of railroads. Their life was cut short by the maturation of the automobile, but for a time they were all the rage in innovative railroad construction.

From this comprehensive history of the Colorado-Kansas Railway will emerge an example of a shortline railroad that enables us to see how these forgotten links in America's railroad past helped integrate the rural landscape with the larger urban and economic world through their ability to adapt to ever-changing economic forces and conditions.

This book, ostensibly, is a history of the Colorado-Kansas Railway, but it is so much more than that. It is the story of countless schemers and dreamers, losers and winners. It is the story of political battles in an era of reform. It is the story of the development of geographic and economic connections in landscape of the American West. It is the story of the hardscrabble existence of a twentieth-century company mining town, home to many employees and their families. And it is also the story of a woman who found herself in a position by happenstance that seems precedent setting in the modern era.

A thematic element throughout this narrative is adaptability, the flexible nature of shortline railroads and their existence on the margins, on the economic edge, and their management adaptability that allowed shortlines to change with the market. Within the theme of adaptability, Part I of this history will explore the Progressive Era political and economic reform movement at the local level, for the Colorado-Kansas Railway found itself immersed in battle for its very existence against the entrenched political machine. Part II will examine a shortline railroad from an environmental perspective, providing a context for the landscape of the railroad and its relation to the environment through a look at its physical characteristics, the areas it served, and its connections to a much larger world. Part III focuses on Stone City, the objective of the railroad builders, and the lives of the people who called it home for several decades. Finally, the issue of gender, of Irma MacDaniel's role in the company and her management of the line in a male-dominated profession, will be explored in Part IV, further demonstrating the flexibility of the railroad's owners in allowing this company to adapt to changing business conditions.

Even though Frederick Jackson Turner declared the frontier closed in his famous 1893 thesis, much of the land of the American West remained undeveloped or underdeveloped at the time of his address. More so than back east, the landscape of the American is a significant actor in tragedy and farce of western development. The landscape dictates its terms to humans as dictatorial directives, such as where limited resources are to be found, which crops will grow in marginal conditions, and, ultimately, what settlement patterns will emerge from its narrow permissions. Until the 1860s, the landscape of the American West controlled its own fate, limiting human incursions to explorers, fur trappers, traders, and those just passing through. Only the Indigenous peoples had found a way to exist in the beautiful but harsh landscape, their population numbers bound by a hunting-gathering way of life. After 1860, however, that control would change.

Science and technology were able to overcome the limitations placed on humans by the landscape, opening the West to development only dreamed about in earlier decades. These advancements created a newfound, infectious optimism in the future of the American West. The second wave of industrialization in the United States in the late nineteenth and early twentieth centuries provided opportunities for industrialists, capitalists, and entrepreneurs to jump into what they saw as the relatively untouched virgin landscape of the West and bring the manifest destiny of economic progress. Industrialization made this progress possible, certainly on a scale that would not have been possible in the first half of the nineteenth century. Advancements in science and technology provided the means to open these lands to mineral and agricultural development. Railroads, steel, coal, oil, electricity, large-scale irrigation, agricultural mechanization—these were the tools and resources that would open these lands to human habitation and economic prosperity. And capital to fund these speculative ventures seemed to be readily available to anyone with the vision to make it come to life. The sky was the limit; it truly was a Wild West for developers.

The reality, however, is that both the physical and economic landscapes were unforgiving. Many ill-timed or ill-planned ventures faltered aborning. Others struggled for several years, never quite turning the corner into any definition of success. Rarer still were those ventures that actually achieved some measure of completing their organizers' vision.

So, while this may be the story of the Colorado-Kansas Railway, it is also a study of the economic development of the American West from within the microcosm of Pueblo County, Colorado. The beginning of the twentieth century marked a time of boundless confidence on the part of any entrepreneur who wanted to jump into the fray that was business in the 1910s. Even beyond the nineteenth century, the American West seemed wide open to exploitation of seemingly unlimited plant and mineral resources. Indeed, industrialization of the American West in the early twentieth century is what made settlement and possible, and it was the schemers and dreamers of the early twentieth century that helped bring this all about, connecting cities with the hinterlands and their resources for a rapidly industrializing country. Between 1890 and 1920, men from all over the country descended upon Pueblo, just as they did on many other counties around the West, some with experience, many with access to capital, and all with big dreams and schemes. When those halcyon days of grand visions were over, some men lay broken. Many men had failed. A handful persevered. This is a story about failure as much as it is about perseverance, if not outright success.

A. B. Hulit, Robert K. Potter, and Charles E. Sutton all represent these schemers and dreamers who helped build the Colorado-Kansas Railway. Other schemers and dreamers—such as John J. Burns, John C. Teller, and George H. Paul—with their own ambitious business plans, would have smaller roles to play in the development of the Pueblo region, representative of the multitudinous similar stories playing out during the industrialization of the American West during the early twentieth century, but while most of the schemes within the pages to follow ended in abject failure, the Colorado-Kansas Railway and Stone City would survive the longest. In the end, it was not the schemers and dreamers that kept the railroad and the city going, however; it was a woman, level-headed Irma MacDaniel, who guided them through their most desperate years.

While most of these schemes and dreams faded, one vision played out in a rather ordinary way, which unexpectedly looks extraordinary when seen in the context of its birth and the many schemers and dreamers who surrounded it in life. This, then, is a story of the American Dream as many saw it a century ago. This is the story of a little railroad that affected the lives of many individuals throughout its history in nearly every conceivable way. This is the story of the Colorado-Kansas Railway, the Little Railroad That Could.

PART I

The Wild West Frontier
of Enterprise

1

Progressive Era Reform and "The Pueblo Road"

The twenty-five-mile entirety of the Colorado-Kansas Railway, from inception to completion, took four years to construct. This duration was not due to an excessively difficult geographic landscape through which the railroad had to build but, instead, was the result of an excessively difficult political and economic landscape in the early twentieth century. In its own way, the Colorado-Kansas Railway is emblematic of the political and economic concerns and reforms of the Progressive Era. While it was not directly a reform-related enterprise, the nascent Colorado-Kansas Railway was caught up in the battle against government corruption, a fight pitting local boosters and outsider investors against an entrenched political machine that threatened to derail the project. Ultimately, the Colorado-Kansas Railway's legal troubles would help bring about in Pueblo the Progressive Era political reforms that were being sought nationwide.

Many Progressive Era reforms concentrated on government, particularly at the city and state levels, where "unaccountable political party bosses manipulated elected officials and ran city and state governments."[1] Efforts to give

DOI: 10.5876/9781646421282.c001

the government back to the people included restructuring city government with mayors and city councils elected directly by the people, rather than by wards or districts controlled by the party machinery. Even further reforms had city councils appoint experts to be city managers, who would administrate the city efficiently and economically and, more important, remove corruption in city governments. These professional managers, rather than political puppets, could develop "new methods of budgeting, contracting, and administration," as well as demand "lower rates and better service from traction and utility companies" and promote "party primaries for city offices or nonpartisan municipal elections to minimize political influence in city management."[2]

By revising city charters, reformers hoped to remove control of city government from the party bosses and their political machines controlled by companies and special interest groups (such as the immigrant or ethnic groups) and place power directly in the hands of the people. At the very least, they hoped to give more power to the middle classes and skilled professionals who, they believed, could more effectively run the city.[3]

As historian John Chambers points out, "By exposing municipal corruption, personal graft, protection peddling, contract padding, and collusion between city officials and utilities, streetcar companies, and other firms doing business with the city," reformers hoped to bring about change for the better.[4] This is certainly true of Pueblo. The political boss in "collusion" with the city, in this case, was John F. Vail, general manager of the Pueblo & Suburban Traction & Lighting Company.[5] Vail had been in the street railway business since 1879, first in Detroit, then Denver, and finally, in Pueblo in 1888. These were all horse-drawn street railways, but Vail would help form Pueblo's first electric utility and later become general manager and purchasing agent for the Pueblo & Suburban Traction & Lighting Company.[6] Vail viewed his electric utility and streetcar company as having a lock on the city. The proposed Colorado-Kansas electrified railroad and electric power company was an obvious threat to this economic lock and, by extension, a political threat to his dominance in the city.

Into a quagmire of reform stepped the Colorado-Kansas Railway. The railroad's construction drama played itself out in the newspapers and courts of Pueblo. Newspapers deliberately placed themselves on the front lines for the reform battles. Investigative journalism, or "muckraking" as it was called in the Progressive Era, propelled reform efforts by exposing the dishonesty in business and in politics and the corrupt connections that bound them, raising a "spirit of indignation" among their activist readers, and calling for more honesty and democracy in both institutions.[7] During this fight over the right of the railroad to operate within the city, the city's newspapers took sides, as was often the case with reform issues. The *Pueblo Sun*, and after the *Sun* folded, the *Pueblo Leader*, stood on the Progressive side, and to them, the Colorado-Kansas Railway represented not just another business enterprise but also another battle against corruption in the city of Pueblo. The *Pueblo Sun* was a typical newspaper of the Progressive Era, touting itself as "the only enterprise newly established in the city that has encountered the boss and his commercial and political lieutenants, carried on an aggressive campaign against graft and selfish corporation rule, and defied the allies in efforts to dictate its policy or crush it out."[8] The *Sun's* motto was "The ONLY Client of the Sun is the People."[9] The *Pueblo Leader* billed itself as "An Independent Newspaper," whose motto was "Read A Little! Think A Little!"[10]

Before the Colorado-Kansas Railway met with political and economic strife, the concept that eventually bore this railroad as its fruit was well received in western Kansas and eastern Colorado. It did not begin, however, as a plan for stretching rails from horizon to horizon, linking towns up and down the Arkansas River, nor was it even first conceived of as a railroad. In fact, it was born from water, or more precisely, a lack of water. The Colorado-Kansas Railway began life, modestly enough, as an irrigation project. Building a railroad was purportedly not on the mind of A. B. Hulit when he came to western Kansas from Wisconsin in 1908.[11]

Andrew B. Hulit Jr., or A. B. Hulit as he was commonly known, was a schemer and dreamer. His father, Andrew B. Hulit Sr., was selling railroad subscriptions in Illinois to build a narrow-gauge railroad in 1876, so it is perhaps not surprising that his son would later on get involved in a similar venture.[12] While A. B. Hulit Jr. styled himself a farmer, he was also a newspaper publisher, political activist, contractor, and promoter. He helped pave the streets in Topeka, Kansas, in 1889.[13] In 1895, still living in Topeka, he was publisher of a newspaper, *Modern Mexico*, which he distributed in both the United States and Mexico.[14] In 1896, he helped form the Republican Silver League, an organization that supported the idea of the 16-to-1 coinage ratio of silver to gold, as opposed to the Populists' and Democrats' stance on the free and unlimited coinage of silver.[15] That same year, he was creating an association of merchants in Mexico and the United States to promote exclusive trade between the two countries.[16] In 1897, he was publishing *El Tráfico Internacional*, an "illustrated monthly journal, printed in Spanish, having a general circulation in all the Latin-American countries."[17] By the end of 1897, he had hatched his most audacious scheme to date: the relocation of 26,000 Cherokee, Choctaw, and other members of the "Five Civilized Tribes" from Indian Territory in Oklahoma to land set aside for them in Mexico. He helped set up the Mexican Land Company, which would purchase land for the tribes from the Mexican government and allow the tribes to set up their own independent state, away from the detrimental effects of the Dawes Act. Hulit assured people that President Porfirio Díaz of Mexico was fully apprised of the situation.[18] The plan meant buying more than 3 million acres of land in Mexico along the Rio Grande Valley for the sum of $3 million and relocation of up to 5,000 Indigenous families. The Choctaw were reluctant at first, according to Hulit, but their treatment at the hands of the US Congress, and the ability to have their own nation in Mexico, convinced them to go along with his plan, especially after Hulit took a few Choctaw representatives to visit the proposed new nation.[19]

In February 1898, Hulit married Martha A. Badger, of Sedalia, Missouri, and the two set off for Mexico for a working honeymoon.[20] As secretary, Hulit helped charter the Inter-State Investment Company at $3 million for the colonization scheme. Foreshadowing Hulit's role in Pueblo, the company was also given the power to build railroads, sell lands, and found colonies.[21] The scheme rapidly unraveled when the Cherokee, who were also pressured by Hulit to participate in his scheme, inquired of Mexico whether this was a legitimate deal. The response from a Mexican envoy that Hulit had not purchased any land and that, furthermore, any Native Americans relocating to Mexico would not be allowed their own independent government, doomed the scheme, as no more of it was heard.[22]

In 1902, Hulit was a founding member and secretary of the National Reciprocity League, organized to encourage the US Congress to make reciprocal trade agreements with other nations.[23] Hulit had taken up the raising of goats in Springfield, Missouri, by 1904, and was reported to be the "largest breeder in the Middle West." He convinced physicians with the St. Louis Medical Society to buy a breeding farm in the Ozarks, stocked with between

700 and 1,000 of the best goats from Europe. Goats would be leased to families in St. Louis to provide fresh goats' milk to the infants of St. Louis. If families were too poor to lease the goats, they would be provided free of charge.[24] Hulit was simultaneously promoting the building of a sanitarium in the Ozarks for tuberculosis patients, who would be housed in comfortable tents and, if able to work, would be gainfully employed at the goat dairy farm.[25] Apparently, this close approximation between goats and tuberculosis patients caused some concern, because Hulit had physicians in Chicago conduct experiments to prove that tuberculosis could not be transmitted through goat's milk.[26]

By 1908, A. B. Hulit was an agent of the Northern Electrical Manufacturing Company of Madison, Wisconsin. Founded in 1895, the company's chief concern was manufacturing electric motors and dynamos for industrial and agricultural use that would eliminate or reduce the power lost through mechanical transmission. A. O. Fox, one of the four founders of the company, had an interest in agriculture dating back to his childhood, and he heavily promoted the use of electrical machinery for farm use.[27]

It was this potential agricultural business that Hulit sought to gain for the Northern Electrical Manufacturing Company when he arrived in Kansas and Colorado. Nearly 70 percent of the plains of eastern Colorado remained uncultivated, and there was a need for affordable irrigation in the dry lands of the West.[28] Irrigated lands would increase property values and bring economic prosperity all around, and railroads were no strangers to developing irrigated lands as a way to increase traffic and revenue.[29] Hulit and Fox were well aware of the need for irrigation and knew their electric equipment would be just the thing the farmers could use to pump groundwater to the surface. If the pump and power stations that supplied this prosperity belonged to Northern Electrical, then so much the better.

Upon investigation of the situation, however, a couple of problems became apparent. Suitable sources of fuel needed for the steam engines to produce the electric power were too far away, and thus prices remained high in Kansas. Also, since irrigation demands were seasonal, what would be done with the power generated during the rest of the year? Further consideration of the latter problem revealed to Hulit many more uses for electricity than just irrigation. Although commercially available electricity had been around for decades, electrification of the rural West was still ongoing. Industrial and residential uses were many, and so the second problem lessened in severity. As for the high prices, Hulit looked westward to the coalfields located near Cañon City and Florence, Colorado. At its source, the coal was affordable. Transportation costs, though, would be prohibitive in bringing the coal down the Arkansas River to western Kansas. One alternative was to build the power generation plant near Cañon City or Florence, but transmission of electricity over several hundred miles presented its own set of problems.[30]

Extrapolating further, Hulit conceived of a series of power plants constructed down the entire Arkansas Valley from Cañon City to Dodge City, supplied with coal by an electrically powered railroad. This attractive idea essentially killed three birds with one stone. The electric railroad created a more regular demand for power year round, not just during irrigation season. The coal could be brought in at lower rates by the entrepreneurs' own railroad, which helped the bottom line for the electrical generation plants. Affordable electricity meant more irrigation for more lands, which would result in more farmers raising more crops for the railroad to haul during harvest. With fruits and melons, sugar beets, alfalfa and flour, there would be plenty of freight to be shipped and land to be irrigated. To Hulit, it looked like a win-win situation from whichever angle he examined the idea.[31] This was vertical integration, the combining of enterprises to control both the means of production and the means of distribution, and the same integration process that helped to create the first large, modern corporations in the United States.[32]

Hulit's interstate railroad project, however, came at a time in America's history when the days of long-distance railroad construction were nearly over. The early years of the twentieth century were years of consolidations of existing lines and upgrading for higher capacity, safety, and efficiency. The American rail network was essentially complete.[33] New construction was rare, and while grand schemes such as Hulit's still arose, the financial wherewithal was critically lacking. The last major railroad construction in Colorado was David H. Moffat's Denver, Northwestern & Pacific Railway. Moffat spent his last dime trying to build a railroad that headed directly west from Denver, through the mountains, to Salt Lake City, Utah. He died penniless in 1911, his railroad languishing uncompleted, operating merely as a branch line to the northwestern part of the state, until the construction of the Moffat Tunnel in 1927 and the Dotsero Cutoff connection with the Denver & Rio Grande Western in 1934 turned the railroad into a transcontinental bridge line.[34]

In early 1908, though, financial and construction difficulties still lay in the future for Hulit's ever-developing project. The simple power plant had grown into an electric railroad and generating facilities that would span over 300 miles of the Arkansas River Valley. The fact that the Denver & Rio Grande Railroad, the Atchison, Topeka & Santa Fe Railway, and, to a lesser extent, the Missouri Pacific served the same territory did not seem to factor into Hulit's estimations. In this era of reform, he knew people would go for the idea of cheaper rates brought on by increased competition. Pueblo, in particular, was interested in cheaper electricity.[35] Progressives in the American West focused some of their reforms on industries such as mining and railroads, which had transformed, in public opinion, from industries necessary to economic growth, into greedy monopolies that overcharged for their products and services.[36]

The people in Garden City, Kansas, were most interested in the irrigation aspect of the project. Colorado, particularly the cities of Pueblo and Colorado Springs, along with the Colorado Fuel & Iron Company (CF&I), controlled the majority of the water in the Arkansas River, leaving the people around Garden City feeling helpless.[37] In the 1907 United States Supreme Court decision, *Kansas v. Colorado*, the state of Kansas failed to show how Colorado's rights of prior appropriation of the river hurt them economically. Stung by this decision, Kansans in Garden City began looking for new ways to acquire the water necessary for irrigation.[38] Hulit's plan called for pumping the subsurface underflow of the Arkansas River, which skirted the issue of prior water rights for the river itself.[39] This idea must have seemed awfully attractive to western Kansas farmers. In the absence of electrification, most farmers in the area continued to rely on the use of gasoline-powered pumps to bring up the groundwater. Prior to the development of gasoline-powered pumps, most irrigation in the region was achieved through ditches promoted by out-of-state investors looking for quick profits in speculation.[40]

With Fox's backing and blessing, Hulit set out to convince the peoples of western Kansas and eastern Colorado to invest in his idea. On April 18, 1908, a general meeting was held at the Grand Hotel in Pueblo to formally announce the Kansas-Colorado Power and Railroad project. Representatives from towns all along the proposed line were in attendance; Scott City, Dodge City, Garden City, and Syracuse in Kansas; and Granada,

Lamar, Las Animas, La Junta, Manzanola, Fowler, Pueblo, Cañon City, and Colorado Springs in Colorado. The project was met with encouragement in the form of a resolution passed by the attendees, who "endorsed and recommended to the people of the Arkansas valley [the project] as worthy of their support, and [whom] we earnestly ask for the co-operation in carrying through this project."[41]

As if he were running for election, Hulit campaigned up and down the Arkansas River. He spoke to the Cañon City Merchants Association on the afternoon of April 23, and the Pueblo Business Men's Association that evening. With considerable optimism, Hulit told the group that three power plants could be up and running, selling electricity, within a year's time. Attempting to entice the men into buying stocks and bonds in the project, Hulit explained how the shipping cost of coal would be far more reasonable from the Kansas-Colorado company than from the area's existing railroads, which was a point of contention that the people in the Pueblo area could not get resolved. As for irrigation, under Hulit's plan, the investor could purchase stock equivalent to the water rights price at $10 per acre. Thus, if the investor owned 160 acres of land, a $1,600 stock purchase would also net him or her the water rights for 160 acres as well as $1,600 in bonds in the new company.[42]

Hulit continued his campaign throughout the rest of April and into the first part of May, meeting with potential backers at Rocky Ford and again at Cañon City in Colorado, and Coolidge, Syracuse, and Garden City, Kansas. At each meeting, the crowd greeted him with enthusiasm. Ironically, a special excursion train from the Atchison, Topeka & Santa Fe Railway (the new project's preexisting competitor) took investors on a tour of the route of the new Kansas-Colorado project.[43]

La Junta, Colorado, played host to a convention for the project on May 14, 1908. Attended by 355 delegates representing the towns along the proposed line, and over 300 nonappointed boosters, the convention provided much pomp as brass bands played while delegates made speeches and passed resolutions. A thirteen-member committee, consisting of a representative from each town along the line, as well as a former governor of Colorado, was selected to begin drawing up contracts for surveying and calculating cost estimates.[44] This committee evolved into the board of directors for both the Kansas-Colorado Electrical Transmission Company and a separate company, the Kansas-Colorado Railroad Company.[45]

As the largest city along the line, Pueblo became headquarters for both companies. Preliminary expenses for the company were apportioned throughout the towns along the proposed line, and Pueblo was slow in raising its portion. Some of the project's boosters expressed concern that Pueblo had been reticent about the entire project, with not as much enthusiasm shown by its Business Men's Association as in the other towns. The association reasoned that they had seen similar projects before that had fallen through and were waiting for the money to appear before fully backing this venture.[46] Concern over funding was certainly a valid reason for hesitating to jump on the bandwagon and would come into play in the near future, but political forces were also at work in Pueblo that threatened to derail the project. Both companies were incorporated June 12, 1908, in Denver; the electric company capitalized at $3,500,000 and the railroad at $5,000,000.[47] Over 350 miles in length, the Kansas-Colorado would have been one of the largest electric railways in the country under single management. The Northern Electrical Manufacturing Company would not be involved in the management of the line, hoping instead to secure the contracts for all the electrical and pumping equipment.[48] Little did the directors know that it would be exactly four years to the day before the railroad would celebrate its grand opening.

2

Construction and the Fight
for the Franchise Begin

Railroad promoters were active in the early twentieth century, especially in
the Midwest, and their hot ticket item was the interurban. Interurban electric railways seemed like the up-and-coming technology destined to replace
steam railroads as a cleaner and cheaper alternative; the rural communities
of the region jumped on the bandwagon. Investors and managers of these
lines saw the opportunities to provide cheaper fares and shipping, combined
with more-frequent service to rural communities.[1] Since electric interurbans
generated electricity from their own plants to power their trains, they usually
sold any surplus power to customers in their service region. After the railroads were abandoned, the power plants often continued as privately owned
utilities.[2] This was the concept for the Kansas-Colorado Railroad, but the
electrification of western Kansas and eastern Colorado was the driving argument. Electrification came first, primarily for purposes of irrigation, and a
railroad as a secondary beneficial concern.

The rise of electric interurban railways coincided with the rise in popu-
larity of the automobile, with both modes of transportation competing for

DOI: 10.5876/9781646421282.c002

passengers against the conventional steam-powered railroads. Essentially electric streetcars that ran between cities, interurbans offered the passenger increased flexibility and convenience to live further outside the city center, but they soon lost out to the complete independence offered by the automobile.[3] The inception of the Kansas-Colorado Railroad came at the very end of interurban construction in the United States. An investment boom and a flurry of construction occurred in the first decade of the twentieth century, but by 1918 interurban mileage began declining rapidly. Few other American industries enjoyed such a short life cycle.[4] In 1908, however, the future for interurbans seemed bright.

Grandiose projects were far from unusual during this era. No interurban scheme of the era was more ambitious than the Chicago–New York Electric Air Line Railroad. Envisioned as an undeviating high-speed electrified railroad with parallel tracks and no grade crossings for roads or railroads, passengers were promised a ten-hour trip between the two metropolises for the convenient price of $10. Stretching nearly 750 miles, the Air Line would have been over twice as long as the Kansas-Colorado Railroad as conceived. Financing seemed to be in place, and the first construction took place on September 1, 1906; success seemed inevitable. Unfortunately, between a reduction in investing during the Panic of 1907 and the slow pace of construction of a line with exacting standards, the Air Line only built about twenty-five miles of track in Indiana before going bankrupt in 1915.[5]

Nationally, electric interurbans had enough success to continue spurring future dreamers and schemers into conceiving, promoting, and trying to birth their nascent lines. By 1916, their peak year, interurbans operated over 15,580 miles of track.[6] Many more schemes died in the planning stages than were constructed. Some interurban railroads saw their charters fulfilled, while most languished in the promotional stage or underwent limited construction before abandonment.[7] Indeed, southern Colorado saw no fewer than thirteen electric railway projects between 1890 and 1920. Some of these were completed as electric lines, others transitioned to steam prior to completion, and still others were built as steam and proposed later to become electrified. In May 1909, an ambitious electric railway that would stretch 115 miles from Denver to Colorado Springs and south to Pueblo reached the incorporation stage, though the promoters would scrap the idea a month later.[8] An identical plan would be resurrected five years later but never get beyond the announcement stage.[9] Just west of Pueblo up the Arkansas River, the Florence Interurban Electric Railway incorporated in 1911 to connect Florence to the neighboring coal-mining towns of Rockvale, Williamsburg, Coal Creek, and Lincoln Park, as well as the concrete company towns of Portland and Concrete. These communities were already served by the Atchison, Topeka & Santa Fe and the Denver & Rio Grande, so the duplicate line was never built.[10]

Successfully completed interurban electric railways in southern Colorado were concentrated around both Colorado Springs and the Cripple Creek Mining District. In 1890, the Colorado Springs Rapid Transit Railway linked its namesake city with Manitou Springs to the west.[11] A group of eastern capitalists later attempted to start a competing railway from Manitou Springs to Cripple Creek in 1911, to no avail.[12] The Cripple Creek District Railway was an electric trolley line that connected the numerous towns in that mining district in 1898.[13] That same year, an electric railway was incorporated to connect Colorado Springs to the Cripple Creek District thirty miles away.[14] While never electrified, the Colorado Springs & Cripple Creek District Railway connected the two terminals on April 28, 1901.[15] The Cripple Creek Short Line, as it was known colloquially, entered receivership in May 1919.[16] By July the railroad announced it would electrify, a pronouncement that would never come to fruition.[17] Operations ceased in 1920; it then entered bankruptcy and was scrapped in 1922.[18]

The Kansas-Colorado Railroad wasn't even the first electrified interurban railroad proposed for Pueblo. That distinction goes to the Pueblo & Beulah Valley Railway, incorporated in July 1902. John J. Burns, former superintendent of the Denver & Rio Grande Railway, organized the Pueblo & Beulah Valley Railway, which would be an electrified rail line from Pueblo, westward to Beulah, and perhaps even beyond, to Custer County. Burns, the line's vice-president, published a beautiful prospectus to entice potential subscribers.[19]

On April 28, 1902, John J. Burns and Francis Meston entered into an agreement with W. A. Beatty, of St. Louis, to finance the Pueblo, Beulah & Western Traction Company, an electrified railroad. Burns and Weston would receive 10 percent of the stock, while Beatty would receive 90 percent, plus 90 percent of the bonuses to be paid by Pueblo, Florence, and any individual subscribers. This return was contingent on obtaining the franchise and right-of-way through Pueblo, westward to Beulah, with a branch to Florence—all of which would total about forty-five miles of track. In return for the franchise, the city of Pueblo would receive 2 percent of passenger revenue from the railroad.[20] A subsequent agreement appointed Burns general superintendent of construction and general superintendent of operations after construction was complete.[21]

J. Ed Rizer, a silent partner and the Pueblo & Beulah Valley's general counsel, commented in a letter to Burns on April 29 that he even though he had drawn up the articles of incorporation of the company and the franchise for the line, he thought it highly unlikely that the "present Council will grant the franchise over all of the streets asked for, as they seem to be of the opinion that rival street car companies cannot successfully operate in the same town, largely on account of it being impossible to have a system of transfers from one to the other."[22] This concern foreshadowed the trouble the Kansas-Colorado would encounter with certain citizens in Pueblo later in the decade. As judge, J. Ed Rizer would go on to play one of the most important roles in the future of the Colorado-Kansas Railway, but that was still a few years away.[23]

By May 17, 1902, the railroad's official corporate name had been changed to the Rapid Transit Company. The articles of incorporation included James N. Carlile, a longtime railroad contractor; John J. Burns; H. R. Holbrook; and Charles Henkle, all from Pueblo, along with William A. Beatty, of St. Louis. The stated goal was to build a steam or electric railroad from Pueblo to Beulah, with a branch to Florence, along with the requisite electric power plants. The railroad was to be capitalized at $1.5 million, divided into 15,000 shares at one $100 a share. Three thousand of those shares would be preferred stock, with 12,000 common stock.[24] The Pueblo City Council passed the franchise on July 21, 1902.[25]

Continuing to foreshadow the Kansas-Colorado Railroad project, financial and franchise difficulties arose early on. Beatty wrote to Rizer on August 8, 1902, complaining that it had taken three months to get the railroad's franchise, instead of the promised three weeks, and had already cost Beatty $1,000 in expenses. Beatty insinuated that improprieties with the stock issuance by Burns had jeopardized Beatty's ability to raise the needed capital. Beatty insisted that Burns and Rizer comply with the contract to which they had entered into:

I want you to be frank and say what is the trouble and who is to blame for it, and whether you are going to comply with our contract, and I will know how to set. You are temporizing by your action and I do not consider this business, and you will agree with me. I am going on with the work on the project, but can only go so far until this is settled. I can put this through, and when I fail there in no use for you people to try. If I have to protect myself [I] will expect to be reimbursed for time and money. I trust that no such action will be necessary, and at a loss to account for the action of you people.[26]

Financial progress was slow, as 1903 brought a new president of the project and a new financier, George Peck, of Cincinnati. Peck entered into an agreement to fund the railroad project with the Business Men's Association of Pueblo, which included C. W. Crews and Asbury White, two men who would also later be associated with the Colorado-Kansas Railway. If the railroad was not financed and built by March 1, 1904, Peck was to refund up to $30,000 of the subscription money put up by the Business Men's Association.[27] Perhaps sensing trouble ahead, Carlile and Henkle had sold their interests in the line by early 1903.[28] Things were looking up, however, for grading on the project started on September 28, 1903, with Margaret Lyle Burns, daughter of John J. Burns, handling the plow in the dirt south of Pueblo. A large parade of wagons, carriages, and automobiles, carrying business men and the Morris Military Band, left the line's downtown terminal location on Fifth Street and headed south of Lake Minnequa for the groundbreaking ceremony.[29]

Ambition was not lacking for the fledgling railroad. In a March 27, 1903, letter to George Peck, Beatty suggested their road extend itself southward to connect with the Chicago, Rock Island & Pacific at Dawson, New Mexico, and even further on to connect to the Atchison, Topeka & Santa Fe. Another branch would connect with the Colorado & Southern at Walsenburg, Colorado. These were hefty goals indeed for a roughly thirty-mile shortline railroad between Pueblo and Beulah that had yet to be built.[30] Beatty even wrote to Peck about the Saint Louis & San Francisco Railroad, or Frisco, being interested in their line as a connection from Oklahoma to Pueblo.[31] But such were the dreams in the first decade of the twentieth century in the American West.

By October 1903, George Peck encouraged Burns to keep the grading teams to an affordable fifteen in number.[32] The *Pueblo Chieftain* reported that

FIGURE 2.1. *Groundbreaking for the Rapid Transit Company, Pueblo, Colorado, September 28, 1903. John J. Burns Photos. Courtesy of History Colorado–Denver.*

as of January 1, 1904, fourteen miles of line had been graded, all paid for with stock subscriptions.[33] An audit in September 1904 showed that the railroad had spent $13,612.84 in expenses to date, compared to receiving $13,396.50 in stock subscriptions. With this small debt, not a single tie or rail had been laid.[34] Peck remained extremely skeptical, however, about the involvement of Beatty and a handful of others, writing to Burns, "I doubt if the whole outfit together could dig up more than a few hundred dollars. The idea of their building a railroad is ridiculous."[35]

An ambitious plan, in May 1904 it was announced that the line would be running from Pueblo to Beulah by September 1. Bonds were reportedly sold, and the railroad capitalized at $1.5 million by a European syndicate. The same syndicate also pledged to invest $2 million to $3 million more in Beulah and the surrounding area to increase business.[36] Throughout 1904 and into 1905, Peck continued to seek funding for construction of the railroad, even seeking eastern and English investors.[37] As of 1906, by-now Judge J. Ed. Rizer wrote to Burns that Peck was lying about seeking capital in the eastern United States or Europe, indicating he had done nothing of the sort.[38] Despite this grandiose idea of these eastern and European investors, the biggest wave the railroad ever made was the announcement that passengers would be charged according to their weight.[39]

In the end, the railroad was never built. This scheme of Burns's perhaps explains some of the reticence on the part of the people of Pueblo to fund a new, and even more grandiose, electrified railroad, the Kansas-Colorado Railroad. Still, the desire to connect the hinterlands to Pueblo was great. In the case of Custer County and the Pueblo & Beulah Valley Railway, it was about the silver and other ores that were being mined in the Wet Mountain Valley. After reading about the railroad possibly building to Custer County, M. L. Moore of the Terrible Mine wrote to Burns in April 1903 about the financial potential for the railroad hauling ore from the Terrible and other mines in the district.[40] Burns was already invested in Custer County and probably did not need to be convinced of the financial benefits of extending the line. In March 1902, Burns had formed the Custer Mining and Realty Company with an investor from St. Louis, Charles W. Walters.[41] The culmination of Burns's Custer Mining and Realty Company came on June 10, 1902, with a large celebration marking the foundation of Custer City, about halfway between Rosita and Querida in Custer County. The *Pueblo Chieftain* prophesied, "With much pomp and some circumstance a new town was today added to Colorado's list. With no past, and with a future that looms before it as brilliant as a rainbow, Custer, Custer county, Colorado, has begun an existence that bids fair to be as prosperous as any other city in the great Centennial state."[42] A large contingent of people traveled from Pueblo by train to Westcliffe, where they were met by Francis Meston, one of the investors in the Custer City project and the Pueblo & Beulah Valley Railway. From nearby Silver Cliff, a procession of carriages and wagons carrying the guests toured the mining district on their way to Custer City, including the famous Bassick Mine at Querida.

Although only a few months old, Custer City was of respectable size. The newspaper counted around twenty houses, a restaurant, post office, assay office, and newspaper office, among other business, as well as a "good hotel," where a big dance was held later that evening.[43] Custer City had an underground municipal water system including fire hydrants at intervals along the platted streets. Besides the park in the center of town, the east end of Custer City featured a ballpark for the residents' amusements. Custer Mining and Realty had also opened two mines in the district, the Toledo, and the First Colorado.[44]

At Custer City, lunch was served in a large tent while a band entertained the guests. John J. Burns opened the celebration with a brief speech. Guest speakers were many, including Governor James B. Orman and former governor Alva Adams, both of whom had lived in Pueblo at one time, as well as H. W. Foss, representing the Grand Army of the Republic, and Dr. O. E.

Sperry, of the Confederate Veterans' Association. Veterans from both the Confederate and Union Armies participated in a review at the celebration. America's pastime was also represented when the Pueblo New Yorks and an unnamed Custer County team played an exhibition baseball game, to the delight of the crowd, though the *Chieftain* did not bother to mention the winner. The highlight was the unveiling of a statue of General George Armstrong Custer by Miss Myrtle Rants, of Silver Cliff. The *Chieftain* noted, "The statue stands in what will eventually be the very center of town and is of heroic size. It depicts the soldier in his fighting clothing, just as he was when he laid down his life with his men in the terrible massacre of 1876."[45] Custer's widow, Elizabeth B. Custer, along with William F. "Buffalo Bill" Cody, were both invited to the celebration, but politely declined the invitation.[46]

Custer City was a flash-in-the-pan town, similar to the boomtowns of the late nineteenth century that quickly went bust, but with twentieth-century flair. In January 1903, the *Wet Mountain Tribune* reported that the house at Custer City were rapidly filling up with miners and their families.[47] By April, however, things were looking grimmer. The *Silver Cliff Rustler* reported, "The town having no need of an electrician at this time, Mr. Morse, who has charge of the Custer City light plant, took Monday's train for other quarters."[48] Ever the skeptic, the *Rustler*, responding to a competitor newspaper, pointed out "the *Guidon* says 'Isn't it remarkable what fools are allowed to run loose in the valley?' There aren't many fools remaining at Custer City. Only a few who can't get away."[49] The financial situation took a turn for the worse. A levy was placed on the property of the Custer Mining and Realty Company, on December 31, 1908, and the entire town was put up for auction by the Custer County sheriff early the next year.[50] Jude T. Stroehlke purchased the entire town, with electric light plant and waterworks, for the satisfying of a $715 judgment.[51] By December, the Custer Mining and Realty Company had redeemed the property from Stroehlke.[52] Mining was still being attempted as late as 1911, but Custer City was nearly a ghost, its promise long since broken.[53]

The Pueblo & Beulah Valley story, along with that of Custer City, parallels the story of the Colorado-Kansas Railway in many ways. There are the similarities of the promotional ambitions of their two of their respective founders and supporters, John J. Burns, and Robert K. Potter. Both were initially quite involved in their railroad, mining, real estate, and town formation

FIGURE 2.2. *A. B. Hulit loading first scraper of dirt and Pueblo mayor John T. West driving the team, July 30, 1908. Courtesy of Pueblo City-County Library District.*

schemes, and both wanted to exploit the natural resources of Pueblo County. Around the Beulah area, limestone, building stone, marble, fireclay, and ganister were touted as potential sources of income, for the Pueblo & Beulah Valley, much like the Stone City Region would be touted a decade later for the Colorado-Kansas. But whereas the Pueblo & Beulah Valley Railway and Custer City were both failures, the Colorado-Kansas Railway and Stone City managed to endure through great hardships for several decades.

Perhaps not surprisingly, the interest in a rail line to the mining districts in Custer County around the towns of Querida, Rosita, Silver Cliff, and Westcliffe was briefly revived in 1909 by none other than Hulit, who investigated the possibility. Because of its proximity to the San Luis Valley, it was enthusiastically supported by businessmen in Alamosa, who were currently only served by the Denver & Rio Grande Railway. Even though they pledged $20,000 to the project, Hulit did not move forward with it, his hands being tied with the Kansas-Colorado project, which would soon devolve and spiral out of his control.[54]

Kansas-Colorado company engineers entered the field in early June for preliminary surveys of the land for the railroad and locations for the power plants. Hulit was so enthused that he anticipated passengers would be traveling between Cañon City and Pueblo by Christmas.[55] At the same time, the directors met for their first official session to elect the officers of the company.[56] The energy level heightened as proposals from two potential

FIGURE 2.3. *Surveyor J. G. Todd and crew at work locating the line near Pueblo, June 1908. Courtesy of Pueblo City-County Library District.*

contractors soon came to the company headquarters in Pueblo, one for cross-ties for the entire 350-mile railroad, and the other for the grading of the railroad from Pueblo to Cañon City.[57] Kansas-Colorado president S. H. Atwater, of Cañon City, signed the contracts on July 24.[58] A week later, Atwater signed contracts for the grading east from Pueblo to Garden City, Kansas.[59]

Railroad officials, politicians, and businessmen witnessed the groundbreaking on the new railroad at a short ceremony on Thursday, July 30, 1908, on Robert K. Potter's ranch at Turkey Creek, west of Pueblo.[60] Potter, in fact, provided the linchpin to the whole railroad deal, so into our cadre of schemers and dreamers Robert K. Potter must be placed. Potter's father, Wellington Potter, like many dreamers, served in the Civil War in the Union Army but remained in Pennsylvania until his death. Robert, though, was a man of ambition, and at the age of twenty-seven he relocated the Potter family to Nebraska, in 1879. In that plains state, he farmed, along with raising cattle and hogs, but the Cripple Creek gold rush of the 1890s proved to be a siren's call. He moved to Cripple Creek, Colorado, in 1892, spending the next ten years building up his business prospects. He ran a sawmill business in Cripple Creek but also farmed further south along Beaver Creek. He later sold all those interests and moved to the Penrose area, just up the Arkansas River from Pueblo. Not long into the twentieth century, Potter purchased land in the northwest corner of Pueblo County, where he enters the railroad's story. He filed on the site of what would eventually become the Teller Reservoir, planning to irrigate lands below it along Turkey Creek but later sold the water rights John C. Teller. He also purchased lands that would become his ranch, as well as lands on Booth Mountain that looked to prove lucrative in the quarrying and clay business. With the prospect of a railroad running near or through his lands, it was an easy decision to become an investor. Potter would go on to become vice-president and general manager of the Colorado-Kansas Railway.[61]

3

Boss Fight

The railroad line as surveyed by J. G. Todd crossed Turkey Creek on its way west to Cañon City.[1] By investing in the railroad, Potter convinced the company to construct a spur from that point to his stone quarries operating up on Booth Mountain. This extension would provide the railroad with revenue from the outset, which the company deemed sufficient to meet operating expenses.[2] Potter had started the Turkey Creek Stone, Clay & Gypsum Company with its attendant quarries prior to 1908, but exactly when is unclear, as the sandstone on Potter's land was identified for building stone as early as 1902.[3] By 1908, however, the quarries were supplying stone for the new Pueblo County Courthouse under construction, and Potter considered a rail link to be a necessity to his operations.[4] Because of the long financial and legal tribulations the railroad faced during construction, it probably carried very little, if any, stone for the new courthouse, as both were completed in 1912. The quarries originally utilized wagons drawn by four-, six-, and eight-horse teams, but later upgraded to a Daniel-Best 110-horsepower, steam-driven road locomotive, capable of pulling wagons of twenty-ton

DOI: 10.5876/9781646421282.c003

FIGURE 3.1. *Freighting camp at Stone City for hauling quarried stone to the railhead at Cabin Springs, July 1, 1908. Author's collection.*

FIGURE 3.2. *Freighting quarried stone to the railhead at Cabin Springs, circa 1908. Courtesy of Pueblo County Historical Society.*

capacity each.[5] The wagons hauled the stone south to the Arkansas River bluffs, transported down to the river, where they transferred to the Atchison, Topeka & Santa Fe Railway at Cabin Springs for shipment to their stone mill located between C and D streets in Pueblo.[6]

A rail connection due south to either the Atchison, Topeka & Santa Fe Railway, or the Denver & Rio Grande Railroad on the Arkansas River, would have been logical, but by investing in a new railroad, which both ran across his ranch and serviced his quarries, Potter could maintain more control and earn a better profit. To that end, he convinced Hulit and the investors to build to the quarries.[7] This would be a small branch line, to be sure, but it had to look attractive to the investors, as it would provide almost instant revenue, and nearly twenty-three miles of track would look imminently feasible

FIGURE 3.3. *The Daniel-Best steam engine hauling stone down to Cabin Springs, circa 1910. Courtesy of Pueblo County Historical Society.*

with what funding they did have. Little did anyone suspect at that point that the line to the quarries was all the railroad that would ever be built and that it would operate as a subsidiary company for the quarries.

By August 10, the grading crews had finished the first mile of grade.[8] Two weeks later, Hulit added thirty additional teams to hasten the work, and grading continued throughout the autumn of 1908.[9] Forty-five Pueblo businessmen took an auto tour along the new grade, and saw firsthand the 80 teams and 125 men hard at work, as well as "one of those famous Panama canal grading machines doing the work of a host of men and teams."[10] Grading began at Garden City on October 19, led by company president S. H. Atwater.[11] W. J. Davis, the electrical engineer in charge of construction of the power plants, arrived in Pueblo in late September to look over the plans before construction started on the Garden City, Cañon City, and La Junta electrical power plants.[12]

FIGURE 3.4. *The Cabin Springs transfer station for Turkey Creek stone on the Atchison, Topeka & Santa Fe Railway, circa 1908. Photo Courtesy of Denver Public Library, Western History Department, X-28161.*

FIGURE 3.5. *Turkey Creek Stone, Clay & Gypsum Company's stone mill in Pueblo between C and D Streets northwest of Lamkin Street, July 1, 1908. Author's collection.*

FIGURE 3.6. *Postcard of Pueblo County Courthouse advertising Turkey Creek Stone, 1912. Author's collection.*

FIGURE 3.7. *Excavating a cut near Pueblo, 1908. Courtesy of Pueblo City-County Library District.*

Although much of the railroad crossed Robert K. Potter's land, and others sold their land to the concern, not everyone was on board with the idea of trains running through their property. Thus, condemnation proceedings began in

FIGURE 3.8. *Grading a fill near Turkey Creek, 1908. Courtesy of Pueblo City-County Library District.*

district court on October 10, 1908, to acquire the remaining 100-foot-wide right-of-way for construction, with over twenty-five defendants named in the petition.[13] The *Pueblo Sun*, however, reported over eighty realty defendants in the condemnation proceedings.[14] The proceedings were swift, with settlements made and the right-of-way secured by November 6.[15]

On the surface, progress appeared to be smooth and steady. The Pueblo City Council passed the franchise for the railroad, though it was not without controversy. The ordinance had to be publicly read three times before it could pass, usually a simple procedural matter. After the first reading, though, the Pueblo & Suburban Traction & Lighting Company and Vail's newspaper, the *Star-Journal*, vowed to fight the Kansas-Colorado Railroad if it came through the city. On Monday, November 2, at 7:30 in the evening, fifty Pueblo business leaders gathered anxiously to hear the third and final reading of the franchise and witness its passage by the city council. The ordinance had been referred to the public works committee, but so far no report had been turned over to the city clerk. By 8 p.m., the crowd was restless. City council president J. D. King, who had been sidelined with an illness, managed to make it to the meeting, but only three aldermen had shown up. Four aldermen were

FIGURE 3.9. *Grading about halfway between Pueblo and Stone City, 1908. Pikes Peak is in the background on the left. Courtesy of Pueblo City-County Library District.*

missing, and no quorum was possible, much less a two-thirds majority. It was remarked by the *Pueblo Sun* that this was "a condition that had never before obtained during the present administration."[16] The rumor mill kicked into overdrive, with much speculation that the traction company had gotten to the missing aldermen and convinced them to stay away from the meeting to avoid a quorum. As the progressive *Pueblo Sun* reported, "Soon the word was whispered and passed quickly among the people present that paper had been cut, job presses made ready, horseback riders and bill distributors engaged by certain Republican workers, and that before daylight circulars setting forth the failure or refusal of the Democratic council to pass the ordinance so vitally important to the city, would be placed in every Pueblo home and distributed at every one of the twenty-nine country precincts."[17]

The implied threat prompted Mayor John T. West and other city officials to round up the four missing aldermen, and by 9 p.m., all were assembled for the reading of the franchise. After an hour and a half of private debate in the mayor's office by the involved parties, the city council gathered at 10:38 p.m. The public works committee recommended that the ordinance pass, with the amendment that the railroad must repair and maintain the levee through the city. Upon the third reading, the franchise passed, unanimous except for Alderman Zink, who left prior to the vote. Vigorous applause resounded throughout the council chambers after the vote. The railroad had won its first major political victory.[18]

The situation could not have looked rosier for the grand project. Both Finney and Kearney Counties in Kansas voted bonds for the project.[19] On October 31, the Kansas-Colorado Railroad Company purchased the assets of the defunct Cañon City & Royal Gorge Interurban, which was building an electric railway from Cañon City to the top of the Royal Gorge in anticipation of hauling tourists, bringing the added benefit of tourist traffic to the Kansas-Colorado project.[20] This line was never completed, but if you drive west out of Cañon City on Highway 50 and look left, to the south of the highway as you climb up out of the Arkansas River Valley you can spot the railroad grade in places as it worked its way to the top of the Royal Gorge. Perhaps ties were laid along the graded line, but steel rails never were. There was even talk about extending the line to the gold camps in the Cripple Creek District, utilizing connections with the Beaver, Penrose, & Northern and the Florence & Cripple Creek Railroads. Both lines were narrow gauge, however, so the connections would not be direct.[21] Overall, the outlook for the railroad looked rosy, but by the start of the new year the situation took a decided turn for the worse.

The first real public report of trouble came on November 7, when the *Pueblo Sun* published a rumor of graft being involved in the city franchise won by the railroad the week before. The paper reported that a former alderman, acting as a go-between, demanded of a Kansas-Colorado Railroad official, "You will have to put up some money for three aldermen if you get your franchise ordinance passed Monday night."[22] The railroad official replied that the company would not pay the graft money. During the anxious wait for the missing aldermen, Frank S. Hoag, press agent for the traction company through Vail's *Star-Journal*, frantically kept checking on the situation all evening, first through repeated phone calls and finally by a hurried visit to city hall, raising more suspicions against the traction company. Mayor West and council president King reportedly railed at the tardy alderman once they were rounded up, threatening to go public with the statement about graft in the council chambers if they didn't participate in the vote. Responding to the allegations of graft, Mayor West stated, "In the three and a half years that I have been mayor there has not been a charge of graft placed against this council or any of its officers, and there will be no graft now without my announcing publicly who are the guilty parties."[23]

The initial fallout from the franchise vote was slight, but the trouble was not over by a long shot. Mahlon D. Thatcher, owner of the Pueblo &

Suburban Traction & Lighting Company, which operated the electric street railway in town, had on several occasions given his "cordial support" to the Kansas-Colorado project.[24] However, John F. Vail, general manager of the Traction Company, must have seen the newcomer as a direct threat to the Traction Company's monopoly on electricity and the street railway system, because in the coming months he would fight the Kansas-Colorado project tooth and nail.

The franchise appeared, on the surface, to be the last real obstacle standing in the way of construction of the railroad and power plants. A couple of days after the city council awarded the franchise, the Kansas-Colorado board of directors signed the contracts with Hulit for the powerhouses, transmission lines, and rolling stock for both companies.[25] The laying of crossties and rails on the line to Turkey Creek would soon begin, with trains running to Turkey Creek by Christmas 1908.[26] The company ordered $1.5 million in rails from the Colorado Fuel & Iron steelworks in Minnequa, to the southeast of Pueblo, with crossties coming mainly from New Mexico.[27]

Plans for a large hotel and depot connected with the railroad surfaced. Built with Turkey Creek stone and standing eight to ten stories tall, it was to be "the best hotel in the Rocky Mountain region." Kansas-Colorado electric trains would use the bottom level as their terminal.[28] This hotel never came to pass, but four years later the company planned another grand depot for the same area. This time it was going to be a Union Station, utilized by all the railroads of Pueblo. Sitting right behind a hotel built in 1912 by John Vail and just east of the Kansas-Colorado terminal, this massive structure would have spanned the Arkansas River, with passenger trains utilizing subways on either side of the river to access the depot. The Santa Fe's main line ran directly through Pueblo's business district, and the numerous grade crossings had long plagued the growing city. This $6 million project was part of the long-running plan to eliminate these grade crossings throughout the city center.[29] One option open to the Santa Fe was to run on the Kansas-Colorado tracks through the city, thereby freeing up valuable real estate for the business district and eliminating troublesome grade crossings.[30] The railroad never built the proposed depot, and the grade crossing problem would not be resolved until the 1950s.

Contractors expected to complete the Dry Creek Bridge just north of Pueblo around the middle of December, which boosted the company's optimism.[31] The company also expected to begin laying rails at the same time.[32] This optimism was premature, for it would take almost another year to drive the first spike. Meanwhile, engineers continued locating the line to the east as far as La Junta, Colorado, and north to near Colorado Springs. They had already finished locating the line from Dodge City, Kansas, to Holly, Colorado, near the state line.[33] Additionally, the *Pueblo Sun* reported stock sales were going well.[34] This assessment was far from accurate, though, for even as late as April 1909, the company had raised only $266,000 from stock sales, far short of the $8,500,000 needed by both companies.[35] Hulit, Fox, and other local representatives went to New York City seeking more financing for the company.[36] This endeavor was, perhaps, an exercise in futility, as there was likely reticence at investing in such speculative ventures following the Panic of 1907, the effects of which were finally easing by early 1909.[37] Nationally, the depressed markets caused by the Panic of 1907 were only temporary.[38] However, the Kansas-Colorado would have to rely on investment from those two states if they were ever to be built.

By February 1909, internal strife over finances came to a head. Investors must have been concerned that work was progressing very slowly on the railroad and realized that financing for the entire project was not going to be feasible. They scaled back their plans accordingly, for the company officers gave assurances that the work would "go ahead to the completion of at the least the western division."[39]

Contractors filed two lawsuits, one against Hulit and Fox, seeking a judgment of $161.50, and the other against the attorneys for the railroad, McCorkle and McCorkle, for $750. The company did not reveal the details of the suits to the public, but they were certainly an outward expression of dissension within the company.[40] Within days of the lawsuits, other creditors came calling on the company offices, seeking settlement in cash or, in some cases, accepting stock in the company.[41] The directors still claimed that once the line to the quarries at Turkey Creek was complete, the railroad would begin paying for itself, and the company would construct the rest of the line all the way to Garden City.[42] The Kansas creditors all signed off on the creditors' committee plan to settle the debts, but some of the Colorado contractors refused to go along with it.[43] Hulit once again headed east to find more investors to help finance the project, but he apparently had difficulty convincing investors to buy into the company, difficulty that one newspaper editor blamed on the "Vail conspiracy."[44] An editorial in the *Pueblo Sun* suggested that Thatcher and Vail were behind the dissension within the company and had conspired to block the funding from eastern investors in the project. "Checkmated again, Johnny Vail and Money Daffy Thatcher," read the *Sun*. "The Kansas-Colorado road is not so dead as you thought your backcapping and dissension stirring had made it." Behind this, suggested the newspaper, was an attempt to gobble up the railroad's franchise.[45] The other railroads that served Pueblo might have had something to do with the inability of the Kansas-Colorado to obtain financing. The president of the Santa Fe served on the boards of bonding companies in Chicago, while George Gould of both the Denver & Rio Grande and the Missouri Pacific questioned whether the railroad bonds should even be sold.[46]

The Kansas-Colorado company reorganized with the arrival of these eastern capitalists. In this instance, eastern meant Kansas.[47] One of these men was John F. Springfield, a consulting engineer in the railroading business since 1887. In 1909, Springfield was a vice-president and general manager of the Hutchinson, Kansas public utilities, which is probably where Hulit ran into him. Springfield would be instrumental in getting the railroad financed and would later go on to become the company's president until his death in 1955.[48]

The new company, the Kansas-Colorado Construction Company, organized in Topeka, Kansas. Congressman Justin D. Bowersock was elected president, R. C. Johnson, secretary, and Charles E. Sutton, treasurer. Sutton would remain with the railroad for many years. Rumors abounded that they would be buying a majority interest in the stone quarries as well.[49] A. O. Fox was still an investor in the railroad at this time.[50] R. C. Johnson arrived in Pueblo near the end of June with enough cash to settle the claims against the railroad at fifty cents on the dollar. Johnson expected to pay off the other half of the claims with revenue generated from the railroad.[51]

Apparently sensing that the railroad would never be the electrified interstate line that Hulit and Fox originally envisioned, the directors of the company requested a change in the city's franchise that specified the railroad must operate electrically. Instead, the company wanted the option to use steam locomotives if needed.[52] The Business Men's Association and the city council called a meeting with the company to discuss the matter. Additional changes to the franchise included adjusting the freight rates for coal and extending the deadlines for the railroad's completion.[53]

The railroad presented to the city council for a vote on the recommended changes to the franchise that came out of that meeting. A spirited debate, including "hisses and hoots," ensued, with both supporters of the road and opposition attending. Only Alderman Norbert Zink protested the changes, but Alderman T. E. Gill did not like the fact that the railroad might not be electrified, as he thought the new railroad would take passengers to parts of the city where the street railway did not already run.[54] In fact, Zink had inserted an amendment that would have prevented the railroad from building east of Victoria Avenue in Pueblo, cutting off any independent access for the railroad and forcing them to ally themselves with the Santa Fe, which R. C. Johnson did not want. Johnson refused to sign such a franchise, if amended this way. Zink testified that he felt the railroad would never be more than a shortline to the stone quarries, and possibly extending on to Cañon City, and did not want to see the franchise through the city go to a company that could not make good on their promises to build east to Kansas. Alderman J. P. Martel seconded the amendment, but when the time came to vote for the amendment, he sided with the railroad, and so Zink's amendment failed. When the council put the franchise to a final vote, only Zink voted against it.[55] Mayor "Honest" Abe Fugard signed the franchise the next day.[56] For a time, the franchise issue appeared to be settled, but things were far from over for the fledgling railroad company.

4

Troubles Continue

Feeling as if the worst were behind them, the Kansas-Colorado Construction Company began ordering materials for construction of the line. Johnson went to Colorado Fuel & Iron for the twenty-five miles of seventy-pounds-to-the-yard rails.[1] Contractors had nearly finished grading to the stone quarries by this time, and work progressed on the bridges and culverts needed. Crews had reportedly laid some ties on the grade west from Garden City, Kansas.[2]

Meanwhile, A. O. Fox returned to Pueblo to meet with the Kansas-Colorado directors, followed shortly by a financial agent from General Electric. As the Northern Electric Manufacturing Company was a subsidiary of General Electric, the directors were apparently still considering building the electrified railroad and irrigation project in its entirety.[3]

With the grading of the line completed to the quarries, the next step was the actual laying of rails. On November 22, 1909, a special Santa Fe train carried distinguished guests to the site where the railroad would connect with the Santa Fe.[4] Railroad contractor J. A. Chezik had placed a few lengths of CF&I "Pueblo-rolled" rail on site. At two o'clock in the afternoon, after

DOI: 10.5876/9781646421282.c004

FIGURE 4.1. *Postcard of Fourth Street Bridge and Arkansas River, Pueblo, 1912. Colorado-Kansas Railway tracks are on the far left. Author's collection.*

much fanfare, officials gave Mrs. Andrew McClelland, a popular booster of the railroad project, the honor of driving the first spike on the railroad.[5]

As a requirement of their franchise, the Kansas-Colorado needed to raise and maintain the Arkansas River levee over the portion on which they were building. Part of this process also involved raising the north end of the Fourth Street Bridge and its approach, and the installation of a fifty-foot arch to allow the tracks to pass underneath the bridge.[6] This north end needed to be raised an additional nine feet.[7] Contractors raised the levee and placed jetties at weak points as added protection.[8] This work was called into question in January 1912 by the commissioner of highways and the city engineer, who both argued before city council that the railroad's work had weakened the levee, leaving the city vulnerable to floods caused by seasonal ice gorges and the danger of resulting overflow. The railroad raised the levee about 600 feet south of the Fourth Street Bridge, and continuing to Victoria, but lowered the grade by up to four feet to pass under the Fourth Street Bridge, and failed to raise the levee at all north of the bridge.[9] Rails headed south and east from the Santa Fe connection, snaking along the river levee toward the center of town by February 1910. Tracklayers installed a standard crossing where the Santa Fe line from Pueblo's Union Depot crossed the river and headed east. From there, it was little work to

FIGURE 4.2. *First Train on the Kansas-Colorado Railroad, near Victoria Avenue, February 28, 1910. Author's collection.*

lay the tracks up to Victoria Avenue, the temporary end-of-track until construction could push east to Kansas.[10]

The last day in February 1910 saw the first official train on the Kansas-Colorado Railroad traverse the section from Victoria Avenue, down the mile and a half of track to the connection with the Santa Fe's Cañon City Branch. With twelve hours to spare in the race to meet the requirements of the franchise, the track crews laid the last 160 feet of rails to Victoria Avenue. While the track was not ballasted and was "a bit rough and sagging in places," the railroad hastily borrowed a locomotive, six flat cars, and a caboose from the Santa Fe, as they had not yet purchased any rolling stock, and ran a special train from Victoria Avenue up to the connection with the Santa Fe. Local dignitaries and citizens were invited to ride by the officers of the railroad, which left Victoria Avenue at 5 p.m.[11] The tracks extended through the Kansas-Colorado yards, which were still under construction, and beyond for another mile, though they were not in any shape to allow the train to pass. The train backed up the same way it had come, returning the hundred or so guests to Victoria Avenue.[12] Track laying progressed faster than the rails could come from CF&I's Minnequa Steel Works on the southeast side of Pueblo, delaying construction.[13]

At a meeting of the stockholders, the company voted to issue $3 million in bonds to construct the rest of the Western Division, from Pueblo to Cañon City.[14] The franchise came up for discussion near the end of April. The amended franchise passed the previous year stipulated that the road had to be built to the Turkey Creek quarries by June 1, 1910. With the deadline fast approaching and only a couple of miles of track having been laid, the railroad needed to have the franchise extended.[15] This time, the franchise would nearly be their undoing.

At the meeting of the city council at the Business Men's Association, John Vail and Alderman Zink again opposed the franchise; Vail against it in totality, and Zink against the amendment to extend the completion date. The Business Men's Association adopted a resolution to present it at the next city council meeting. Addressing concerns that the road would not have enough funds to complete any phase of the project, John F. Springfield's representative assured the crowd that the company would place sufficient funds to complete the road to the quarries—around $250,000—in a local bank, and that the road would be running by September 1.[16] John Vail lobbied against the franchise at the city council meeting, but the council accepted the recommendations for an amended franchise and referred it to the Street and Bridge Committee. Two of the three men serving on the committee had voted against the franchise.[17]

Vail had sold five subscriptions of $25,000 apiece for the construction of his new hotel near Victoria Avenue, one of them to himself. It is possible that Vail wanted to build his hotel to spite the railroad company, as he would build it in the same area where the Kansas-Colorado had earlier planned their hotel and headquarters. The day after the franchise meeting, the *Pueblo Sun* reported that Vail decided to withhold his $25,000 and prevent the construction of his hotel unless the city council killed the Kansas-Colorado project. The newspaper commented that he had been trying to get out of the hotel business anyway and possibly did not have the $25,000 he claimed.[18] Two days later, the *Sun* claimed victory over Vail: "After a story recounting the start of his bullying tactics appeared in The Sun Wednesday, Vail quieted down and has been like an oyster ever since. As a result of this victory of The Sun, it is not likely that the Vail hotel proposition will be used as a club over the K-C franchise, and in consequence the franchise application will be heard on its merits . . . The club which Vail has so often swung over business men and politicians, came down on his own head."[19] Despite the *Sun's* self-congratulatory mood, Vail was by no means out of the fight.

In anticipation of the coming franchise vote, Robert K. Potter took the mayor, city councilmen, and the city attorney on a tour of the railroad, including the graded portion toward Turkey Creek.[20] Springfield, Sutton, and other investors offered a $25,000 bond to the city, which they would place with the city treasurer and forfeit to the city if the railroad was not built within the specified time.[21]

John F. Springfield stated to the people of Pueblo, "I stand ready to put sufficient money into the Kansas-Colorado railroad project to construct and put into operation the road to Turkey Creek as soon as the city council of Pueblo grants the extension of the franchise asked by that company upon the terms proposed therein." Pressed further, he expressed his reticence, adding that unless the situation was met fairly by the city council, "[he does not] care to have anything to do with it."[22]

All the lobbying efforts were for naught. Supporters of the railroad turned out in large numbers at the council meeting, but when the time came for a vote on the amended franchise, John F. Vail won. Vail and several of his employees showed up at the council meeting to lend their backing to the antirailroad faction, giving rise to two hours of "oratory, sarcasm, cutting rebuke, rapid-fire repartee, argument and animosity such as has perhaps never crept into a Pueblo meeting."[23] Vail must have felt there was too much at stake, for he openly led the fight, something for which he was not known. "It was in striking contrast with the manner in which the traction boss used to sit in his own office and dictate the manner in which his vassals should make the council members perform. Last night he had come with his hired men and personally superintended the job of obstruction; and then only after the hardest possible fight was able to handle but half the votes," the *Sun* reported.[24]

The *Sun* chalked up Vail's second victory within a few months as a demonstration of the power of the political boss. Vail's previous victory was defeating the city's charter convention, which would have cleaned up "corrupt" politics in Pueblo. Vail stymied political progress then, and commercial and business progress was the victim this time. According to the *Sun*, this was the third railroad the "moss backs" chased out of Pueblo, the other two being the Chicago, Rock Island & Pacific, and the Florence & Cripple Creek, though the Rock Island had eventually reached Pueblo by way of Colorado Springs and trackage rights south over the Denver & Rio Grande. Both Colorado Springs and Fowler, east of Pueblo, offered their assistance to the Kansas-Colorado if Pueblo did not want them, but the fight for the Kansas-Colorado had only just begun.[25]

Some thought Vail might have gone too far this time, for there were rumblings of dissension among members of his own party, specifically, the anti-corporation Democratic leaders who spoke out "against the despotism that Boss Vail has established over party machinery, and the continual swaying of official acts by corporation influence." Progressive Democrats charged that Vail "used Democratic votes in the city council to prevent progress in civic matters" and kept the charter from coming to a vote of the people.[26] The Vail political machine was showing signs of vulnerability.

As a result of the failed franchise vote, contractor J. A. Chezik filed a $25,000 lawsuit against Hulit. The railroad expected bankruptcy proceedings and more lawsuits to follow. "Vail's Folly" was the name the *Sun* gave to the miles of deserted grade and rusting rails. According to the *Sun*, Vail ran surveys down the Arkansas River along the projected Kansas-Colorado right-of-way, and the paper hinted that he was planning to pick up the pieces of the Kansas-Colorado power and railroad project and make it his own. When someone purchased the La Junta Electric Company in October 1910, rumors flew that Vail was behind the sale.[27]

R. C. Johnson filed suit in the district court, asking that the assets of the Kansas-Colorado Construction Company be sold to satisfy creditors.[28] Judge J. Ed Rizer granted the request, ordering the sale of the property at a receivership auction by Receiver Asbury White on November 28.[29] As the auction commenced at ten o'clock, two bidders appeared for the property. One was Charles E. Sutton, treasurer of the railroad, representing the previous investors. The other was George McLagan, who claimed he represented local interests but not Vail's Traction Company. Bidding started at $12,000, the minimum required to satisfy the creditors, and increased in $100 increments until Sutton had bid $15,000 and won back the property.[30]

By this point, A. B. Hulit and A. O. Fox, originators of the scheme, had bowed out of the picture. Hulit, the "greatest dream artist who ever 'worked' Pueblo," went on to other schemes. After Hulit's failed work on promoting the Kansas-Colorado Railroad, he continued to promote land development in the West through the "Back to the Land" movement, designed to encourage unemployed in the cities to move west to farm. This pursuit also turned his attention to the problem of immigration. By this time, he had moved to Chicago, and with unemployed immigrants flooding the cities back east, Hulit claimed to have set up committees in thirty-one states to develop lands for farming by those unemployed immigrants. Hulit's movement resulted in the formation of the National Association of State Immigration Officials, with Hulit being named commissioner-general. The states' governors and presidents of their agricultural colleges would work together to develop agricultural practices specific for each state, which would be published by Hulit's organization in Chicago for distribution to immigrants. All publications would be printed in twelve languages and would be free of charge. Additionally, the agricultural colleges would develop classes to teach students how to farm in their state, with the course of twenty-four lessons costing only a dollar or two.[31]

As part of the movement Hulit also founded the American Agricultural Association, which would be headquartered in Chicago in a permanent agricultural exposition building providing social and educational services for those wanting to get into agriculture. Participating states would have to help pay to maintain the exposition. Governor Robert S. Vessey of South Dakota was the association's president. The *Chicago Tribune* leaked a prospectus that Hulit had provided them in confidence, causing an uproar regarding the proposed directors, prominent names who had not been first consulted, and the accusation by the paper that the association was only in this for its own interests. Hulit's scheme crumbled beneath him.[32] Hulit had even provided the Turkey Creek Stone, Clay & Gypsum Company with blueprints for his exhibition building so they could put in a bid on the construction stone, but it was not to be.[33] He rebounded two years later with an idea for a new exposition scheme, but instead of one building headquartered in Chicago, each exposition would be housed in mammoth tents in the various states.[34]

Hulit's flirtations with immigrants continued into his old age. In 1935, in the midst of the Great Depression, Hulit dreamed up the idea of a $50 annual tax on all immigrants, plus a "substantial fee for the privilege of sending money back to 'the old country.'" He estimated that this would bring in $400 million a year, financing an old-age insurance, which would be divided among the states according to their population.[35] His idea became pointless once Congress passed the Social Security Act later that year.

Hulit concocted a plan in 1934 for reclamation in the West. At a meeting of the Mid-Continent Reclamation Association, representatives from nineteen states met in Chicago to endorse Hulit's plan to request of Congress a survey regarding the practicality of a building canals and dams to form a massive flood control and soil erosion program stretching from northern North Dakota, south through Texas, to control waters flooding down from the Rocky Mountains.[36]

During the debacle, Hulit got into an argument with a reporter, who argued, "If that Arkansas Valley irrigation project and your 300-mile electric railway from Cañon city, Colo., to Dodge City, Kas., with the scheme for supplying electricity to all the industries along the line, had been successful, you wouldn't be here promoting this scheme, would you?" The reporter further reminded Hulit that after Pueblo, he "stung" Chicago businessmen with a "National Land Journal," intending to sell worthless land to immigrants.

Hulit was hurt by this verbal reminder of his failure in Pueblo and Chicago. He rebutted:

> I made a fool of myself promoting this land journal, and some money was lost. Let us forget about it. But along in February, 1909, I was sent to Pueblo, Colo., by my employer, the Northern Electric Company of Madison, Wis., to sell electric supplies. You know there was talk about a pumping plant at Garden City, Kas. The farmers met and I showed them that instead of hauling coal from Cañon City to Dodge City, 300 miles, at a cost of $6 a ton, we could stretch a wire, establish our plant at the terminus, and have the coal put into our bins at 40 cents a ton. It was all black. Yes, we lost thousands of dollars.
>
> My wife became ill and I had to leave that climate. Senator Vilas was my principal backer. He had invested $40,000. Foolishly, I didn't have a contract with him, and when he died, the thing stopped. We owed the workmen money. They were satisfied with my word. I raised more money, then my creditors attached it and got me into the courts. There was nothing dishonorable about it.[37]

The death of A. B. Hulit's dream to build an electrified railroad and irrigate the Arkansas Valley ended with two deaths. Senator William F. Vilas, of Wisconsin, passed away on August 27, 1908, and with it went Hulit's funding, prompting the initial reorganization of the company. Martha Hulit's illness in Pueblo was due the miscarriage or stillbirth of their daughter, on November 22, 1909, the same day that the passenger excursion traveled on the AT&SF to the proposed connection with the Kansas-Colorado Railroad. It is unknown if the two events were related. Lilian V. Hulit was buried in Pueblo's Roselawn Cemetery.[38] It is not surprising that Hulit abandoned Pueblo and the project to the destinies of other men and one woman.

5

The Colorado-Kansas Railway

The railroad reorganized as the Colorado-Kansas Railway. The name change better reflected the road's focus: Colorado first, Kansas later. Charles E. Sutton, trustee for the railroad, sold the property to a syndicate of fourteen subscribers for $499,775 worth of stock in the new company. The new owners were essentially the same as the old owners.[1] The total original Kansas-Colorado subscriptions and the Colorado-Kansas bond issue came to $439,850. J. F. Springfield, as himself and as a trustee, held a combined $189,250 worth of bonds in the company, while Charles Sutton held $55,445, J. R. Greenlees held $40,000, and C. W. Crews held $27,000. As for stock, altogether, there were 20,000 shares of stock divided among twenty-eight individuals.[2] Two of the owners and managers—E. W. Wilson, of Lawrence, Kansas, and F. G. Kelley, of Pueblo—would later get out of the railroad business in 1913 by swapping their interests in the railroad and quarries for Pueblo-area ranches owned by Charles Sutton, John F. Springfield, and Robert K. Potter. C. W. Crews, of Pueblo, the third manager, retained his interests in the line.[3] The new owners invested heavily in Pueblo real estate. Between 1909 and 1910,

DOI: 10.5876/9781646421282.c005

according to Colorado land sales records, the railroad's investors in both Colorado and Kansas, including familial relations as well as the Pueblo Land & Irrigation Company, purchased over 15,000 acres of land in Pueblo County, split between the railroad right-of-way and agricultural land. All total, their real estate holdings cost them over $124,000.[4]

Charles E. Sutton, of Lawrence, Kansas, also qualifies as one of our twentieth-century schemers and dreamers. While the Colorado-Kansas Railway and the Turkey Creek quarries became a primary focus, they weren't his only projects. While involved with the Colorado-Kansas construction, he also developed the Pueblo Land & Irrigation Company, a real estate development company that first developed 5,000 acres of land twenty miles east of Pueblo, which he called Orchard Park. After placing the development under irrigation, the company initially charged $100 per acre of land.[5] Sutton's Pueblo Land & Irrigation Company later filed a map with the county clerk of Pueblo for the proposed Pumpkin Hollow Reservoir, with a dam sixty-five feet high and a capacity of 107,750,150 cubic feet of water, supplied by Pumpkin Hollow and Turkey Creek.[6] Neither Orchard Park nor the Pumpkin Hollow Reservoir ever appears to have made a significant impact on Pueblo County.

The nascent Colorado-Kansas Railway Company drew up a new franchise, this time eliminating any mention of completion dates. The franchise was even endorsed by prominent Pueblo businessman Andrew McClelland.[7] With a new mayor and city council taking over on April 17, 1911, the Colorado-Kansas promoters must have feared that the new regime would be friendlier to Vail and would not pass their revised franchise. Determined to win at any cost, the railroad company somehow convinced Mayor "Honest" Abe Fugard to call a special council meeting on Saturday, April 15, to consider the franchise. The *Pueblo Chieftain*, which had been strangely silent on the entire affair, suddenly cried foul, printing rumors that several of the lame-duck council members, who had previously voted against the franchise, were going to vote for this new franchise. This change was highly suspicious, and the newspaper threatened a legal fight if the railroad company had bought the vote with graft. The new franchise, the *Chieftain* editorialized, promised nothing for the city of Pueblo since it contained no requirements to build to the quarries or the coalfields in Fremont County, and would prohibit any other railroad from utilizing the right-of-way if the Colorado-Kansas should fail to build anything.[8] After a lively debate and the addition of a couple of amendments, the city council granted the franchise by a vote of 6 to 2. The mayor then rushed to the city clerk, demanding of him to sign the new franchise, but Clerk Frank G. Duke refused, noting that he had forty-eight hours in which to turn over the ordinance to the mayor for signing. Duke planned to file his paperwork by the book.[9]

On Monday evening, April 17, Duke announced at the council meeting that outgoing mayor Fugard had "forcibly taken from him" the ordinance earlier in the day. Fugard, he claimed, handed the document to the railroad's attorney, J. H. McCorkle, while Fugard forcibly detained Duke. Then, both Fugard and McCorkle locked themselves in Fugard's office, where Fugard signed it into law. After Duke's speech, incoming Mayor John T. West immediately vetoed the ordinance. The new city council backed him up.[10]

The railroad took the matter to court. Judge Rizer issued a writ of mandamus ordering Duke to publish the ordinance as required by law or to appear in court and explain why he would not comply. The railroad asked that the court not include Mayor West's veto in the published ordinance, and Rizer granted the railroad promoters' request.[11] Duke's response to the court was that Fugard's special council meeting was illegal and that John T. West was mayor on April 15, having received the certificate of election and taken the oath of office just prior to that date.[12]

The case dragged on for several months as the court granted the city attorneys delay after delay, until Rizer finally set the date of July 5 for the hearing.[13] By July 19, Rizer had made his decision: Abe Fugard had been the de facto mayor until the new council was sworn in and took office the night of April 17. Therefore, his actions were legal, and the law required City Clerk Duke to publish and record the ordinance. In a final ironic twist, Duke was to publish the ordinance in the *Pueblo Star-Journal*, the newspaper founded and owned by John F. Vail.[14] The sheriff swiftly served City Clerk Duke with the mandamus to publish the Colorado-Kansas ordinance.[15] As ordered by the court, the *Star-Journal* published the franchise ordinance on July 21, and again on subsequent dates.[16]

The Colorado-Kansas Railway case was a test case for the city's political machine and was perhaps even a smokescreen to keep attention away from an important reform measure linked by happenstance to the railway's case. Waiting in limbo with the railroad was an initiative and referendum ordinance, passed by the city council the same night as the franchise vote. Initiatives and referendums were two of the political reforms enacted during the Progressive Era by cities and states to combat corruption in government. In Pueblo's case, the city attempted to enter into a "secret" contract, worth over $150,000, for the construction of a water filtration facility on the north side of town, without taking competing bids. Reform-minded citizens viewed this as an abuse of the city's authority and wanted to give residents the power to vote on the bond issue in an attempt to curtail this activity.[17] As happened with the railroad franchise, incoming mayor West vetoed the initiative and referendum ordinance.[18]

Although the court case only pertained to the railroad, and Judge Rizer's mandamus only ordered publication of the franchise ordinance, both the reformers and their opposition knew that the initiative and referendum ordinance would also have to be published. However, after arranging for the publication of the Colorado-Kansas Railway franchise ordinance, Duke promptly left town.[19] Duke's friends claimed he had merely gone on holiday to Almont on the Western Slope for ten days and had not skipped town to prevent the publication of the initiative and referendum ordinance. In Duke's absence, the city claimed the acting clerk had no authority to publish the ordinance.[20] The reformers sought a temporary injunction to stall any further action on the filtration contract until the publication of the ordinance.[21] Duke returned August 7, surprised to find his character called into question while he was on vacation. He promised he would publish the ordinance at once.[22] In the end, it did not matter whether or not Duke's vacation was a stalling tactic by the reform opposition, as the injunction proceedings tied up the case in court.

Meanwhile, Vail and others filed an injunction against the railroad to block construction and started a quo warranto action against the company that challenged their charter.[23] The railroad had filed its acceptance of the franchise on April 20, within thirty days of the vote, and had resumed construction, only to find construction halted by the restraining order on July 19. Vail's argument was that the railroad company was not incorporated at the time of the franchise vote and therefore had no right to the franchise. The railroad responded that they had been incorporated since April 1, 1911, that the city council had legally granted the franchise, and that they had every right to continue construction. It was up to Vail to prove that the railroad had obtained the franchise illegally.[24] The case went back and forth in Rizer's court for a few more months until November, when Vail was either unable to prove his allegations, or withdrew his case.[25]

While the Colorado-Kansas Railway's actions seem a little suspect at best and perhaps questionably legal at worst, it is apparent that the railway promoters felt they had no recourse when it came to fighting Vail's political machine and that Vail left them no choice but to fight back. The fact that Judge Rizer sided with the railroad company in the end upheld the legality of the company's actions, as no charges of graft came out during the court proceedings.

Lost in the fallout was the idea of an electric railway. Although talk persisted for several years about continuing to Kansas as originally planned, the first 22.8 miles of track, plus 2.4 miles of additional track for the yard and sidings, became the whole of the railroad. Farmers along the Arkansas River Valley still hoped they could get electricity for irrigation, going so far as to petition the Atchison, Topeka & Santa Fe to electrify to Dodge City, completing what the Kansas-Colorado Railroad / Colorado-Kansas Railway could not. The Santa Fe did not take up the idea.[26]

The local street railway and electric utility company, Pueblo & Suburban Traction & Lighting Company, asked in July 1911 for a franchise to build from Pueblo down the Arkansas Valley to La Junta, a likely bid to disrupt the Colorado-Kansas.[27] H. M. Byllesby & Company, out of Chicago, incorporated the Arkansas Valley Railway, Light & Power Company to consolidate the Pueblo Suburban Traction & Lighting Company with the Colorado Light & Power Company of Cañon City.[28] The company would ultimately serve electric customers from Cañon City, the Cripple Creek Mining District, Pueblo, and the agricultural district of the lower Arkansas River Valley all the way to La Junta, thus fulfilling some the Kansas-Colorado Railroad's projected goals. In 1915 the Arkansas Valley Railway, Light & Power Company announced intentions to construct an electric railway line from Pueblo through La Junta to the Kansas state line, which would have completed even more of the Kansas-Colorado Railroad's original plans, but this plan never moved any further.[29]

In the Colorado-Kansas Railway affair, the reform movement in Pueblo had won a major victory against the entrenched political machine, and local boosters and venture capitalists won the economic freedom to pursue their enterprise. Vail's undoing in the Colorado-Kansas fight was his reliance on his influence, which did not reach to Judge Rizer's court. The victory sealed Vail's political fate, for after confounding the city charter movement for years, Vail, with his political machine, was unable to prevent the election demanded by reformers. As the court battle was winding down, Puebloans voted to change the city charter on September 19, 1911, replacing the council of aldermen with five city commissioners selected through examinations by a three-member civil service commission. It was not until 1949 that the charter finally called for a fourteen-member city council elected from districts and created a new position of city manager.[30]

Following the purchase of the Pueblo & Suburban Traction & Lighting Company by H. M. Byllesby and Company, John F. Vail retired as their treasurer, general manager, and purchasing agent, receiving a diamond stud as a parting gift from his employees.[31] Still, Vail managed to leave his permanent mark on Pueblo, for the Vail Hotel still stands at the intersection of Grand and Union Avenues, right across the street from Pueblo City Hall, as if a reminder of who once ran the city.

Free at last of any legal entanglements, the Colorado-Kansas Railway vigorously resumed construction around the beginning of December 1911. Perhaps not coincidentally, chief engineer of the Colorado-Kansas Railway was Edward Forrister Rizer, nephew of Judge J. Edward Rizer.[32] With funding firmly in place, the railroad ordered the rails and crossties needed to complete the line to the Turkey Creek quarries. Five cars of ties, with six more on the way, waited in the company's yard, along with sixteen cars of bridge materials and track hardware.[33]

In December 1911, the Colorado-Kansas Railway purchased their first, and only, steam locomotive, Colorado-Kansas No. 1.[34] Locomotive No. 1 was a heavily used Class 93 4-6-0 locomotive from the Colorado Midland (CM), built by Schenectady in 1887. Renumbered by the CM from builder's No. 2437 to No. 24, the locomotive was part of a class of three 10-wheelers, numbers 23–25, that were the lightest road engines the Colorado Midland owned.[35] The engine weighed in at 117,000 pounds, or 58.5 tons, or 70 tons when including the loaded tender. The Class 93 engines were delivered with fifty-two-inch drivers and eighteen-inch-by-twenty-six-inch cylinders, but even with 17,031 pounds of tractive effort, they did not fare well on the steeper mountain grades of the Midland. Their light weight ultimately limited them to operations on the lighter grades on the Western Slope of Colorado, operating in

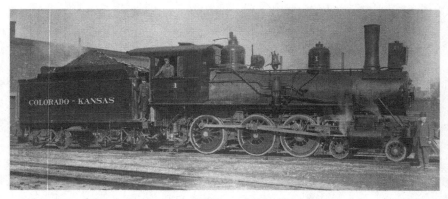

FIGURE 5.1. *Colorado-Kansas Railway No. 1 at her Pueblo debut, December 1911. Author's collection. Courtesy of Allan C. Lewis.*

passenger service out of Basalt, Cardiff, and Grand Junction. After 1903, the Midland rebuilt all three to be lighter and faster, with sixty-inch drivers and seventeen-inch-by-twenty-six-inch cylinders.[36] This rebuild would be more than enough for the Colorado-Kansas. For some unknown reason, the tender was swapped out, perhaps at the point of purchase, for the Baldwin-built tender from Colorado Midland No. 38, as later photos of Colorado-Kansas No. 1 reveal a faded "38" peeking through the paint. The Colorado-Kansas Railway paid $7,000 for the used locomotive but would continue to accrue heavy repair costs over the next decade and a half.[37] With their own locomotive purchased, the laying of rail commenced in earnest, and the Colorado-Kansas operated as a railroad for the first time.

A record snowfall on December 19 failed to halt construction, though it slowed it down somewhat, as the Colorado Fuel & Iron's Minnequa Steel Works delivered 500 tons of rails, which construction crews laid into place for yard sidings. Locomotive engineer S. J. Bowen was anxious to get the main line started, so he could really try out No. 1.[38] By January 11, 1912, crews had laid six miles of rails, with Minnequa having delivered 800 more tons; by the end of the month, the railroad stretched a total of eleven miles.[39]

Work progressed into the spring, as the railroad decided it required eight miles of new grade alignment from Turkey Creek to the quarries. The company deemed the earlier grade built up the east side of Turkey Creek by the Kansas-Colorado Construction Company as inadequate due to the elevation,

FIGURE 5.2. *Builder's photo of Colorado Midland sister Locomotive No. 23, 1887, showing how Colorado-Kansas No. 1 would have looked as CM no. 24. Author's collection.*

and so grading crews pushed a new grade across the creek at a more southerly point before turning north up the west side of Turkey Creek to the quarries.[40]

By March 29, 1912, the track had almost reached Pumpkin Hollow, at the rate of 4,500 feet to 6,400 feet of track a day. Construction had to be halted briefly because of a shortage of ties, though builders had enough rails to reach the station of Rio (Turkey Creek). Additionally, the railroad had to wait on CF&I to roll 400 tons of steel into rails before they could continue, but at least surfacing of the track could continue.[41] Construction crews laid the last rails into Booth Gulch at the terminus on April 15, 1912, a year to the day from the final frantic franchise vote, and almost four years to the day after A. B. Hulit first presented his ideas for a railroad and power company to the peoples of Colorado and Kansas.[42] The first carload of Turkey Creek stone to be handled by the railroad arrived from Piedra (later renamed Stone City) at the Irving Place yards on April 25, 1912, even though workmen were still busy ballasting the tracks.[43] The railroad had finally reached Stone City, but it was not complete. The switch tracks to the quarries were not completed until November. The company then also opened their fireclay mines, and the first shipments were sent to laboratories back east for testing.[44]

Pueblo's manufacturers decided to hold a "Home Industry Week" in April 1912 to showcase the production of Pueblo companies. Exhibits of manufacturers' wares were showcased in storefront windows along Main Street and Union Avenue, including a display of Turkey Creek Stone, Clay & Gypsum Company products.[45] The week kicked off on Saturday, April 13, but the real start was a grand parade at 8 p.m. on Monday night, which featured a procession of vehicles and floats two miles long.[46] A second parade was held on Thursday, April 18. On April 13, 1912, just days before the parade, Charles Sutton wrote a letter to the syndicate managers in Pueblo with his ideas for the railroad's float in the parade: "Gentlemen, Mr. Crews I believe requested me to think out an attractive banner for our float. A big stork presenting Pueblo with a little R. R. would be 'catchy'—a real 'Heir' (not Air) and contributor to Pueblo['s] future prosperity. Watch me grow. If this pleases you—get a good cartoonist to work it out." In the letter, Sutton drew a representation of his idea for the float. The stork is holding a baby bundle with a train in its beak, with the bundle dated April 14, 1912. In a cartoon balloon, the stork is saying, "Our own make, let's name him or we call him Colorado-Kansas. The kind you don't push . . . a real producer." Comically, in an apparent political statement, Sutton added a bandage around the stork's head, representing the legal headaches the railroad had come through. Added as an afterthought, the stork also says, "It's a rough road I've traveled but we're here and it's a Dandy." Indeed, the letter almost reads like a stream-of-consciousness projection of Sutton's excitement for the railroad:

> I bring you a Summer Resort, Building Stone, Fire Clay, Tile Clay, Brick Clay, Gannister, Dolomite, Gypsum, Gypsite, Lime Rock, Hematite, Glass Sand, Iron Ore, and other minerals. I bring with me best of all, Prosperity . . . A Real "Heir" Line . . . A Contributor to Pueblo's prosperity.
>
> Pueblo can be a distinguished dame—and say—We welcome "Our million dollar baby." Mrs. always wanted a baby R.R., Dr., but we never believed it was such uphill business—and maybe I am afraid the baby never would have been born if I had not taken my wife to the Springs—Cabin Springs.
>
> On the float—should be the 1st stone hauled to Pueblo over the line.—It should be retained by the Quarry Co. and placed as a marker later on in an appropriate place. Turn everybody upside down but finish the laying of steel to the franchise limits by Apr 15th. Then we can take our time.
>
> We should furnish clay and have brick made for Mr. Allen's test—at once—He will return to Pueblo next week.
>
> In haste, Sutton.[47]

The float did not turn out as Sutton hoped, probably because the timing was too close to the parade. The *Pueblo Chieftain* described the Colorado-Kansas

FIGURE 5.3. *Turkey Creek Stone, Clay & Gypsum Company window display during Home Week, April 1912. Photo courtesy of Pueblo City-County Library District.*

FIGURE 5.4. *Turkey Creek Stone, Clay & Gypsum Company window display during Home Week, April 1912. Photo courtesy of Pueblo City-County Library District.*

Railway's float as being a truck carrying a section of track, and on the track was a regular section car. Sutton's idea of carrying the first piece of Turkey Creek stone didn't come to fruition, and there is no mention of the stork banner.[48] While the *Chieftain* gave good coverage of the events of Home Industry Week, it was overshadowed by the sinking of the *Titanic*.

It was a long fight for twenty-five miles of track, but the people of Pueblo celebrated on June 12, 1912, in grand fashion with a special excursion train to the newly renamed town of Stone City at the end of the line, where they held a barbecue picnic to celebrate. Showing a remarkable lack of foresight, the railroad's officers christened the line with the moniker "The Pueblo Road" and renamed Turkey Creek Stone as "Pueblo Stone." Neither name stuck. Still, the guests of the Colorado-Kansas Railway adopted a resolution commending the railroad, noting it had added "another spoke to Pueblo's wheel of progress."[49] In a last gasp of Progressive boosterism, the *Pueblo Leader* proclaimed that railroad would "mean so much to Pueblo's future development" and would mean millions of dollars for the city, bringing in "new industries, new factories, new people."[50] Indeed, every outward appearance suggested the newspaper was correct. Public business nearly came to a halt for the entire day on June 12 so city and county officials could partake in the special excursion and celebration at Stone City. Even John Vail's newspaper, the *Pueblo Star-Journal*, congratulated the railroad and its builders though could not resist a parting shot. The editorial truthfully pointed out that the railroad could have been built years earlier, and its builders have saved a lot of expense, if the Colorado-Kansas Railway had not sought a franchise to build *through* the city but instead sought to earn their money *outside* the city limits, as was the case with the present railroad.[51]

The Colorado-Kansas Railway had officially opened for business. While the railroad may not have been a great industrializing force, may not have electrified and watered the Arkansas Valley, and certainly did not live up to the hype it generated, it still played an important connecting role between smaller businesses and the rest of the nation. The point of a railroad is to service customers, whether it is one or many, for without customers there is no need for a railroad. The customers that the Colorado-Kansas Railway cultivated are typical of the customers found along any shortline railroad. Although they may be smaller enterprises, those customers still contribute to the local and national economy—growing, waning, and evolving—specifically through the feeder connections offered by shortlines. For the Colorado-Kansas Railway, these connections between the railroad, its customers, and the landscape through which it operated came to define its relationship with Pueblo and the nation.

PART II
Economic Development in the Great American Desert

6

Connecting Tracks

Pueblo, Stone City, and the Railroad

While the Colorado-Kansas Railway never achieved the success its founders dreamed of, it still played an important role in the local, national, and even world economy. The model of metropolis and hinterland, argued so elegantly in *Nature's Metropolis* by William Cronon, works well to illustrate this argument. Like Chicago and the Great West, Pueblo has a symbiotic relationship with its surrounding area, a relationship between *nature* and *metropolis*, between metropolis and hinterland. In this case, Pueblo serves as the metropolis, and Stone City serves as the hinterlands, where resources are extracted and transported to the metropolis. By connecting Stone City to Pueblo, a distance of over twenty-two miles, the railroad served as a small link in a vast national rail network of rail linkages.[1]

The burgeoning metropolis of Pueblo functioned as a gateway to the hinterlands, from the plains to the east and the rugged mountains to the west, and as an entrepôt, a "processing, collection, and redistribution center" that connected the hinterlands to the outside world.[2] Originally established in 1842 as a trading post serving Indigenous tribes, Mexican settlers, and

DOI: 10.5876/9781646421282.c006

Americans, and later a bona fide settlement founded at the beginning of the 1859 gold rush, Pueblo quickly developed into a major industrial center in the American West.[3] By 1910, Pueblo had 44,395 residents, and by 1930 that number had grown to 50,996.[4] Railroads turned the city into a hub, with lines running in all four compass directions. With large coal deposits to the west and south, vast mineral resources coming down from the mountains on the railroads, and a ready supply of water from the Arkansas River, ore-processing smelters and a large steel mill greatly expanded the industrial character of Pueblo. These industries defined the city both by employing thousands of men who turned out products necessary for the continuing industrialization and modernization of America and by filling the sky with a black, smoky pall, and covering the city in a layer of grime and soot. Pueblo was a blue-collar town with a blue-collar reputation.[5]

In 1912, a new railroad stretched across the prairie, a new connection to the hinterlands for Pueblo, and a path for raw materials to flow outward and to bring recognition and economic gain to the region. Those twin foundations were only a middle step in a series of connections to the region-at-large. Take the steel rails, for instance, rolled in the open-hearth furnaces of the Colorado Fuel & Iron company.[6] Their composition came from iron ore mined in Wyoming or Colorado; the coal, and subsequently, coke, used in the steelmaking process, most likely came from CF&I mines near the Colorado towns of Trinidad or Crested Butte; and the limestone necessary for converting iron into steel probably came from Monarch, Colorado. The untreated yellow pine crossties were cut from trees growing near Cimarron, New Mexico.[7] If records still existed, they would tell that the lumber for the railroad's two depots, or the corrugated iron used for its engine house, themselves were connected to far away locales. Even steam locomotive No. 1, purchased secondhand from the Colorado Midland Railway, traced its nativity to Pennsylvania.[8] The list is practically endless. Already, before the first trainload of stone ever made its way from Stone City to places distant, the railroad had connections to the land that stretched north and south, east and west. The economic reality of 1912, however, focused the Colorado-Kansas Railway owners on one thing: getting stone and clay to market.

A railroad does not stay in business without a steady source of revenue, and this was the case with the Colorado-Kansas Railway as it struggled to stay financially solvent throughout its existence by finding new sources of

FIGURE 6.1. *View of Victoria Avenue and the Arkansas River from the roof of the Vail Hotel, circa 1912. The Colorado-Kansas Railway's depot and station tracks are partially visible on the left. Courtesy of Pueblo County Historical Society.*

revenue when its old ones dried up. Although stone and clay were the initial impetus for building the railroad as it came to exist, other sources of revenue had potential. One way to examine the different business opportunities along the line is to take an imaginary ride on the Colorado-Kansas Railway.

The Colorado-Kansas Railway had its passenger depot on Victoria Avenue, in Pueblo, Colorado, on the north bank of the Arkansas, just across the river from the power plant of the Pueblo & Suburban Traction & Lighting Company. Its depot was originally designed to be constructed of fine Turkey Creek stone. The owners of the railroad and quarries could not have asked for a better advertisement for their product than their own public façade, the passenger depot.[9] Slated to cost $25,000, the grand depot was apparently too much cash for the little railroad to spend, so the owners settled for something less grand, a former blacksmith shop along their tracks at Victoria Avenue. The structure originally belonging to blacksmith John A. C. Kretschmer, the railroad tore down the brick portion of it but retained the wood-frame building directly adjacent to their tracks. Kretschmer's father was a pioneer of Pueblo, arriving in the city from Germany about 1870. The senior Kretschmer opened a blacksmith shop, where John learned his craft of wagon making and blacksmithing

FIGURE 6.2. *The Kretschmer blacksmith shop prior to being repurposed for the Colorado-Kansas Railway's Victoria Avenue depot, 1912. Courtesy of Pueblo County Historical Society.*

under his tutelage.[10] After demolition of most of the buildings on the site, the repurposed depot was fifty-seven feet long, a one-story wooden structure with a false front, across which was sprawled the railroad's name in large, flowing letters.[11] From this depot, passengers boarded the railroad's only passenger car, a combination baggage and passenger coach, at 10:30 in the morning. The train would return from Stone City at 4:30 in the afternoon.[12] One dollar bought a round-trip ticket.[13]

Pueblo has always had a relationship with the Arkansas River. Founded first as a trading post in 1842 at the confluence of the Arkansas River and the Fountaine qui Bouille, or "Boiling Fountain" (now known as Fountain Creek), Pueblo served as a hub of trails along the Front Range of Colorado, and though the rivers were not navigable, they still functioned as sources of irrigation and landmarks.[14] The town grew up on both sides of the river, to the effect that the river cut through the middle of Pueblo's business district. Following the damaging floods of 1893 and 1894, the residents of Pueblo attempted to confine the river into a levee channel, hoping to contain its fury and limit destruction. As an improvement, Pueblo designed the new channel to handle 40,000 cubic feet of water per second.[15] Pueblo, however, had not seen the worst the river had to offer.

FIGURE 6.3. *Victoria Avenue depot, circa 1912. Author's collection.*

On the afternoon of June 3, 1921, torrential rains to the west had swollen the river beyond its banks. Pounding thunderstorms upstream sent a wall of water crashing through Pueblo, unleashing a force that caused over $10 million in damage, destroying 500 buildings and claiming a confirmed 156 lives from Pueblo to La Junta, with an additional 147 persons missing.[16] From the Denver & Rio Grande's railyards along the bluffs, to the new downtown area on the north, the river, rushing at more than 100,000 cubic feet per second, crested at over twenty-seven feet above flood stage, removing wooden structures and weakening stone buildings.[17] All of the railroads suffered massive amounts of damage to tracks, locomotives, and other rolling stock. The Colorado-Kansas lost 6 percent of its existing trackage, along with its passenger depot at Victoria Avenue. This track was rebuilt in 1925, along with spurs to reach customers for the Pueblo Terminal Railway, for whom the Colorado-Kansas did the switching.[18] A flood map produced in 1921 shows that their yards and engine house would have been awash from the Dry Creek overflow but were situated far enough north of the Arkansas that there was little irreparable damage.[19]

The railroad soldiered on during the remainder of the summer, rebuilding the levee and clearing debris from the flood.[20] Its depot was gone, washed away, and its trackage through Pueblo lay in ruins. Pueblo rebuilt the levee, but the railroad's depot remained missing in action, a casualty of the flood, never to be rebuilt. In 1925, crews went to work on the line destroyed by the flood, grading the right-of-way south to Victoria Avenue in preparation of relaying steel to the Victoria station site.[21]

Following the flood, proposals appeared to ensure that a disaster of this magnitude would not happen again. The final solution to the problem is remarkably similar to one proposal from the Colorado-Kansas Railway, published in the *Pueblo Chieftain* in July 1921.[22] The river channel was removed from the business district and rerouted to the south along the bluffs, where the Rio Grande yards were located, and placed inside a giant earthen and concrete levee, much taller than the previous one, and twice as high as the floodwaters had crested. Subsequent completion of the Pueblo Reservoir in 1976 effectively tamed the Arkansas and put an end to the floods in Pueblo.[23]

By channeling the river away from the city's center and confining it within a concrete barrier that kept it from view, Pueblo suffered a geoenvironmental disconnection from the river—in essence, out of sight, out of mind.[24] The people had lost what had once been an important relationship between themselves and the river. In an effort to revivify this relationship and to revitalize Pueblo's historic district, the city has renewed the original river channel through town, turning it into a park, with green space and miles of trails. It is an effort designed to not only recall the past but reconnect Puebloans with the river, a connection to bridge nature and urban and human. The incongruity is that the river is a built environment, long since taken from its natural state, and the relationship, while renewed, could never be the same as that with the first settlers to the region. In the general location of the former Colorado-Kansas Railway depot now stands a large, steel gazebo, a cultural gathering place for the people of Pueblo to celebrate life and all its changes, while overlooking Lake Elizabeth in the former river channel.

Continuing on its journey, the little Colorado-Kansas locomotive and train would travel along the winding, cottonwood-lined river levee the railroad company had built up, passing under the Fourth Street Bridge, which crossed over the river. Just past the bridge was a short spur track to a sand and gravel pit.[25] From there, it skirted Peppersauce Bottoms, an area of small truck

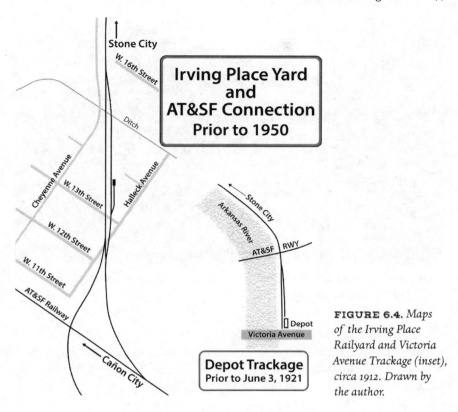

FIGURE 6.4. Maps of the Irving Place Railyard and Victoria Avenue Trackage (inset), circa 1912. Drawn by the author.

farms, before running along the south edge of the Colorado State Insane Asylum and, after a mile and a half of travel, reached its junction with the Santa Fe's Cañon City Branch Line.

From their all-important connection with the Santa Fe, empty cars moved from across the nation—from railroads such as the Missouri Pacific, Colorado & Southern, and Rock Island, even the Reading from far-flung Pennsylvania. The Colorado-Kansas brought these cars back to the Santa Fe, or sometimes the Rio Grande, loaded with cut, decorative stone, or with clay. Although only directly connected to the Santa Fe, interchange rights gave it connections to the other railroads in Pueblo: the Denver & Rio Grande Western, the Missouri Pacific, Colorado & Southern, and Pueblo Terminal Railway.[26] With the major railyard relocation in the mid-1920s to make the Pueblo Conservancy District improvements, the Colorado-Kansas also gained a

FIGURE 6.5. *The Baker Steam Motor Car manufacturing plant, circa 1918. Courtesy of Pueblo County Historical Society.*

direct connection with the Denver & Rio Grande Western.[27] Records from 1923, for example, show cars coming in from the Santa Fe, Chicago, Burlington & Quincy, Missouri Pacific, Southern Pacific, Union Pacific, Western Pacific, New York Central, Pennsylvania, and Reading. By far, the largest number of cars came from the Santa Fe and the Missouri Pacific.[28]

Just beyond the Santa Fe junction was Irving Place, site of their railyard and locomotive service facility. Three tracks, each over 1,000 feet in length, stretched between West Twelfth and West Sixteenth Streets and gave plenty of room for the cars to be set out and shuffled around. A seventy-foot-long engine shed made of corrugated iron dominated the site, as well as a standpipe for watering the thirsty iron horse, and a thirty-three-foot-long coaling dock to feed it.[29] A small toolshed might have served double duty as a station in the early years, but the railroad later replaced it with a retired boxcar. A shed also served as the garage for the railroad's Model-T Ford railway maintenance car.[30] The railroad owned a section house next to the yard, where the section hands who maintained the track lived. In later years, when the railroad did not need so many section hands, they rented out the house.[31]

From the yard the train traveled northwest, up the center of Tuxedo Boulevard for about half a mile alongside Dry Creek, before turning due

FIGURE 6.6. *Dry Creek Trestle north of Pueblo, circa 1930. Courtesy of Pueblo City-County Library District.*

north. This was the outskirts of town in 1912 and remains nearly so today. The prairie begins here, stretching away westward to the bluffs of the Arkansas River and beyond to the mountains' gate at Cañon City, thirty-five miles distant. From here, the train crossed Twenty-ninth Street, past the large, long, cinder-block factory of the Baker Steam Motor Car & Manufacturing Company. The company, which existed from 1918 to 1924, built a steam-powered motor car, similar to the better-known Stanley Steamer. The factory would have provided revenue for the railroad hauling the materials in and finished cars out, but the steam car idea never took off. Baker ended up building only a couple of dozen automobiles in total.[32]

In 1922, Baker equipped one of its trucks to run on rails and ran an excursion for distinguished guests on the Colorado-Kansas from his factory, out to Stone City. Baker intended his rail trucks to replace steam locomotives for short hauls on shortlines and larger railroads as a cost-cutting measure. According to the *Pueblo Chieftain*, the entire population of Stone City turned out to witness their arrival.[33]

In later years, the old Baker factory would be the home of the Pueblo County Shops, with a spur built into them from the main line. Still later, after World War II, the Chicago Freight Car & Parts Company built their plant on the other side of the tracks from the County Shops. Chicago Freight Car became the source of a majority of the railroad's revenue and will be discussed in chapter 16.

Beyond the Dry Creek Bridge, the first substantial wooden trestle on the railroad, the tracks passed through a platted subdivision known as Wiley Heights, but nothing was ever developed in this area until the end of the twentieth century. It then crossed what would later become US Highway 50 and turned northwest again. At this point, the railroad skirted the northern edge of over 16,000 acres of shortgrass prairie. Considered unsuitable for agriculture since the area only received twelve to fifteen inches of rain a year, it would soon be put under irrigation.[34] The land through this stretch of the Colorado-Kansas line is categorized as Great Plains Dry Steppe. Known as shortgrass prairie or semidesert—consisting mostly of sagebrush and rabbitbrush—buffalo, grama, wheatgrass, needlegrass are about the only grasses that can survive the aridity. Prickly pear and cholla grow as well but are sparser.[35] The dry, rolling prairie supports jackrabbits, coyotes, antelope, and mule deer, as well as numerous rodents such as black-tailed prairie dogs, ground squirrels, hares, and pocket voles. Coveys of scaled quail flurry around while western meadowlarks fill the spring air with their cheerful songs, and horned larks, lark buntings, and red-tailed hawks call the skies their home. Burrowing owls occupy abandoned prairie dog towns. Plains spadefoot toads serenade the clouds on the rare rainy nights. On the creepier side of life, giant desert centipedes, with their bright orange bodies and black stripes, crawl around with tarantulas, while bull snakes vie for territory with rattlesnakes. These multitudinous inhabitants of the land would soon find themselves sharing their home with humans in another grandiose, but ill-fated, venture.

7

Tales of the Teller Cousins

The agricultural history of the lands of northwest Pueblo County exemplifies the problems with trying to earn a profit in the "Great American Desert." Between Pueblo and Stone City lay tens of thousands of acres of desert prairie, seeming not useful for anything other than cattle ranching. Whether or not the Colorado-Kansas Railway would carry a lot of livestock remained to be seen. However, in a flurry of activity coinciding almost exactly with the planning and construction of the railroad, grandiose plans were afoot to turn the pastureland into a veritable garden for agriculture. In what is now Pueblo West, 16,000 acres of land went through a tumultuous few years of development schemes in an attempt to profit off of it. If successful, the schemes would have increased the traffic of the railroad and assured its continued existence in a more stable fashion.

The story of this particular tract of land began in 1885 with one of the most famous names in Colorado history. Fresh off his tenure as secretary of the interior, in March 1885, Henry M. Teller resumed his seat in the United States Senate, having been reelected for his second term. By that fall, he

DOI: 10.5876/9781646421282.c007

began acquiring land patents from the United States government. Thirty-five of them, between November 1885 and October 1886, granted him 11,886.05 acres, and an additional two patents for nearly 500 acres in April 1888 and February 1892, respectively, brought his landholdings in Pueblo County to 12373.83 acres. Most of this land was in Township 20 South, Range 66 West; essentially, this is all of the modern community of Pueblo West south of US Highway 50.[1] In December 1885, Teller deeded these lands, along with acreage in Township 20 South, Range 67 West, to Willard Teller, Harper M. Orahood, and William Fullerton.[2]

Prior to his political career, Teller ran a law firm with his brother, Willard, in Central City, Colorado. The Teller brothers were joined in 1873 by Harper M. Orahood.[3] Teller, along with his law partners, Willard, and Orahood, organized the Turkey Creek Land & Cattle Company, on June 22, 1887.[4] In September they transferred ownership of these lands to their new company.[5] The Teller tract, as it came to be known, was used for raising cattle. Senator Teller had considered a series of reservoirs extending from Turkey Creek on land owned by the Turkey Creek Land & Cattle Company, and he even filed a survey map in March 1886, for the Turkey Creek Ditch and Reservoir System, about six miles due south of where the Teller Reservoir would eventually be built.[6] This filing might have opened up some of the land for agriculture; however, no reservoirs appear to have been constructed.[7]

On March 9, 1892, the Turkey Creek Land & Cattle Company sold 15,644 acres in Pueblo County to John C. Teller for $200,000.[8] This sale included the land, associated water rights, and leases from the state of Colorado. Harper M. Orahood held the deed of trust for promissory notes worth $112,500 at a 5 percent annual interest rate.[9] To help pay for the land, Teller took out a mortgage on the 15,644 acres, along with several lots in the city of Pueblo, from Joseph A. Thatcher of Denver for $50,000 on March 29, 1895. The promissory note was payable in one year.[10] Teller lost the 9,900-acre state land lease in 1903 for failure to pay $1,300 in rental fees, a sign that his business ventures were, perhaps, chronically underfunded.[11]

John C. Teller was a first cousin to Senator Henry M. Teller, though his junior by twenty years. Their grandfather was Remsen Teller, of Schenectady, New York.[12] John C. Teller's father was Isaac Teller, the first-born son of Remsen and Catherine Teller.[13] Isaac's younger brother, John, was born February 15, 1800.[14] Isaac later moved to Canada, where his son, John C., was born to him and his wife, Anna.[15] Teller moved to the United States by the time he was twenty, where he found work as a boatman in Buffalo, New York.[16] He lived for a few years in Bay City, Michigan, in the early 1880s.[17] It was perhaps his cousin Henry who convinced John C. to move to Colorado, for by 1885 he was living in silver boom town of Aspen, Colorado, working in mining operations.[18] It was also in Aspen, where, perhaps trying to follow in his cousin's footsteps, John C. Teller ran unsuccessfully for state senator in 1886.[19] The Denver City Directory lists him as a railroad contractor in 1888, the first year he shows up in Denver directories.[20]

John C. Teller first made his name in the West in the timber industry, supplying railroad ties for the rapid western railroad expansion. The Union Pacific proposed and began construction in 1886 on an abortive rail line from Fort Steele, Wyoming, to Aspen, Colorado. The Blue River Division would have run approximately forty miles from Dillon to Aspen.[21] The Union Pacific awarded John C. Teller the railroad tie contract to supply 5,009,000 standard gauge railroad ties for their new Blue River Division.[22] Even though the Union Pacific abandoned the idea, Teller did not give up. As late as 1897, he was still determined to build a rail line from Fort Steele, Wyoming, that connected with the Colorado Midland.[23]

Over a decade before John J. Burns attempted to build an electrified railroad from Pueblo to Beulah, John C. Teller had been connected to a similar scheme. In September 1889, Teller and J. F. Drake, an attorney in Pueblo, sent a corps of engineers into the field to begin surveying the Pueblo & Western Railroad, which would build from Pueblo to Beulah, on to Red Creek Springs, and into the Wet Mountain Valley by way of Rosita and Silver Cliff.[24] The Pueblo & Western scheme, later referred to as the Pueblo, Beulah Springs and Rosita Railway, died out for lack of money, though capitalists in Silver Cliff attempted to revive it in 1891.[25] John J. Burns would bring the idea back again in another ten years. Teller doesn't appear to have any connection to Burns's attempt, though because they worked on other ventures, it is quite possible there was some relationship there.

For a brief year or so, John C. Teller was president of the J. C. Teller Envelope Company in Denver, incorporated in 1895.[26] The company produced regular envelopes, but their specialty was an envelope with a thread to open the envelope without a knife or letter opener. Robert O. Brigham, of Denver, invented and patented an attachment for an envelope machine to produce these special envelopes.[27] Teller expected to eventually enlarge his factory enough to turn out 3 million envelopes a day using paper made in Denver and to employ about 100 people.[28] In 1896, though, Brigham bought out Teller's interest in the company and later moved the business to Nebraska and, finally, Illinois.[29]

Teller had mining interests in Carbon County, Wyoming, among other places in the region, though his Carbon County connection was built through the timber industry.[30] Much of Teller's career was spent cutting timber for railroad ties for the Union Pacific Railroad, and it is this industry that may have cost him much grief and money for court fees. Teller gained infamy by unlawfully cutting railroad ties from timber on government land. He was often able to get out of trouble, perhaps by leaning on his government contacts, such as Senator Henry M. Teller. In 1898, Teller illegally cut 350,000 for the Union Pacific and was threatened with legal action, before intervention at the highest levels allowed him to avoid prosecution. As the *Salt Lake Herald* described it on August 6, "Through strong influence in Washington, Mr. Teller was permitted to dispose of his ties to the Union Pacific, but not until he signed a contract with Uncle Sam to pay, at any time he is called upon to do so, the full market value of the ties. Mr. Teller relies upon his Washington 'pull' to extricate himself from his present difficulties. The steal of this timber from government land was one of the boldest in the history of the west, and Mr. Teller is lucky if he escapes punishment."[31]

The timber contractor was not yet out of the woods, though. Teller brought suit against the US government seeking to recover damages for 47,000 railroad ties cut unlawfully on government land. The government seized them in July 1898 and subsequently sold them, but only after Teller had signed the agreement with the general land office to pay for them and they had been released to him. Teller won in federal court and was awarded $18,843 in compensation. However, promptly at the close of the trial, Teller and his foreman, L. V. Bruce, were arrested for unlawfully cutting timber on government land.[32] The government appealed the jury's award decision, but it was upheld in appeals court.[33] As a result of the trial, Teller was convicted November 17, 1900, in the District Court of Wyoming and fined $1,000.[34] The United States also instituted a civil suit against Teller in the Circuit Court of Colorado in June 1901 and secured judgment against him for $27,964.[35] The Eighth Circuit Court reversed the judgment.[36] Teller seemed untouchable, though the $1,000 fine plus various court costs hung over his head until President Theodore Roosevelt granted him a remission of the fine and costs on November 7, 1905.[37]

The government was still out to get the scofflaw. In 1901, Teller was still cutting over 500,000 ties for the Union Pacific from lands in Wyoming.[38] On May 8, 1905, a federal grand jury handed down two indictments against Teller for unlawfully cutting 100,000 railroad ties, worth $39,000 on government land in Carbon County, Wyoming, between fall 1901 and spring 1902. Teller, along with his cousin Henry, appeared before the judge in May 1907 to agree to John C. Teller's $1,000 bond. The indictments were dismissed July 15, 1907, when Teller was allowed to avoid criminal liability by paying for his trespass a rate of $2.50 per acre, or roughly $1,700.[39] The government brought a civil suit against Teller and the Union Pacific in 1908 for the same crime, seeking $390,000. Teller was again allowed to pay the $2.50 per acre cost.[40]

Within a few years, in November 1895, Teller leased 3,200 acres of his Pueblo County land for $100 a year, plus 10 percent royalties, for possible oil and gas production to E. C. Kurtz. The *Colorado Weekly Chieftain* in Pueblo speculated that Kurtz might be representing the Standard Oil Company, based upon earlier rumors, but this allegation was not confirmed.[41] No work was ever done, however, and the lease lapsed after a year.[42] Then, the Arkansas Valley Oil Company incorporated in Denver on May 14, 1901. J. C. Teller was one of the investors, along with H. P. Vories and J. W. Purdy of Pueblo, and H. S. McFall, of Pittsburg. The company capitalized at $250,000, with investors from back east, as well as from Colorado Springs, Denver, and Pueblo. They leased the Teller ranch and additional land west of Pueblo, 45,000 acres' worth, to prospect for oil. McFall had experience in oil development in Pennsylvania and West Virginia, and he would lead the drilling of a 3,000-foot well.[43] Nothing came of this venture. On October 8, 1915, Teller leased to Columbine Oil & Gas, the president of which was Robert K. Potter, the rights to drill for oil and gas, as well as to construct pipelines.[44] Even when this lease played out, Teller and others were convinced there was oil on the property. Shortly before his death in 1917, Teller leased the rights for gas and oil to the Big Eight Oil Company.[45]

John C. Teller had considered building a canal on the Teller tract as early as 1903. On February 14 of that year, Teller, along with Senator Henry M. Teller, visited the US Geological Survey in Washington, DC, and presented his proposal to F. H. Newell, the bureau's irrigation expert, to construct an irrigation canal in the Arkansas Valley. It was Teller's hope that the government would be willing to allow the canal to carry floodwaters to storage in potential reservoirs at government-owned land along the proposed canal. Newell suggested this plan was feasible, and both Tellers left the meeting pleased with the interview.[46]

In a surprising turn of events, in December 1904, the *Pueblo Chieftain* reported that Teller sold his 15,600 acres, which was "for many years recognized as one of the great cattle grazing operations of the county, and at different times has been stocked with many thousands of head of livestock," to the Turkey Creek Land & Cattle Company. In one of the rare instances of truth surrounding this property, the paper noted that "very little can be used for agricultural purposes." The paper noted the sale was for an undisclosed sum, but the truth was far more telling.[47] Teller had paid only a part of the indebtedness on the land by 1904, so he returned the land he had bought back to the Turkey Creek Land & Cattle Company in exchange for being released from the mortgage.[48]

John C. Teller would not be gone from the property very long, for in September 1908 the Turkey Creek Land & Cattle Company made an offer to sell the same land to Teller and John J. Burns, the man who had previously tried to build the Pueblo and Beulah Valley electric railway. The Turkey Creek Land & Cattle Company offered to sell approximately 15,648 acres in Pueblo County, with associated water rights, to Teller and Burns for $93,888, but upon the condition that they sink one or more artesian wells on the property, invest a minimum of $5,000 to improve the land, and pay $5,000 to the company within six months. The notes payable would be $10,000 on or before 6 months from March 1, 1909, and then three equal payments of $26,296 on or before 12, 18, and 24 months, respectively. Interest would be 6 percent per annum, payable semiannually, in deferred payments. Conditionally, if these terms weren't met by the aforementioned dates, then the Turkey Creek Land & Cattle Company could repossess the land.[49] This was half the price of the first purchase, but the Turkey Creek Land & Cattle Company may have taken previous payments into account when they offered to sell it again.

The impetus for Teller to pursue this same land in Pueblo County a second time likely has to do with two significant developments in 1908: first, the announcement of the construction of the Kansas-Colorado Railroad and, second, the location of a dam and reservoir on Turkey Creek simultaneous to the railroad planning and construction. These two enterprises would make the land far more valuable and open to development than it had ever been. Teller had the land, but he lacked the water for irrigation. He lacked a reservoir and a ditch system and needed to rectify the situation with haste. A lot of work had yet to be done to make the land usable for agriculture and settlement, and with the railroad seemingly on its way, time was of the essence.

8

Dam Troubles

In 1890, the US government located and surveyed land along Turkey Creek in northwestern Pueblo County, reserving portions of sections 19, 20, 20, 30, and 31 of Township 18 South Range 66 West for a potential reservoir. These 1,000 acres of land were segregated on February 27, 1891, and designated Reservoir Site No. 21.[1] As early as January 1901, Richard S. Fuller, of Denver, filed for a dam on Reservoir Site 21. Maps and statements for the reservoir site were approved by the secretary of the interior on June 30, 1903.[2] Between March 4, 1907, and September of that year, Fuller carried out a work site survey and tests of materials on the property, but whether he began constructing a dam in not known.[3] In fact, Robert K. Potter would create a competing claim by also filing for the Potter–Turkey Creek Reservoir on Reservoir Site 21 in September 1908. According to the filing plat, Potter's first survey and soundings on the reservoir site took place on July 30, 1908, the same day as the groundbreaking for the Kansas-Colorado Railroad and as A. B. Hulit's tour to the dam site. Potter originally projected the dam to be 100 feet in height, with a capacity of 425,000,000 cubic feet, though he revised this figure in 1909

DOI: 10.5876/9781646421282.c008

FIGURE 8.1. *A. B. Hulit and party inspecting the future site of the Teller Reservoir, July 1, 1908. Author's collection.*

to a capacity of 634,317,891 cubic feet. The construction cost was estimated to be \$200,000.[4] On October 12, 1908, Potter bought 320 acres of land, situated in the middle of the segregated reservoir site, from John Palmer and the estate of Thomas J. Tong for \$1,600.[5] The forty-acre-wide strip of land along Turkey Creek previously belonged to the Raynolds Cattle Company, though Thomas J. Tong, John Palmer, and Fred Bean purchased it January 5, 1895.[6] John Palmer deeded the land to Potter October 12, 1908.[7] Potter's filing was approved by the secretary of the interior on August 22, 1910.[8] Although known in the present day as the Teller Reservoir, its official name in government records is still the Potter–Turkey Creek Reservoir.

Potter may have been working alone, but it is more likely he was working in conjunction with Teller and Burns, for it was the Teller Reservoir & Irrigation Company that had the dam constructed and owned the water rights.[9] Potter deeded the reservoir lands and water rights to Teller's attorney, H. E. Brayton, as trustee, on April 5, 1909.[10] Potter and Teller concluded an agreement in writing for the purchase by Teller Reservoir & Irrigation Company of lands and water rights from Potter for \$25,000.[11] Initial plans for the reservoir also included a big resort at the small community of Lytle

FIGURE 8.2. *A. B. Hulit viewing Teller Reservoir dam site from opposite side, July 1, 1908. Author's collection.*

adjacent to the reservoir site. An artesian well had already been drilled on the proposed resort site, with a flow of one cubic foot per second. The resort plans never reappeared after the first mention.[12] Whether anything would come of the latest reservoir plans was questionable. As the *Pueblo Chieftain* noted, "The map of the proposed reservoir takes in a portion of the proposed site of another company which filed last year. Several individuals and companies have been filing on reservoir sites, but so far none of the schemes have been carried out . . . [S]o far no one has secured the capital to construct the irrigation systems necessary."[13] Teller appeared to be the one who could do it.

Richard Fuller's prior claim to the reservoir site came to the attention of the Teller Reservoir & Irrigation Company by September 1909, for John J. Burns arranged for Fuller and Messrs. Monson and Malcom to sell their claim on the "Fuller Turkey Creek Reservoir" filings to the company, for which he would receive a $1,000 commission.[14] Fuller filed a quit claim deed to Teller on June 11, 1909, seemingly ending any potential controversial claims to the reservoir.[15] Teller's claim to the reservoir and lands would later be challenged in court, with the plaintiff, Frank L. Tebow, of Denver, alleging that John

C. Teller took possession of land that Tebow had already filed upon, for the Pueblo Reservoir and Reservoir Site. Tebow claimed in the suit that he had already started construction of a dam, in March 1907, and had continued work throughout 1908 and 1909. Frank Tebow alleged that Teller did this with full knowledge that Tebow already had filed upon and owned the land. Contradicting himself, though, he attested that he did not discover that his claim had been jumped by Teller's company until March 1910.[16] Considering that Teller's contractors had been working on the dam since March 1909, it seems unlikely that Tebow was simultaneously working at the same site, and, if he indeed was working, that he would have been unaware of the other construction work.[17]

Tebow sued to get his land and reservoir back, along with $60,000, but the appellate court ruled that Tebow did not own the land at the time he filed the map and that filing the map did not constitute possession of the land title. Tebow's appeal was rejected by the court, and Teller maintained ownership.[18] It is unknown if the Tebow and Fuller claims are connected, but the fact that both use March 1907 as their filing date is striking, and perhaps not coincidental. Fuller was a civil engineer and Pueblo County surveyor from 1899 to 1904, but by 1907 he was listed a civil engineer living in Denver. It is possible he may have filed on Tebow's behalf, though never turned over the rights to the reservoir site.[19] In any case, in 1909 claim to the reservoir site was firmly in the hands of Teller and Burns.

With no time to waste, John C. Teller; John J. Burns; and Teller's son, Edward C. Teller, organized the Teller Reservoir & Irrigation Company in April 1909.[20] The purchase was divided into two transactions, with the first 5,220 acres sold to the new company on August 17, 1909.[21] At the time of the sale, the Turkey Creek Land & Cattle Company's charter had expired, so the company was reincorporated on March 10, 1910.[22] The sale had to be reentered into the books by the trustees of the former company on October 28, 1910.[23] The final 10,304 acres were deeded to Teller and Burns on April 19, 1911.[24] The Continental Trust Co. of Denver held the mortgage, or deed of trust, of $350,000, which included financing to build the reservoir.[25] John W. Springer organized the Continental Trust Company in Denver in 1902 and was instrumental in financing irrigation projects in Colorado, including the Fountain Valley Land and Irrigation Company in Colorado Springs and the North Platte Canal and Colonization Company. His belief was that "Colorado money should be kept at home and that all Colorado enterprises should be heartily supported by the financial interests of the State."[26] William Fullerton, partner of Henry M. Teller, held the majority of the mortgage bonds issued, with ownership of $136,500 in bonds. The Arkansas Valley Construction Company held $65,500, Continental Trust held $61,000, and Nellie Kinman held $14,000 through J. W. Springer, while Harper M. Orahood only held $5,500 worth.[27] Teller added 260 acres of School Lands, purchased from the state of Colorado for $1,300, on September 22, 1911.[28]

Chief engineer on the Teller project was T. W. Jaycox, who had spent six years as the state engineer of Colorado and thus was well suited to designing and building the project. The earthen and concrete dam, situated in a cañon, would be 106 feet in height, with a length of 760 feet and width of 22 feet, and consist of 410,00 cubic yards of earth and 3,000 cubic yards of concrete. Two concrete conduits, 466 feet long, would carry the water from the dam intake to the spillway. The basin of the reservoir covered 721 acres and contained 971,317,921 cubic feet of water, or 23,000 acre-feet.[29] Jaycox wrote to Teller, "I am willing to stake my reputation as a Hydraulic Engineer, that when the Turkey Creek Dam and Reservoir is completed it will be one of the very best, and the canals will have a carrying capacity sufficient for the proper irrigation of these lands."[30] Since water in irrigation systems is lost through seepage and breaks, state engineer Welles estimated that the short length of the canal would prevent much loss.[31] Plans for the reservoir and dam were approved by the state on July 29, 1909.[32] Jaycox expected the cost of the dam, reservoir, canal, and laterals to be $240,000. The main canal would be 12 miles in length, 4 feet deep, 16 feet wide at the bottom, and 24 feet wide at the tops and have a carrying capacity of 240 cubic feet of water per second.[33]

On April 22, 1909, at the same time that John C. Teller was organizing the Teller Reservoir & Irrigation Company, he entered into a contract with the Mesa Land Company to market and sell the land.[34] Mesa Land Company would begin selling the land from offices in Chicago, Kansas City, and Pueblo.[35] While details of the contract have not come to light, it was limited in the amount of land for sale. The general selling agent for the Teller tract, Vernon J. Rose, of the Mesa Land & Trust Company in Kansas City, Missouri, wrote to Teller on August 9, 1909, reporting that his company had sold over 1,000 acres, at $80 per acre. The price would be rising to $100 on September 1. The company ran its first excursion to the Teller tract, marketed as "Pueblo

Gardens," on June 17 and had been getting "quite a good response to our advertising, considering that it was midsummer and the farmers were busy with their crops."[36] The *Rocky Mountain News* reported that many eastern men "were taken in automobiles today on an extensive trip over the property. Many of them expressed themselves as highly please with the prospect, and some big sales were consummated, one of the visitors making a $9,000 purchase."[37] Rose was hopeful that Teller would extend the contract to the entire amount of the land, but that did not happen.[38]

Senator Teller and Harper M. Orahood wrote to John C. Teller in August 1909 to express their approval of the progress to that point and that they would be investing in the bonds of the company, as well as conveying the deed to the remaining 10,644 acres of land.[39] Through the Mesa Land Company, the Teller Reservoir & Irrigation Company planned to sell the land to prospective farmers using advertising in newspapers across the Midwest, as far away as Indianapolis, touting the availability of 10 to 160 acres of land, ready to plow and plant alfalfa, wheat, oats, barley, sugar beets, potatoes, and cantaloupes, along with various fruits and berries, all grown in abundance in the region.[40] Colloquially known as "Teller's pasture," the company renamed it to the more enticing Pueblo Gardens. Small farmers could purchase 10 to 20 acres for fruit and truck farming, or larger 80- and 160-acre farms.[41] The company described the soil as "rich and fertile, from five to twenty feet deep," though anyone who has ever watched a house being built in Pueblo West can attest to the layer of rock just under the topsoil.[42] Stone quarries near the future site of Stone City offered fine-yet-inexpensive building stone, at seventy-five cents a yard, for the most affordable houses in the "middle states." They even promised to throw in a free set of plans for a house and barn to the purchaser of property.[43] By June 1910, however, Teller changed his mind about doing business with Mesa Land Company, for he withdrew his land from sale and was reportedly converting 2,000 acres into an experimental farm to "demonstrate the productiveness of the land," once the dam was complete.[44]

William Olson and John Olsen, representing the Arkansas Valley Construction Company of Denver, entered into a $200,000 contract with the Teller Reservoir & Irrigation company in March 1909 to begin construction of the dam, along with the main canal and laterals of the Teller Ditch. Work on the dam commenced on April 28, 1909, and by August, $50,000 in work had been

FIGURE 8.3. *Concrete conduits of the Teller Dam during construction, circa 1910. Courtesy of the Pueblo County Historical Society.*

completed. A force of sixty teams were working to get the dam completed enough to hold water for the next spring's irrigation purposes. By August 15, they expected to have a large force of teams and men working on the main canal.[45]

With the dam still under construction, on July 12, 1910, a flood on Turkey Creek breached the structure, tearing away a section on the west end of the dam. As the deputy state engineer's report noted, the damage was caused not by faulty construction of the dam itself but by the simple fact that the floodwaters crested the incomplete top of the dam. The dam was sixty feet high at that point, forty-six feet short of its ultimate height. Unfortunately, the company believed that flood season had passed, so the conduit valves were closed to allow retention of some water for upcoming irrigation. Several hours of heavy rains began filling the reservoir. When the water reached within five feet of the top of the dam, the workers tried to open the outlet gates to relieve the pressure, to no avail. At noon on July 12, the water breached the west end of the reservoir, creating a chasm 100 feet wide that reached down to the bedrock. To make matters worse, the concrete facing slipped down into the reservoir, blocking the left conduit.[46] Although this turn of events

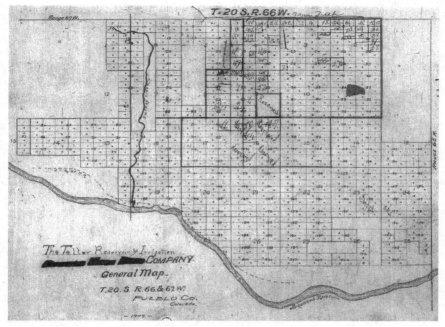

FIGURE 8.4. *Map of the Teller Reservoir & Irrigation Company's lands, 1909. "Pueblo Mesa Land" has been blacked out. John J. Burns Papers, History Colorado-Denver, Colorado.*

was devastating to the construction schedule, homesteaders and about seventy construction workers camped downstream were given enough warning to make harrowing escapes.[47] No deaths were reported, but Teller estimated the damage to be between $25,000 and $40,000.[48]

Teller briefly considered consolidating the Teller Reservoir & Irrigation company with the Colorado Southern Irrigation Company—also known as the Cañon City, Florence, and Pueblo Water Company—but ultimately decided that his plans were too far along to make the consolidation worth it for him.[49] Teller did join with other regional irrigation system owners to form the Colorado Water Conservation Association, to "gather data with a view to prevent unnecessary loss of water available for irrigation purposes . . . , to promote legislation which will have for its object the conservation of the water of all streams in the state, and to promote economical use of the water."[50]

After completion of the Teller Dam in April 1911, John C. Teller announced that a campaign to sell the land to settlers and farmers would start at once. Excursions would run to Pueblo from Kansas, Oklahoma, and Nebraska, bringing in hundreds of farmers, according to the *Chieftain*, "in a manner that will settle up the 16,000 acres in short order and bring to the Pueblo markets the products of this great heretofore barren tract."[51] But this task must have proven daunting to Teller, for by late summer, he turned to outside help to sell off the Teller Gardens.

9

Geo. H. Paul, Boy Wonder

Excitement was brewing in Pueblo at the end of August 1911 as John C. Teller turned to George H. Paul, of Washington, Iowa, a renowned real estate dealer, to market and sell his property in Pueblo County. George Harvey Paul, or Geo. H., as he preferred to be called, can, without a doubt, be added to the list of schemers and dreamers in the Pueblo area.[1] Paul, a man of medium height and slender build, with black hair and blue eyes that looked out from a cherubic face, fit the profile Teller needed to sell his land, a man successful in agriculture, real estate, and business.[2] Paul's projects spanned the North American continent, from Saskatchewan and Alberta in Canada, south to Wyoming, Iowa, Oklahoma, and Corpus Christi, Texas.[3] His Texas operations—which included starting new towns or subdivisions in adjoining towns in Nueces, San Patricio, and Bee Counties in Texas—"were quite imposing."[4] Paul, as he described himself, was "just a farm boy with no business experience, and little education, until," as he put it, "I got my education right in that development Land business, and I went from a very poor farm boy to the head of that large business, in such a short time it was really

DOI: 10.5876/9781646421282.c009

astonishing. It was the largest thing of its kind ever in the United States, and for a country boy that was some leap."[5] This land business had made Paul a millionaire in his thirties.[6]

Geo. H. Paul's father, James Paul, immigrated to Pennsylvania from Ireland in 1827, where he worked on a rented farm. In 1859 he moved his family to Washington County, Iowa, in 1859, where he was able to fulfill the American dream by buying his own farm.[7] It was there that Geo. H. Paul was born on May 6, 1877.[8] Paul was the youngest of twelve children, the first eight from his father's first marriage, followed by four more from his second marriage. His father was sixty-one when Geo. H. was born.[9] At the age of fifteen he went to work as a farmhand. Life began to turn in a different direction, however, when Geo. H. married Eva J. Hunter on July 24, 1899. By 1901 Paul's ambitions grew beyond working on a farm.[10] He and Eva moved into the town of Washington, Iowa, in 1901, where he worked in a grocery store for $25 per month.[11] In 1902, Paul traded a house in Washington for a farm in Washington County. He continued to trade land in 1903, making more money each time. Paul had found his true calling in real estate. He went into business in the spring of 1904 with the friend from whom he had acquired his first farm, and together they expanded into the Canadian land business. Their initial foray in Canada failed, but Paul was undaunted. He acquired the entire operation from his partner and continued selling Canadian land through 1906.[12] Geo. H. even dabbled in the railroad business, deciding in 1907 to build an electric interurban line between Iowa City and Fort Madison, which would bring the rails through Washington. Paul was well into the planning stages for his fledgling railroad, having negotiated for the right-of-way and secured funding for the bond issue with Knickerbocker Trust Company of New York, when the Panic of 1907 dashed his railroad dreams. Knickerbocker's collapse helped create the banking panic, ensuring that Paul would be unable to fund his railroad.[13]

His focus remained, however, on land development, this time in south Texas. Paul made an investigative trip to Texas in January 1907, and upon his return jumped into creating the Geo. H. Paul Company and the organizational infrastructure needed to sell land. His first employee was hired to select the agencies for the various territories across the Midwest. These agencies would receive 15 percent on all sales in their territories. The territorial agents then could subcontract with smaller local agents, or "Bird Dogs," as

Paul called them, at a 10 percent commission. Paul figured it averaged out to about $100 per sale for the Bird Dog. At its height, the Geo. H. Paul Company had between 1,000 and 1,200 agents working on its behalf. To keep track of all of these agents and their territories at the home office, Paul set up what he called the Map Desk, which had sliding boards instead of drawers. When pulled out, each board held maps of the states where they had agents in operation. Colored strings attached with thumbtacks were strung out across the maps, marking the agents' territories to which they were contracted so that one could tell at a glance the geographic coverage of each agent.[14] When he opened his office in Washington, Iowa, Paul hired a woman who was "considered top in the community" and compensated her accordingly, paying her $35 per month. Within two years he was paying all twelve women working in the home office $50 per week. Comparatively, when Paul had hired out as a farmhand in his youth, he had earned between $15 to $18 per month.[15]

With the organization coming together, Geo. H. ran his first prospective buyers' train in March 1907. He only had enough passengers for one private car, and business grew slowly at first, but by the end of the year Paul had required an entire a special train for each excursion.[16] Paul purchased three private passenger cars for his company: the Wamduska, the Etta, and the Taft. All were combination dining and sleeping cars and always used for each excursion. The special trains usually required more cars, which the company rented from the Pullman Company in numbers necessary to handle the potential buyers.[17] The Pullman company required a minimum number of 150 paying passengers for renting a special train.[18] Paul estimated that he regularly carried, on average, between 25 and 28 passengers per car, or between 325 and 364 passengers per train.[19] Paul was especially proud of Wamduska, purchased from James J. Hill, the famous "Empire Builder" of the Great Northern Railway. Paul claimed he bought the best car, Wamduska, which reportedly was an Indigenous word that meant "home finder."[20] Paul ran special trains on the first and third Tuesdays of the month, with a round-trip ticket costing $23 from north of Kansas City and St. Louis. Pullman charged the Paul company $45 per day, so each car cost Paul $450 for the ten-day trip.[21] Winter proved to be the time of heaviest business. Buyers might show interest in the summer but would head south in the winter months to purchase land.[22]

Paul was quite particular about the way he and his agents handled the buyers, refusing to use pushy tactics. This approach even extended to the

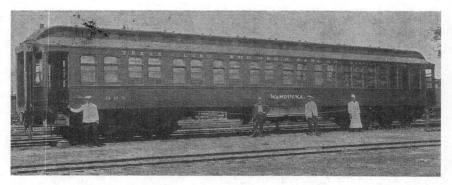

FIGURE 9.1. *The Geo. H. Paul Company's private car, Wamduska, 1909. Author's collection.*

name of his company. Paul never allowed his company to be called the Geo. H. Paul Land Company in any publication, or even have the word "Land" anywhere in the name because of so many "men with bad reputations" who, he felt, had sullied the land business with their dubious and aggressive selling tactics. It was thus always promoted simply as the Geo. H. Paul Company.[23] Every agent was instructed to tell their prospective customers that "Mr. Paul would never ask them to buy land," and he never did. When the agents sensed a customer might be interested in actually buying land, they would lead them back to the Wamduska, where Paul would greet them. His personal sales tactic involved talking about the topography of the area in which the prospective buyer was interested, showing him maps of the property for sale. He would then ask if the customer had noticed that particular piece of land was unsold. "If he showed the least bit of interest, I would ask him what sort of terms he would want, if he were going to buy—if he were able to make the necessary first payment, etc., and before any of us knew, he would have purchased a piece of land. I NEVER asked them to buy as I had learned that no pressure was actually the very highest pressure one could use," Paul recognized.[24] As they continued to discuss the land and terms of purchase, Paul would be furiously writing out the contract as they talked, enough to make his hand cramp. Before turning the finished contract around to the buyer, Paul would first sign his own name as a show of good faith.[25]

The land business was sluggish throughout 1907, with Paul struggling to find sellable land he thought was suitable. His first trains ran to the area around Hebbronville on the Texas Mexican Railway, where the land was good for little more than ranching. Good word-of-mouth brought in more business, though, and by 1908 Paul no longer had to search out more land on his own. "Instead of me looking up lands, it turned the other way, and people with lands for sale looked me up," he reported. "By this time we were making enough stir that we were known as the livest thing that had hit Corpus in years, so I did not have to look for land to handle." Boswell and Speath, land agents for Colonel Robert Driscoll at Robstown, Texas, had little success on their own in selling the Driscoll ranchland, and contacted Geo. H. Paul. After meeting with Paul and his agents, as well as requesting bank references of Paul, Driscoll agreed to turn the land over to Paul to sell.[26]

Seeing Paul's success at selling Driscoll land, Joseph Green, manager of the Coleman-Fulton Pasture Company, approached Paul about a possible deal.[27] The Coleman-Fulton Pasture Company controlled around 265,000 acres of Texas ranchland at its peak, with much of it in San Patricio County. By 1900, Charles P. Taft, half-brother to William Howard Taft, began managing the company. Ownership of the company and its lands had passed into the hands of Taft's wife, Anna, upon the death of her father, David Sinton, a millionaire from Cincinnati, who had purchased the lands from its founders.[28] On Friday, March 13, 1908, Paul entered into a contract to sell a portion of the Taft Ranch lands of the Coleman-Fulton Pasture Company land. Paul was not superstitious about the date. "We made that contract of Friday the thirteenth of March, 1908. It was one of the best deals I ever made, so I have always since told people to not be afraid of Friday the thirteenth."[29]

Paul bought all of the Taft land south of the San Antonio and Aransas Pass Railroad, though "bought" is not exactly the best word to describe the deal. "Of course I purchased without any cash, but the land was to be paid for as sold," Paul acknowledged. He was permitted to sell half of the land within two years, after which he could then sell the other half.[30] Paul purchased the land for $20 per acre and sold it for $35.[31] Sales were so successful that by July 1908, just four months into his contact, Paul and Joseph Green traveled to Taft's headquarters in Cincinnati to request that Taft release the other half of the land to sell. Green did not expect Paul would get the opportunity to meet directly with Charles Taft, but luck was on Paul's side:

> I was 31 years old in 1908, was five foot six and weighed 107 pounds, so looked like some school kid, and when I met Mr. Taft he sure thought I was a prodigy

of some kind . . . We happened to be in the outer office when Mr. Taft came in, so Mr. Green was forced to introduce me to Mr. Taft and took me right into his private office and [except] taking us both to his club for lunch, he and I were alone in his private office all day, and when it came time for him to leave for home in the evening, he and I were sitting together with our feet propped up on the radiator.[32]

Well, he called me "The Boy Wonder" and said ever so many nice things, but was more interested in what made me tick, even than I was overshadowed by his wealth. Well, during that afternoon, when he let all his other matters go for the day, and just visited with me, he laughed and said to me, "You know my brother Bill is running for President this year—of course I am financing his campaign, and we are going to run a campaign special train out through the middle west during the campaign, and we may even go to California, but I was wondering if it would do you any good if I would take that train down to the ranch in Texas, and time it just so as to have [it] arrive when you had one of your trains there."[33]

Now he knew there was no chance of them carrying Texas in those days, so he did this just for me and we had a Barbecue and Rodeo on the ranch, and all my prospective buyers and agents were able to meet the candidate for President, and we pulled in there with two special trains on adjoining tracks at Gregory. That was one of the times my train was large enough that it had to run in two sections on some divisions on the Railroads on the way.[34]

Paul used the Taft name to good effect in his promotional materials. Their circulars printed "TAFT" in a large typeface at the top, hoping to attract voters to see what was being said about the candidate. On the next line, in a smaller typeface, was printed the word "LANDS." This "little joke," as Paul referred to it "was really worth a small fortune to me just at that time."[35] He estimated the Geo. H. Paul Company had sold between 90 to 95 percent of its Taft lands by the end of 1908.[36] According to his best recollection, he had settled about 250,000 acres in the South Texas area, with an estimated sales success rate of 85 percent[37]—not bad for a millionaire "ignorant farm boy, having a lot of fun."[38]

The Geo. H. Paul Company's Texas operations came to a bitter end in 1910, after Paul "got pretty deep" into Colorado and was convinced to sell his Texas business to John Shary and his International Land and Investment Company of Omaha. Shary was one of the Paul company's agents with a state contract in Nebraska. Shary convinced Paul to sell him the Texas lands, wherein he would handle all the business and divide the profits with Paul. Paul agreed, with the stipulation the name be changed to the "International Land and Investment Company, successor to the George H. Paul Company." Paul even let Ralph E. Shannon, his traveling secretary, go over to the new company, along with selling Shary his private railcars. According to Paul, Shary then immediately "told all his help to kill off all reminders of the Paul company, and instead of staying with the lands I had bought, he went to the Valley and contracted for lands down there, and in his story down there, he mentioned that he had settled three hundred thousand acres in the Corpus Christi country, before coming down there." Paul declined to pursue a civil case against Shary, saying, "Of course I was badly hurt financially and in my heart too, but I did not do the obvious thing, and take John into Court, but I had loved all my men and they had all loved me, or so I thought until John showed me different so I just let things go." Disillusioned, Ralph Shannon rejoined the Geo. H. Paul Company in Pueblo, becoming his closest, lifelong friend.[39]

Paul placed a lot of faith in his fellow man and their word: "Speaking of a man's word being good, there was another way that credit was always available then, that people would not think of using today. I ALWAYS just signed Geo. H. Paul on a note and NEVER put up a dime's worth of security, for any amount I borrowed." This worked for him in his deals prior to expanding his operations into Colorado, but he knew things were handled differently out west, so he had to coax the president of the El Paso National Bank in Colorado Springs, one Mr. Hemming, to loan him $25,000 on short notice. After Paul explained how he always handled his loans, Mr. Hemming loaned him the money, security-free at 6 percent interest, as long as he didn't mention it to Hemming's friend, who was paying 8 percent interest "amply covered by security."[40] While this method of conducting business worked well for Paul in his Texas years, it would come back to haunt him in Colorado, leading to his downfall.

10

"Land of Sunshine, Health, and Opportunity"

After his Texas success, Paul set his sights on Colorado. In late 1910 or early 1911, the Geo. H. Paul Company purchased 85,000 acres in the San Luis Valley a few miles southeast of Alamosa, part of the Trinchera tract formerly owned by Denver & Rio Grande Railway founder William J. Palmer. As he had done in Texas, Denver & Rio Grande special excursion trains would bring in up to 300 potential settlers at a time. A reservoir was surveyed to provide water for irrigation, promising to fulfill the land's potential.[1] When Paul turned to Pueblo County, he had a different plan in mind, in that the land would be transformed into orchard tracts instead of farms. This idea possibly came from the successful orchards already growing up the Arkansas River between nearby Penrose and Cañon City.

Geo. H. Paul's relationship with John C. Teller is vague, but Paul and Teller appear to have been talking about a land transaction for several months. Teller intimated in letters that George H. Paul was "interested in some manner, either as agents for sale, as owners, or otherwise."[2] The *Pueblo Chieftain* reported that Geo. H. Paul, of Washington, Iowa, had completed

DOI: 10.5876/9781646421282.co10

negotiations on August 31 to purchase the land and irrigation holdings of the Teller Reservoir & Irrigation Company, including the dam, reservoir, and ditches, along with more than 16,000 acres. Paul would maintain offices in Pueblo and Denver and would be managing the property. In a brief interview for the newspaper, Paul stated, "Just say for me that I intend to begin to make the Teller Gardens the garden spot of that section of the state and intend to begin doing it immediately."[3]

Negotiations had been underway for two months, utilizing the services of Yates & McClain in Colorado Springs. Through the realty company, Geo. H. Paul agreed to buy the property and water rights for $800,000, though no deed, mortgage, or agreement of sale was ever filed in either El Paso or Pueblo Counties.[4] While the exact nature of the agreement may never be known, Paul's modus operandi in other real estate transactions can give a fair estimation of what happened. By way of a verbal agreement, a handshake, or an informal written contract, Paul agreed to sell Teller's land, with associated water rights, to prospective settlers on which Paul was turning it into an orchard. Upon receipt of the completed payments of promissory notes to Paul by the purchaser, Paul would have the deed to the land transferred from Teller to the purchaser. It is unknown if Paul ever paid any kind of a down payment or any money on a promissory note for the land.[5]

In order for Geo. H. Paul to be able to sell the land on Teller's behalf, however, the original mortgage with Continental Trust needed to be modified to accommodate such a transaction. A meeting was called in August 1911 by the Teller Reservoir & Irrigation Company's bondholders to consider amending and modifying certain sections of the deed of trust that had been given to secure bonds of the company.[6] Paul also purchased 3,600 acres north of Pueblo from Horace K. Deveraux for development as orchards.[7]

On October 25, 1911, the Geo. H. Paul Orchard Company filed its articles of incorporation with the recorder's office in Pueblo County. Paul—along with E. R. Howard, J. W. Yates and J. O. McClain (both of the realty company)—capitalized the company for $1.25 million, divided into 12,500 shares of stock at par value of $100 per share, 10,000 of which was common stock and 2,500 shares of which were preferred stock. Besides stating that the company could "acquire by purchase, lease, own, hold, option, sell, mortgage or encumber both improved and unimproved real estate and personal property," the articles also granted the company the right to "act as promoting and selling

FIGURE 10.1. *Plowing on the Geo. H. Paul Orchard Company property, circa 1911. Photo by John W. Floyd. Courtesy of Pueblo County Historical Society.*

agents or brokers in the advertisement and sale of the lands and water rights in the state of Colorado, as well as throughout the United States, Canada, and Mexico."[8]

The first earth was turned in November 1911 by a tractor that could plow up to forty acres per day in good weather. At the same time, a large force of men was busy raising the height of the Teller Dam by an additional fifteen feet to increase the water storage capacity in anticipation of the spring planting and irrigation.[9] George H. Paul planned to offer the land for sale as a cooperative orchard in five-acre tracts, with an easy plan for buyers. "We offer a very attractive form of development contract—in this we agree to plow, plant, irrigate, cultivate and maintain it during the life of the contract which extends five years after the trees are set, or over a period when the orchard is non-productive from apples." As long as the purchaser had paid half the cost of the contract, all fruit grown during that time would belong to the purchaser. If the purchaser of the land wanted to live on it, the company would "pay him annually Ten Dollars for each and every acre purchased

FIGURE 10.2. *Furrowing the soil on the Geo. H. Paul Orchard Company property, circa 1911. Photo by John W. Floyd. Courtesy of Pueblo County Historical Society.*

under the contract, but he must build a dwelling and occupy the same and be under our supervision regarding the care and maintenance of the trees." As an added bonus, if a buyer purchased at least ten acres, the price of his or her train ticket to Pueblo would be refunded. Paul did not publish the prices for land, noting instead that the price changed depending on the location of the tract.[10]

The orchard company's primary advertising literature was *Apples of Gold*, a forty-page, full-color booklet put together by their advertising manager, A. U. Mershon. The booklet, designed to entice buyers to the "land of sunshine, health, and opportunity," praised the agricultural, cultural, scenic, and lifestyle virtues of the area.[11] Distribution of the booklet was so successful that the first 5,000 copies of the original printing of *Apples of Gold* rapidly sold out, and the Geo. H. Paul Orchard Company had to order a second and third printing, at a cost to the company of $1.00 per booklet.[12]

The Geo. H. Paul Orchard Company started marketing in 1912 in a grand fashion at the Kansas City Land Show, held February 26 through March 9. The company targeted "farmers, horticulturalists, and young men from the state agricultural schools of Kansas and Missouri" to visit their booth at

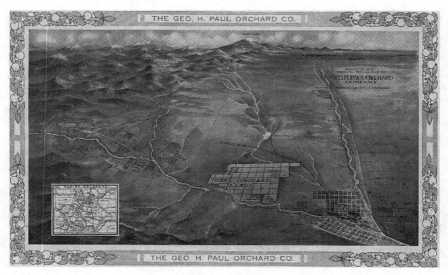

FIGURE 10.3. *Map of the Geo. H. Paul property from the* Apples of Gold *promotional booklet, 1911. Courtesy of Pueblo City-County Library District.*

the show, hoping to entice them to invest in the property.[13] A. U. Mershon designed a visually dramatic booth to showcase the Geo. H. Paul Orchard Company, featuring photographs used in its advertising campaign. It was perhaps a toss-up for the most eye-catching part of the exhibit, though, with either the sample apple orchard of live trees, measuring fifty feet by seventy-five feet at the booth, or Lorena Wade, a young woman selected as Apple Queen of the National Apple Show in Denver, who sat on her throne and passed out apples to the booth's visitors.[14]

George H. Paul also sent out a traveling lecture show to communities throughout Kansas and Iowa. The show used the most modern media of film to try to sell potential customers on the benefits of Colorado generally and the company's lands specifically. Company lecturer R. O. Clark's typical presentation, such as the billed special feature on "Picturesque Colorado" at the Star Theater in Newton, Kansas, on the evening of Thursday, March 14, featured 300 colored slides and 1,000 feet of colored motion pictures. The topics showcased Colorado, more than the orchard lands themselves, including, "The Indians in Sun and War Dances in the Famous Garden of the Gods," "4000 Feet Up a Mountain Side in a Bucket," "Through the Royal Gorge,"

FIGURE 10.4. *Geo. H. Paul button from the Kansas City Land Show, February 1912. Author's collection.*

"Over the Georgetown Loop," and "Cripple Creek, Colo." The only part of the advertised visual media that applied to the company was "Apple Picking and Packing." The presentation was followed by four regular feature films, also included in the ticket price. Clark presented his show Thursday evening, then a matinee on Friday afternoon from 2:30 p.m. to 5 p.m., concluding with another show again Friday night. The show finished with a push to get people to sign up for the first of many special excursion trains to Pueblo on Tuesday, March 19, in the hope that they would buy land.[15]

The train carrying 100 potential "colonists" arrived in Pueblo on the evening of March 20, 1912, on what was to be the first of many biweekly excursions throughout the summer.[16] An unknown number of people invested in property on the Teller tract during the stewardship of the Geo. H. Paul Orchard Company. Charles J. Hobson, a local rancher just west of the Teller

MISS LORENA WADE
The American Apple Queen
WILL ACCOMPANY THE GEO. H. PAUL ORCHARD CO.'S
EXHIBIT TO THE KANSAS CITY LAND SHOW
FEBRUARY 26TH TO MARCH 9TH

FIGURE 10.5. *Apple Queen postcard from the Kansas City Land Show, February 1912. Author's collection.*

FIGURE 10.6. *Geo. H. Paul Orchard Company headquarters, Appleton, Colorado, circa 1912. The barn was built by the author's great-grandfather. Photo by John W. Floyd. Courtesy of Pueblo County Historical Society.*

tract, recalled that maybe fifty families called Appleton home during its brief existence, their homes consisting of little more than shacks because they came out to Pueblo "on a shoe string."[17]

The headquarters for the company resided in Pueblo itself until the construction of onsite facilities, including a large house and a costly barn, in the middle of the orchard lands at the site of the future town of Appleton.[18] Paul had grandiose plans for Appleton. Construction for the summer of 1912 included "stores, school houses, churches, carpenter and blacksmith shops, electric and steam railroad stations, a fine hotel, offices, quarters, stables and store rooms for the operative force of the Company." He also touted that newest luxury: electric lighting for any settler that so desired.[19] Of these proposed buildings, only the headquarters and barn were ever finished over the short life span of Appleton.

Paul expanded his Colorado operations considerably in September 1912 when the Geo. H. Paul Orchard Company purchased thousands of acres of orchard land on the Redland Mesa in Western Colorado from White & Davis, clothing merchants in Pueblo, and their associates on the Western

Slope. Located near Hotchkiss and Delta in Delta County, this was prime orchard land, compared to that west of Pueblo.[20] Paul employed the same sales tactics he had always used, bringing in prospective buyers to sell off the 4,000 acres in five-acre chunks.[21] It is possible that Paul realized the Pueblo purchase was a bust at that point, since by December 1912 the orchard company stopped advertising their Pueblo land in Kansas newspapers and instead advertised the Delta County orchard land.[22] However, the advertising of the Delta County property also ceased in the spring of 1913.

Still the company had not given up on Pueblo. In June 1913, the Pueblo *Chieftain* reported that the orchard company had already planted 2,200 yearling apple trees and a similar number of cherry trees.[23] The trees reportedly stretched in a swath a half-mile wide and a mile long.[24] Apple trees took up to five years to bear fruit, but the cherry trees, interspersed among the apple trees, would bear fruit in only three years, providing a more rapid source of income.[25] County Horticulturist J. N. Salter declared they would "thrive nicely" but would ultimately be proven wrong.[26]

Part of the orchard's downfall may have been due to lack of water, despite the irrigation. A fundamental problem lay in the unlined irrigation ditches, which would have drunk up most of the water that came down from Teller Reservoir, long before it ever reached the thirsty fruit trees. Anecdotally, one estimate is that only a fifth of the water ever made it to its destination.[27] For lack of water, the young trees died, and the families who had invested their life savings in the project were out of luck.

More than likely, however, it was the financial pressure created by Paul's financing methods, the fallout from his trouble with John Shary, and Teller's need for income on the property to pay the mortgage that caused the crash of the orchard company. Whether in Iowa or Colorado, Geo. H. Paul seemed to have lapsed in payments.[28] By March 20, 1913, the Teller Reservoir & Irrigation Company was in litigation with Continental Trust, which was planning to foreclose on the property. This potential catastrophe was due to unfulfilled promises of Geo. H. Paul. In November 1912, Paul agreed to pay "a large amount of money" to Teller on March 15, 1913, and never did. John J. Burns died the week of March 25, 1912, in Pueblo.[29] In a letter to Burns's widow about the possible foreclosure, Teller wrote, "This of course works hardship on everybody. I am working hard and giving my attention to this proposition but cannot tell at the time how we will come out. I presume it is worrying me more than it is you at this time."[30] Teller might not have ever received any money from Paul.

To add to the financial difficulties, the conduit outlets on the Teller Dam failed in the spring of 1913. For repairs, the Geo. H. Paul Orchard Company hired the original contractors of the dam, John Olsen and William Olson, of the Arkansas Valley Construction Company, to repair the conduit outlets on the Teller Dam on May 14, 1913. The repairs were completed on July 23, but following Paul's failure to pay $4112.65 for the materials and labor, the Arkansas Valley Construction Company claimed a lien against the property of the Geo. H. Paul Orchard Company, along with the Teller Reservoir & Irrigation Company, John C. Teller, and the Continental Trust Company, all of whom retained an interest in the property.[31] According to county filings, "The George H. Paul Orchard Company was in possession of said premises and property and exercised dominion and control thereover, as owner although each of the other parties to whom this notice of lien is addressed, had or claimed some right, title, interest, or equity in and to said property."[32]

The conduit trouble with the dam must have spooked Paul into bailing on the project, for as he recorded later:

> My first enterprise after leaving the Coastal Bend, was in Colorado, where
> we had a beautiful layout, in developing orchards, under irrigation, but while
> I had always talked against irrigation, I went into a project where the State
> of Colorado had approved the project, and the largest bank in Denver had
> loaned the money to build the dam, and I had every sense of security, and yet
> the dam went out and I lost at least a million dollars trying to make good with
> my customers. I have so often thought since that if I had stayed in Coastal
> Bend, and developed the St. Paul farm as I once had in mind, I would have
> been so secure and been happier than the big fight, trying to save myself and
> customers in Colorado.[33]

Considering the dam was repaired, a small matter of a $4112.65 repair bill seems hardly enough of a reason to abandon such an endeavor. Geo. H. Paul's decision to walk away from the orchard project is saturated with palpable irony.

Teller and the reservoir company settled the lawsuit by paying William Olson 340 acres of land, plus rights to 340 acre-feet of water, worth $30,600. At the same time, 640 acres plus 640 acre-feet of water were conveyed from the company to John C. Teller to sell in order to pay $600 in taxes for 1913,

$1,300 in supplies and repairs for the company automobile, $800 balance due on reapers, $800 in insurance on wheat, $5,000 to pay off the principal sum plus accrued interest on a note for the plowing and seeds for the wheat, and $1,000 for a working fund for the company.[34] The lawsuit was thus dismissed November 25, 1914.[35]

There is no clear evidence for what finally happened to the Geo. H. Paul Orchard Company, or when it happened. By 1913, Paul had simply walked away from his lands in Colorado, having sold little land. Perhaps he realized the $800,000 deal he reportedly made with Teller was far too generous for the value of the land. Despite his success in Texas, Colorado broke him, financially. Paul lost his millionaire status and never regained the same level of success, despite trying. Life continued to be difficult following the collapse of the orchard project. Mrs. Paul gave birth to their third child, George Harvey Paul, Junior, on January 9, 1918, but the baby only lived four days, and Mrs. Paul passed two months later from complications of the birth. Geo. H. Paul was in Florida on an excursion at the time of the birth and had to rush home to see her in the hospital.[36] While his wife was alive, Paul was either busy at the office or busy at home, which was rare. After her death, he tried "loafing" downtown but claimed he never learned how. "Then I would go home, but Home was not there, so in 1919 I moved to Bismarck, North Dakota, then to Des Moines, then to Florida, and finally, Los Angeles for twelve years." He tried his hand at promotion again but was not successful. After moving to Omaha, he worked during World War II at a Bomber plant.[37] According to a nephew, "In October 1961, at my grandparents' fortieth anniversary party in Washington, Iowa, I was introduced to my father's great uncle, George Harvey Paul. After the party, my father explained to us that George Paul had once been a millionaire but had lost everything on Colorado land." Geo. H. Paul died in poverty August 22, 1965.[38]

The *Pueblo Chieftain* reported that Paul had let the land revert to the Teller Reservoir & Irrigation Company.[39] After the demise of Geo. H. Paul's orchard plan, the Teller company again advertised their land for sale. One thousand acres were already planted in Turkey Red wheat. Eight tracts of forty acres each would be sold for $85 per acre, with only $21.25 per acre required as down payment, and the balance paid off within two years, which the company promised could be paid within the two years by the profits on the wheat.[40] Even this attempt by the Teller company failed.

By the autumn of 1915, the Teller Reservoir & Irrigation Company was in default on its original sales agreement to Robert K. Potter. John C. Teller and his son, Edward, formed a new company, the Turkey Creek Irrigation Company, to take over the holdings of the Teller Reservoir & Irrigation Company. At the same time, with his attorney, H. E. Brayton, Teller financed a new loan for $22,800 at 6 percent per annum rate of interest, to repay Potter. The terms were $2,500 with interest in cash by September 23, 1915, with the balance payable in nine equal installments, the first being due upon July 1, 1916, and then each year thereafter. Teller was also indebted to H. E. Brayton for money he had paid for taxes on the land, court costs, and traveling expenses on Teller's behalf.[41] Water rights were reserved in excess of an amount sufficient for supplying one acre-foot per acre per annum to 10,000 acres H. E. Brayton, trustee.[42]

By 1915, too, the Geo. H. Paul Orchard Company was defunct.[43] On October 30, 1916, the state of Colorado listed the corporation as declared Defunct & Inoperative (D&I). Colorado statutes necessitated that D&I be declared after a corporation had not filed an annual report for five consecutive years, which means that the Geo. H. Paul Orchard Company never fulfilled their obligations to "pay the annual state corporation license tax, and other fees required by law, or to make any report the Statutes require."[44]

The financial hardships caused by the collapse of the Geo. H. Paul Orchard Company perhaps also created physical stress that shortened John C. Teller's life. Teller died on August 4, 1917, at his home in Denver. A glowing obituary from a Pueblo newspaper hints at this possibility:

> He was a broad-minded gentleman who did things on a big scale. He had wonderful confidence in his fellow man, and notwithstanding that this confidence often cost him much money, he would not let go of the idea that all men were not honest until he had positive proof. Probably the worst jolt he ever received in his career came a few years ago when he had a million dollar deal on, that involved considerable property, and also required him to give a bankable reference, which he did. And then this friend turned him and his deal down so heartlessly that we believe it was the beginning of the undermining of his health. He could not understand how a sane business man could willfully go back on a life-long friend and a legitimate and absolutely safe business proposition.[45]

Following John C. Teller's death on August 4, 1917, The Turkey Creek Land & Cattle Company reclaimed their property. On August 23, the District Court of the City and County of Denver directed the Pueblo County sheriff to execute a levy against the Teller Reservoir & Irrigation Company.[46] At the sheriff's auction on September 24, 1917, the Turkey Creek Land & Cattle Company purchased the land for $75,000.[47] After twenty-five years of dealing with the ups and downs of John C. Teller, the Turkey Creek Land & Cattle Company was back in control. The land returned to cattle ranching. As was evident early on, it was only good for that purpose.

Continental Trust filed suit in 1920 against the Teller Reservoir & Irrigation Company, Turkey Creek Land & Cattle Company, Columbine Oil Company, Rock Canon Oil Company, W. K. Oil & Refining Company, Charles E. Sutton, J. T. McCorkle, and other individuals. The court found that Continental Trust was entitled to a foreclosure of the mortgage. The court, however, also found in favor of Cross Complaints filed by Rock Canon, W. K. Oil, Eureka Oil and Charles Sutton, and J. T. McCorkle against the Teller and Turkey Creek companies. The court determined that these companies' oil and gas leases were still in effect once Turkey Creek reclaimed lands through the sheriff's foreclosure. The Teller company had not paid taxes in 1912, and 1914 through 1918, and owed a total amount of back taxes of $3735.51. The company also had not paid interest on the $282,500 in bonds by the February 1, 1913, deadline, a date that was generously extended to 1917 by Continental Trust. After five days the foreclosure would happen, and the sheriff could sell the property in parcels or as one single tract.[48] The land was still tied up in litigation the next year, as the Teller Ditch had been inadvertently left off of the court's decree and the sheriff's sale in December 1919.[49]

Meadow Investment Company purchased the land and the Teller Ditch at the sheriff's sale but had to wait until the judgement against the Teller Reservoir & Irrigation Company by Continental Trust was satisfied before taking title to the property. Once that was complete on January 7, 1924, a flurry of same-day transfers saw the lands deeded from the Turkey Creek Land & Cattle Company to Meadow Investment, then to Pueblo Meadows Land Company, and finally, to Red Rock Reservoir, Inc., all companies associated with Fullerton's heirs and Denver attorney Arthur Ponsford.[50] William Fullerton's widow, Clara, and their son, Wilfred, formed Red Rock Reservoir, Inc., in December 1923 to acquire the Potter-Turkey Creek Reservoir and the

Teller Ditch, which they achieved through the deed transfers. Their purpose was to provide irrigation for the company's own uses, rather than subdividing and selling off the land.[51] The state of Colorado even granted the company additional land for a new reservoir about a mile downstream from the Potter–Turkey Creek Reservoir on Turkey Creek, though they never developed it.[52] The days of major land developments in northwestern Pueblo County were over, at least for the next few decades.

Still, these were grandiose schemes. If the cash flow had been positive, and perhaps if the ditches had been engineered differently, the town of Appleton might still be thriving today. Of all the buildings constructed for the town, including family houses and the company headquarters, none remains today, and of the plan to turn over 16,000 acres of desert into fertile orchards nothing remains but the ghost of the ditch snaking down from Turkey Creek. Instead, the land reverted to sagebrush and grasses until the arrival of Robert McCulloch in 1969. McCulloch and his company, McCulloch Properties, formed the Pueblo West Metropolitan District and began to entice buyers to the property. Much like John C. Teller, the Mesa Land Company, and Geo. H. Paul had done six decades earlier, McCulloch flew potential buyers to Pueblo and showed them the land where they could build their dream homes.[53] Today the town of Pueblo West is home to nearly 30,000 residents as of the 2010 US Census.[54] Poetically, the heart of Pueblo West south of US Highway 50 takes in all of the original Teller property, a fitting testament to the forgotten men who envisioned a burgeoning landscape of human activity.

The Colorado-Kansas Railway's grade cut across the northeast corner of the Teller tract, and so a station siding was vital for both the property owners and the railroad, in anticipation of the bountiful harvests due in a few years. As construction on the railroad progressed across the prairie in the winter of 1911–1912, these businesspeople installed a 1,100-foot-long siding.[55] The railroad later cut this siding back to half that length.[56] The railroad originally named the station Huerto, Spanish for "orchard," following an affinity of railroads in the region to give their stations Spanish names.[57] Once George H. Paul planned the community of Appleton, though, the siding's name changed to match that appellation, and remained as the name of the siding long after the orchard company was gone. It does not appear that a depot structure ever existed at this location, though a crane stood along the siding for the loading and unloading of freight.[58] But in the end, it wasn't cattle, or farming, or even orchards that could settle people on the land, but residential housing. Agriculture along the Colorado-Kansas Railway was a failure. That left the stone and clay products from the Turkey Creek Stone, Clay & Gypsum Company at Stone City as the main source of revenue for the railroad, and upon which the dreams of the builders rested.

PART III
People of Stone and Clay

11

Geology, Geography, and the Town

Beyond the orchard project, the railroad headed west again across the open prairies. As it passed through a cut on the crest of a summit dividing the Dry Creek drainage from the Turkey Creek, small scrubby cedars began to dot the landscape. Along the line here was a station named Cedro, Spanish for "cedar."[1] No depot marked the site, and any potential use for this station soon disappeared along with the name. The station name soon changed to Pumpkin Hollow, after the geographic area it inhabited.[2]

Continuing on graded fills across the rolling prairie, the train reached Turkey Creek proper, a spot first named Rio by the railroad, though the creek is hardly deserving of the appellation of river. A two-hundred-foot-long trestle crossed the creek here, before the tracks turned north, paralleling the creek for the last few miles. Somewhere before the railroad crossed into Booth Gulch, a sixth station existed for a while under the name Guanado [sic], the Spanish word for cattle.[3] In this vicinity in later years, a station and 1,200-foot siding named Myrtle appeared, and it is possible that the two are synonymous. Although ranching was prominent in the region, it does not

DOI: 10.5876/9781646421282.c011

FIGURE 11.1. *Colorado-Kansas train near Stone City, circa 1912. Photo courtesy of Denver Public Library, Western History Department, Z-8902.*

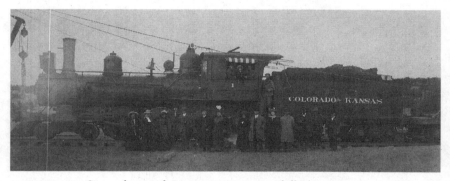

FIGURE 11.2. *Group photo with Locomotive No. 1 on a chilly day, circa 1912. Author's collection.*

appear to have played much of a role in the railroad's revenue, as no evidence has emerged to date of cattle movements on the line.

Over the final few miles, the rolling prairie gave way to more spectacular scenery. The railroad traversed an incredibly long, twenty-foot-high earthen fill along the base of the hogback in order to gain elevation to reach Stone City.[4] Turning into the mouth of Booth Gulch, the train remained on the fill until it crossed the trestle at Booth Creek and climbed the last few feet into Stone City, the final station stop and the promise of an economic windfall. At an elevation of 5,540 feet, Stone City presented the railroad a climb of around 845 feet from Pueblo, or an average grade of 0.7 percent over 22.8 miles from its Victoria Avenue depot.[5]

At Stone City, the Great Plains meet the foothills of the Rocky Mountains. Spanning the eastern side of Stone City, Booth Mountain rises to over 6,400 feet in elevation, dividing the Booth Creek and Turkey Creek drainages.[6]

FIGURE 11.3. *Locomotive No. 1 with unnamed people, possibly some of the owners, circa 1913. Note the size disparity created by forced perspective between this photo and the previous one. Photo by John W. Floyd. Courtesy of Pueblo County Historical Society.*

Clothed by a mixture of juniper and piñons with an undergrowth of Gambel oak, the mountain dominated life in Stone City for the men removing sandstone from its flanks and clay from its depths. Prairie grasses blanketed the area between Booth Mountain and the Hogback while prickly pear and cholla crept up the gulch. Cottonwoods, box elders, and willows grew along the creek, but the valley was nearly barren save for grasses, prickly pear, cholla, yucca, and other brush scattered throughout Booth Gulch. The only trees on the plateau below the mountain were Chinese Elms that the citizens of Stone City planted to beautify their streets. Bison and elk used to roam the area, as well as mule deer, whitetail deer, and pronghorn antelope, and smaller mammals, such as mountain lions, bobcats, wolves, coyotes, foxes, and black-tailed prairie dogs.[7] Semipermanent human habitation in the Stone City area dates at least as far back as 3000 to 500 BC. More recently, the mountain and plains tribes—such as the Ute, Comanche, Cheyenne, and Arapahoe—surely hunted, if not camped, here.[8] In the nineteenth century, explorers, such as Zebulon Pike in 1806, checked out the Turkey Creek area, but settlers were few and far between. The mountains and hills around Stone City gave it a feeling of isolation, but the arrival of the railroad brought with it a sense of connectedness to Pueblo and the world outside of Booth Gulch.

FIGURE 11.4. *Booth Mountain as seen from Stone City Road, 2001. Photo by the author.*

Sticking with their Spanish theme, the company first named the station Piedra, a name it held at least until April 1912.[9] In its application to the United States Post Office, instead of Piedra, the Turkey Creek Stone, Clay & Gypsum Company suggested the English version "Stone" as the name of their town. However, feeling it was too similar to a town in Colorado already named Stoner, the post office gave it the name Stone City instead.[10]

To understand why Stone City existed, it is first necessary to look at how it came to be, and for that we must look back into geologic time. Colorado—and, in fact, most of what would become the western United States—began its formation at the bottom of a shallow sea. Long before the hard granites of the lofty and beautiful Rocky Mountains thrust their way skyward between 28 and 75 million years ago, the Colorado Piedmont formed. Situated between the Arkansas River and the South Platte River, the Piedmont is a plateau of sedimentary deposits laid down during the Cretaceous Period. Beds of this sandstone, belonging to the Dakota and Purgatoire Formations, folded to form hogbacks, part of the foothills of the Front Range on the eastern slope of the Rocky Mountains.

Stone City is bordered on the west by these hogbacks, and on the east by Booth Mountain. The structure of the outcroppings on Booth Mountain results in a beautifully colored sandstone that is strong enough for use in building construction and facilitates the quarrying of large blocks. Buried in layers within the sandstone outcroppings lay seams of clays, which had many uses.[11] The Turkey Creek stone field covered an area of about 500 acres, with ledges ranging in thickness from fifteen to forty feet.[12]

Turkey Creek stone came in a variety of colors, including gray veined, white, flesh tint, gray, turkey egg, and pink. The Colorado Bureau of Mines remarked that the stone "is of unusually close texture, and without doubt possesses the most delicate coloring, which combined with its exceptional crushing strength (12,850 pounds per square inch), makes it the most desirable stone found in America."[13]

While a beautiful building finishing material, the stone only had a market for less than three decades. Besides the courthouse in Pueblo, the Minnequa Bank building and portions of the Sacred Heart Church featured the local stone.[14] The Santa Fe office building in La Junta and the Broadmoor Hotel in Colorado Springs utilized Turkey Creek stone.[15] By 1913, sixteen residences in the city also utilized the stone for construction or decorative purposes, including fireplaces, mantels, and porch columns.[16] A large window display at the railroad's office building on Main Street featured the many products and uses of Turkey Creek stone.

Turkey Creek stone found many markets in the region. Major constructions in Denver included the science hall on the University of Denver campus.[17] The Denver Public Library, as well as the Greek Theater and Voorhies Memorial in Civic Center Park, also made use of the sandstone.[18] Kansas received quite a bit of Turkey Creek stone. In Lawrence, the Perkins Trust Company used the product for construction;[19] so, too, did Wichita's Union Depot.[20] One regular customer, the United States government, utilized the sandstone, in at least two post offices in Kansas, including the one at Ottawa.[21] The stone made its way as far as Bartlesville, Oklahoma, for the courthouse there.[22] The company even put in a bid for supplying stone for the construction of the Utah State capitol, but, not surprisingly, the contract went to a stone quarry local to Salt Lake City.[23] Large sandstone blocks also served as riprap protection along riverbanks and lakeshores, as well as roadbeds.[24] This use was especially important after the 1921 flood, when the railroad remained busy hauling stone for use in shoring up the levee.[25]

Clays were the primary products removed from the mines, and chief among these was fireclay. Turkey Creek fireclays, or more accurately, refractory clays, could withstand temperatures of 3,200 degrees Fahrenheit, which made them ideally suited for the manufacture of firebricks for boilers and

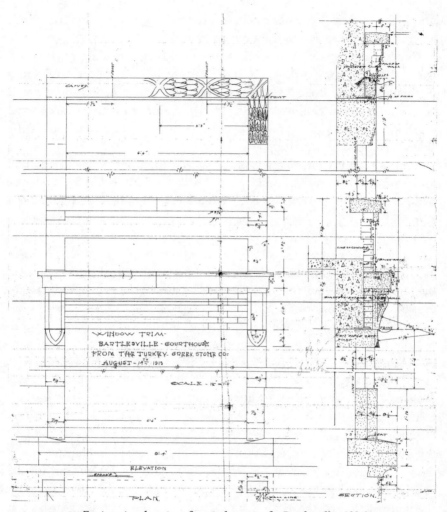

FIGURE 11.5. *Engineering drawings for window trim for Bartlesville, Oklahoma, courthouse, August 14, 1913. Courtesy of Colorado Railroad Museum Collection.*

furnaces in steel mills and smelters, laboratory ware for chemical and metallurgical uses, and insulators for electrical construction.[26] These products found uses all over the nation, and even internationally. During World War II, production of fireclay at Stone City greatly increased for use in the boilers of United States Navy ships.[27]

Turkey Creek clays came in three varieties: plastic, semiplastic, and flint. Flint clay was the highest quality. Light gray or light blue-gray in color, it was the most economically important of the clays, sought after for high-grade refractory products.[28] Semiplastic clays in the Turkey Creek area were black in color, high in carbon, and dense. The local miners referred to it as "black flint" clay.[29] Plastic clays varied in color from light gray to bluish-grey to black. Refractory products used both the semiplastic and plastic clays, but because of their higher quantity of impurities, these grades required more work than the flint clays.[30] The mines at Stone City shipped clay in both the raw and calcined forms. Calcined clay is clay that has been fired in kilns at 2,000 degrees Fahrenheit to remove impurities.[31]

There is little left of Stone City today except for a few foundations and the railroad grade. More relics exist near the mines and quarries, but of the town where people lived even the roads are difficult to discern. Interpretations will have to come from photographs, archaeological evidence, and memories. Archaeologists categorize Stone City as an industrial frontier, which encompasses extractive activities such and mining and lumbering.[32] These industrial frontiers exhibited close economic and cultural ties with a larger nearby community, and because they were so closely linked, their camps were usually temporary, of short duration, and seldom self-sufficient.[33] Their settlement pattern was resource based, grouped in this instance around the stone and clay resources. The impermanent nature of the camps resulted in the construction of transportation systems to industrial frontiers using the least-possible capital expenditures, which usually meant poor roadbed and inexpensive equipment.[34] Stone City and the Colorado-Kansas Railway both certainly fit this model.

Even though the town was founded by a company, it bore little resemblance to other regional company towns, such as those owned by the Colorado Fuel & Iron Company near Trinidad, Colorado. Company houses did not march across the landscape in neat rows, owing to the fact that the Colorado-Kansas Land Company sold town lots individually.[35] Buildings were sparsely located, not crowded together, and featured a very utilitarian architecture. Some houses used the local building stone for construction. Most, however, utilized wood. With the founding of the town in 1912, residences went up quickly. Many canvas tents and unpainted frame houses, evoking a scene reminiscent of the early mining boomtowns of the previous century, greeted visitors to Stone City.[36]

FIGURE 11.6. *Stone City, 1936. View is looking east. Note the stone sawmill on the right. Courtesy of Colorado Railroad Museum Collection.*

The quarry company platted the town in Booth Gulch, a half-mile wide valley that lies between Booth Mountain on the east and the bluffs to the west.[37] Booth Creek only flows for a few months a year and was thus not a major source of water for the town, which explains why the town's founders built it a considerable distance from the creek.[38] One known water source was a well northeast of town on the flanks of Booth Mountain. A modern cinder-block pump house is the only structure remaining at Stone City today, though partial remains still exist near the mines.[39] The city stored water for the residents in a tank on the north side of town.[40]

The layout of the town was roughly linear, west of and parallel to the railroad tracks entering town. Five avenues—four of which (McCorkle, Potter, Crews, and Harvey) received the names of officials of the Turkey Creek Stone, Clay & Gypsum Company—ran east and west, along with the fifth: Hillside Avenue. West Street bordered the town on the west and Candow Street (named after the quarry company's superintendent) on the east. Within those five and one-half blocks, the quarry company marked off 187 lots to sell, but it never developed anywhere near that many.[41]

Most mining towns were concentrated near their mines for reasons of convenience. This concentration is true for Stone City, though the quarries developed first, four years before the company platted and developed the town farther south of the quarries. The town was much closer to the mines and the stone sawmill. This afforded the railroad ease in switching both the mines and sawmill. Additionally, natural springs were located near the mines

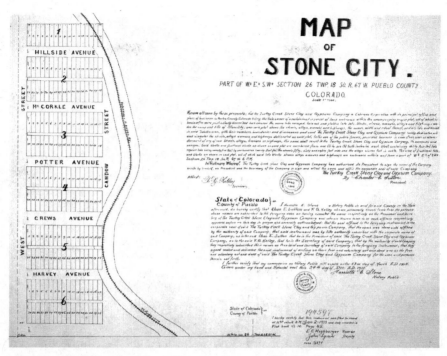

FIGURE 11.7. *Plat map of Stone City, 1913. Courtesy of Pueblo County Recording Department.*

and near the sawmill, which was handy since a reliable source of water was necessary to cool the saw blade as it cut the stone.

Commercial buildings at Stone City were few. The primary commercial building in town, and the center of the "business district," was the depot. The train station was a small, wooden one-room affair, with a gabled roof. For the first three years, it also housed the town's general store and post office. Eventually these operations moved into another building. The post office opened in January 1913, with J. W. Heath appointed as postmaster. The railroad carried the daily mail up from Pueblo.[42] The depot stood at the head of the railroad's wye, a track arrangement that allowed the locomotive to execute a three-point turn so that it could head back down to Pueblo. A water column also stood on one leg of the wye to service the locomotive before heading home, the only railroad-servicing structure available at Stone City.[43]

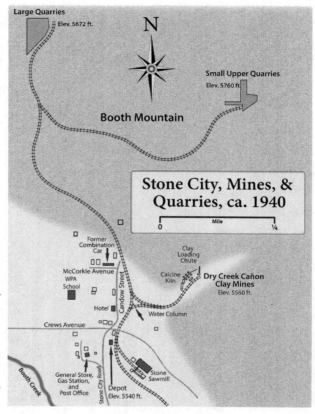

FIGURE 11.8. *Map of Stone City. Drawn by the author, based on a hand-drawn map by former Stone City resident Jerry Waller in the collection at the Cañon City Public Library, and the 1912 Stone City plat map, courtesy of the Pueblo County Recording Department.*

A two-story hotel, built with Turkey Creek stone, was opened for business in 1920. The tallest building in town, its gaunt façade stood watch at the corner of Candow Street and Potter Avenue, north of the depot. It was operated by fifty-five-year-old Margaret Candow, whose husband, William, was superintendent at the quarries. She and William were both immigrants from Scotland.[44] Elizabeth Jasper ran the new general store when it opened, with her husband, Charles, serving as postmaster. By 1921, though, Tacy S. Grant was postmaster, and she would remain so through to the town's bitter end. This was a late-in-life career for her, as she was fifty-one years old at the time. Tacy Grant, a widow, was well known to everyone in Stone City, for she had lived in the district since at least 1910 and by 1918 had purchased a town lot for a home from Robert K. Potter.[45] A chiropractic office located to Stone

FIGURE 11.9. *Stone City depot, circa 1912. Photo by John W. Floyd. Courtesy of Pueblo City-County Library District.*

City in 1928 and appears to be the only medical-related facility. Back injuries were a priority for miners and quarrymen. In 1939, Stone City added a gas station, in combination with a general store and post office.[46] James Mayfield operated the combined store and gas station, with Tacy Grant continuing to serve as postmaster. By this time, however, the railroad had lost the mail contract, so a rural carrier delivered mail three times a week from Pueblo. With the mail delivery came Hostess products, such as Wonder Bread, CupCakes, Sno-Balls and Twinkies, which were adored by the local children, though families could afford these treats only about once a month. Mayfield's store also had the one and only telephone in Stone City.[47]

The only institutional building at Stone City was the schoolhouse, which also served as a church on the occasions that a traveling minister or missionaries would drop in to town.[48] Because Stone City was more of a fledgling mining camp than an actual city in 1912, the first school was a twelve-foot-by-twenty-four-foot tent. The school's teachers relied upon charitable donations for payment of services. In 1913, an actual wood-frame building was constructed, which lasted until 1918, when it burned. It was replaced by a two-room school, which also later burned.[49] This building burned down

FIGURE 11.10. *Stone City Hotel, 1936. Colorado Railroad Museum Collection.*

in 1939 but was rebuilt a year later by the Works Progress Administration as a handsome two-story structure using local stone.[50] The main floor consisted of a large, single room with a partition down the middle. The partition divided the children, with grades 1 through 5 occupying one side of the room, and grades 6 through 10 on the other.[51] A large basement provided additional room for community activities.[52]

Even before Stone City existed, the school district had three teachers, all single women: sisters Elizabeth Mahoney, 32, and Rebecca Mahoney, 29, along with Clara Brown, 18.[53]

The school served as the social center of the town. The community held events both upstairs and in the basement. Schoolchildren held plays in the building twice a year, one at Christmas and the other at the end of school.[54] Several events were the highlight of social activity. Popular were box suppers, in which the women would provide dinner for two in a decorated box, and the men would bid on the boxes without knowing who furnished the meal. The highest bidder would then have dinner with the woman who provided the box. At the end of the school year, residents attended ice-cream socials. Dances at the schoolhouse, featuring a small band, drew people from nearby Penrose. Girls and women received free admission, but the boys and men had to pay. Probably the biggest event of the year was the Christmas party. The local boys would head into the hills for a Christmas tree, which the townspeople decorated with handmade ornaments, such as paper chain garland. The children presented their Christmas play, and afterward everyone joined

FIGURE 11.11. *Stone City Post Office, General Store, and Gas Station, 1946. Author's collection.*

in a sing-along. Santa Claus then visited the children, bringing presents to all of them. Previously, the children had drawn names in a gift exchange and provided the gift, but Santa also brought each child a bag of nuts, candy, and an orange.[55]

Archaeological evidence suggests there were around twenty residential-type structures within the town limits, and as many outside the town limits, though artifacts representing different periods indicate that their occupation varied over the years.[56] Local residents recall about twenty-five houses, and the archaeological evidence supports this.[57] Most houses in later years had electricity and running water.[58] Only one house in town had a lawn, to the envy of the other residents.[59] The houses were small, single-story wooden structures for the most part, though one house was a two-story affair. A few houses were constructed of Turkey Creek stone and tended to be larger in area.[60] One house even utilized another local resource, adobe bricks.[61]

The town established the positions of constable and justice of the peace in 1929, though these were gone by 1931.[62] It is unknown what kind of building served for these municipal purposes. Missing from Stone City were an organized church and any independent saloon or eating establishment, though it is possible the hotel may have had the latter. Unlike many a self-sufficient rural town, these missing institutions reflected Stone City's strong hinterland connection to Pueblo, a dichotomy of both isolation from and dependence on the larger city.

12

The People of Stone City

Like any mining town, the population of Stone City was an itinerant one. Jobs came and went with the fortunes of the products and their markets. By far the greatest number of people living and working in the Stone City area were there in the first dozen years of existence of the quarries, from 1908 to 1920. In 1910—before there was even a Stone City proper but merely a collection of quarrying, mining, and railroad grading camps surrounded by farms and ranches—sixty-seven households, comprising 344 individuals, called the area home. Most of the families were engaged in farming, including three dairy farmers and one fruit farmer. Ranching remained a much smaller occupation, with only with six men identifying as ranchers 1910, a number that would remain fairly consistent over the next few decades.[1]

The Turkey Creek Stone, Clay & Gypsum Company was a large employer in the district, since the quarry had been actively shipping stone for the Pueblo County Courthouse construction since 1908. Eleven men worked as laborers or stonecutters, while a blacksmith and a quarry teamster and three freighting teamsters rounded out the crew at the quarries. The clay

DOI: 10.5876/9781646421282.c012

mines had yet to take off in importance, as only one miner was working a claim in 1910.[2]

By far, the biggest employer in the district was the railroad, deep into construction in 1910 while fighting its political battles back in Pueblo. Sixty-six men were hard at work grading the line or working in tertiary positions. Besides twenty-three grading laborers and twenty-eight grading teamsters, the railroad also employed a section foreman, a section laborer, a grading contractor, both a chainman and a surveyor for the surveying team, a time-keeper, a blacksmith, a steam shovel craneman, and a cook. Between the quarry and the grading, the sounds of horses, mules, wagons, and shouting teamsters would have permeated the camp.[3]

Once the town of Stone City itself was officially founded in 1912, it took on the look of a more permanent settlement. With the grading and railroad construction crews gone, the town would settle into a declining population pattern. Forty families called the town home by 1913.[4] The population fluctuated from 100 in 1912 to a peak of 175 in 1929.[5] Given that many of the buildings outside of the town limits only indicate earlier occupation, the number of houses seems inadequate for the population. In later years, residents would take in boarders for the extra income they afforded, so it is possible that this source of further population occurred during the 1910s and 1920s as well.[6]

By 1920, the population of the area had dropped to 200, though the number of households only diminished from 67 to 64. Some of the decline could be due to deployments in World War I. The difficulties of farming in the region become apparent by census, as the number of farmers plummeted to twenty-six. The failures of both Teller and Geo. H. Paul in the field of agriculture serve as prime examples of farming as a tough existence in the northwest corner of Pueblo County.[7]

Work was ample enough in 1917, and laborers in such demand, that the Colorado-Kansas Railway and the Turkey Creek Stone, Clay, & Gypsum Company both granted substantial raises to their workers. Manager Harry O'Neill lamented that the quarries and clay beds were running to a maximum, and if it were not for the shortage of common laborers, he could have a force of 100 men at work.[8] The good times would not roll on forever, though. The quarries slowed down considerably with the waning days of stone construction by 1920. Seventeen men worked the quarries, two of whom were superintendents. Nine teamsters kept the stone moving out of the quarries to the railroad or stone mill. Four men kept the stone sawmill running. Business, however, had picked up at the clay mines and would continue to show growth over the next two decades. Whereas in 1910 there was only one miner, the mines now had foremen, muckers, trammers, truckers, and miners—nine in all. The railroad kept a track laborer and a station agent employed at the Stone City terminus.

The quarries and stone sawmill were essentially shut down by 1930, overseen by a superintendent and one lonely quarry laborer. The total population in the area was 143, comprising 40 households, but most of those were in Stone City itself.[9] Stone City's population declined to 125 following the closing of the stone quarries and mill but held steady until 1937, when an increased demand for firebrick resulted in the population increasing to 150.[10] A man could always find work at the clay mines, though most families lived payday to payday.[11] The mines employed 10 men in 1930 and 13 men in 1930, which included 10 miners, a superintendent, a foreman, and a trucker. Mining appears to have been relatively steady labor during the Depression years. The clay kilns kept one fireman employed over the next couple of decades.[12]

Beyond the railroad, mines, and mill, Stone City's diversity of employment during its first decade of existence included two woodcutters, four schoolteachers, a postmaster, a hotel keeper, a storekeeper, an electrician, an accountant, a blacksmith, an automotive repairman, a pool hall owner, a lineman for the power company, a clubhouse proprietor and clubhouse servant (though details about the clubhouse are unknown), a salesman, a boardinghouse cook, a boardinghouse operator, a cigar maker, and two men working in nearby oil fields.[13]

Most women in the Stone City environs were housewives, though in the first decade, before the rapid decline in agriculture in the area, many wives assisted their husbands with farming or ranching. By 1920, however, only one woman listed herself as a farmer. Other women worked at jobs commonly open to them. Maud Baty was a cook in her husband's boardinghouse, and by 1930 Beatrice Snowden kept a boarding house, possibly the old Baty boardinghouse. A private family employed fifteen-year-old Bertha Wolfe as a servant.[14] Eighteen-year-old Elsie Daniels worked as a laundress. Lena Potter, wife of clay miner Robert Potter, had one of the most atypical jobs, for she was the Colorado-Kansas Railway's station agent. Robert Potter was not an immediate family member of Robert K. Potter, but it is likely that he is related, considering both Robert Potters have Nebraska ties and that Lena held the respectable job of station agent for the railroad. A Potter connection would have helped her land that job, since often it is all a matter of whom you know.[15]

Today, Pueblo portrays itself as the quintessential melting pot of America because of all the different nationalities and ethnicities that migrated to the city in the late nineteenth and early twentieth centuries to work in the steel mill and various smelters. Stone City was little different, having different ethnicities living and working together but never in as great a number as in 1910. With the quarries and railroad construction, as well as the large number of farmers, thirty-five foreign-born people lived in the Stone City area, representing Germany, England, Ireland, Sweden, Denmark, France, Mexico, Canada, Scotland, Austria, Slovenia, and Bohemia. With the exception of the two railroad section laborers from Mexico, who spoke only Spanish, everyone else spoke English.[16]

With the decline in agriculture and the railroad's completion, and possibly as a result of recent American immigration restrictions, the number of foreign-born people dropped to twelve by 1920. Most were housewives or children, though a handful of the men worked at the quarries. They hailed from Ireland, Italy, Germany, Mexico, and Canada. The few major businesses in Stone City were owned and operated by immigrants. William and Margaret Candow, quarry superintendent and hotel keeper, respectively, were from Scotland. Lou Vitullo, from Italy, owned a pool hall, and Elizabeth Jasper from Wales was the storekeeper at the general store.[17] By 1930, the only resident of Stone City born outside the United States was farmer Joseph Porta, an Italian immigrant who came to the United States in 1908 and had settled outside Stone City prior to 1920.[18] Joe Porta was joined by 1940, though, by Paul Hansen, a clay miner from Denmark, and Flora Hayes, housewife, from Scotland.[19]

While Puebloans acknowledge that tolerance is mostly the case today, in the past it was a far different story. As just one example that relates to the railroad, in September 1919, two section hands of the Colorado-Kansas Railway, both listed as Mexican in the newspaper report, were charged with the murder of Pueblo City Police patrolman Jeff Evans as he was attempting to place them under arrest. They had reportedly been drinking and were alleged to have told a Santa Fe switchman that they were going to start a race riot in Pueblo by killing "every nigger in Peppersauce Bottoms." They were also alleged to have overheard that they had killed a "dozen negroes" in Mexico and were going to kill a dozen more in Pueblo.[20]

Stone City was a "typical poor mining community" and in many respects resembled a nineteenth-century town more than a twentieth-century one, partly due to its relative isolation, but mostly due to the poverty of its residents. Vegetable gardens beside the houses served as major sources of food for the residents, with canning ensuring supplies throughout the winter. Sources of meat included venison taken during hunting season and canned for storage, as well as rabbits, and chickens the residents raised. Bartering was a useful form of payment for anything from doctor's visits to piano lessons, to haircuts.[21]

The people of Stone City maintained a sense of humor and solidarity, even through the bad times. Lee Oldham recalls, "Folks in the community had a laugh over a fellow who drove a big Packard into the village and asked the first person he saw what people did for a living. With a straight face, the man replied that we took in each other's laundry."[22]

Families were important in Stone City. During the Depression, extended families would come to town when down on their luck, and residents would take in boarders to supplement the family income.[23] Within Stone City, families tended to be itinerant, moving from one shack house to another. Rent was $3 to $6 a month. Many former residents share memories of having lived at one time in the railroad's old passenger coach, which the company had turned into a residence and rented out. One former Stone City resident, Shirley Louise Baker, believes her family suffered from being good tenants. Her father and mother, in their thriftiness, fixed up the houses they rented. Her father brought home empty dynamite boxes from the mine, and her mother would make them into kitchen cabinets. Her mother also turned patterned feed sacks into kitchen window curtains. When the owner of the house saw the improvements, the owner would either demand more rent or ask the family to move out so the owners' relatives could move in.[24] Despite its hardships, Baker recalls, "Living in Stone City in poverty wasn't really all that bad as I look back. We had a loving family atmosphere and many great childhood friendships. We had a good education, and our family was very

FIGURE 12.1. *Former Colorado-Kansas Railway Combine No. 1, October 1947, serving as a ramshackle home. Sadly, this is the best photograph of this car. Photo by Albert Knicklebine. Author's collection.*

respected. The entire community cooperated and helped each other out; we all pulled together for basic survival."[25]

Rent problems seemed to be a common issue for both owners and renters. Lee Oldham remembers, "Dad owned several small houses in the community and rented them to the miners who worked for him at $7.00 per month. The larger part of the time, he was not paid the rent."[26]

The impoverished families braved the cold in winter without adequate clothing. Usually, the only heat was from the kitchen stove and a potbelly stove in the living room. To supply their stoves, the residents "borrowed" slack coal from the kilns for heat, until the kilns closed, at which point they had to scavenge wood. Summer brought its own set of problems, such as rattlesnakes. Worse still, the deluge from thunderstorms periodically undermined the bridge into town, cutting off access to Pueblo for several days until the county crews could repair it. At the first sign of big thunderheads, someone would drive their car to the other side of the bridge so that anyone who needed to get to town would be able to, until the repair crews arrived.[27]

Stone City children spent a lot of time roaming the hills. On the bluff to the south, overlooking town, they would gather fossilized sharks' teeth. Because of numerous snakes and other potentially dangerous animals, their parents allowed them to pack guns for protection.[28] With adult permission, they could take off after school and go hunting rabbits for supper in the hills outside of town with their .22 rifles. On weekends, the children participated in horseshoe-pitching contests, baseball games, slingshot games, and dances around the player piano.[29] The children also named and kept track of the many old or lame burros that were no longer able to work in the clay mines. The miners turned the animals loose to wander the town, and the children delighted in catching and riding them.[30]

The families of Stone City pulled together for more than just survival. Grief and patriotism united the town when a young man from Stone City, Lester E. Mayfield, died on the USS *Arizona* during the Japanese attack at Pearl Harbor on December 7, 1941. His death brought a newfound and intense sense of patriotism to the entire town. Residents gathered scrap metal for the war effort, grew "Victory Gardens," and bought war stamps in school trying to save enough to buy war bonds.[31]

Stone City's fortunes continued to wane following the war. By 1950, the population had dropped to 100.[32] Many of the miners who worked the clay pits tended to live in the Florence and Cañon City area and commute into Stone City for work.[33] Some residents who lived in town commuted elsewhere for jobs, such as at the coal mines in Fremont County. When the Stone City Post Office closed for good in 1957, only seven families received mail there.[34]

13

Quarrying and Clay Mining

Business as Usual

The dominant structure at Stone City was undoubtedly the stone sawmill. Built with a timber frame and sheathed in corrugated iron, the sawmill housed seven gang saws, stone planers and lathes, and diamond saws and rubbing beds, all capable of turning out 1,000 cubic feet of finished stone per day.[1] A large, twenty-five-ton Morgan overhead crane would lift the raw blocks from the Colorado-Kansas Railway flatcars the locomotive brought down from the quarries and would later load the finished stone for transport to market.[2] During its busy years, the sawmill kept fifty workers employed.[3]

Quarrying was labor-intensive work. By June 1912, over 100 men were at work in the quarries.[4] To remove the stone, quarry laborers blasted or cut a working face out of the sandstone and then loosened the blocks for removal. Using the natural grain and cleavage of the stone, the laborers drilled multiples holes in a line and then hammered a set of three metal wedges, called plug and feathers, into the stone to split it further. Large cranes, known as guy derricks, maneuvered the stone into position on flatcars for transport to the sawmill.[5] The quarries were equipped with electrically operated

DOI: 10.5876/9781646421282.c013

FIGURE 13.1. *The twenty-five-ton Morgan crane loading stone at the sawmill, December 31, 1912. The Stone City depot and the railroad's only passenger car are seen in the background. Photo by John W. Floyd. Courtesy of Pueblo County Historical Society.*

machinery capable of handling thirty-ton blocks.[6] The railroad hauled its first carload of stone on April 24, 1912.[7]

Robert K. Potter sold the Turkey Creek Stone Quarries to the Lawrence, Kansas, faction in May 1913. Sutton's Pueblo Land & Investment Company traded $248,000 worth of land to E. W. Wilson and associates of Pekin, Illinois, for $118,000 worth of quarry stock, $112,500 worth of railroad bonds, and some city property. This enabled Charles Sutton, J. R. Greenlees, R. C. Johnson, and others to take control of the quarry property. The first stone sent east out of the quarries on the railroad went to Lawrence, Kansas, for the Perkins Loan and Trust Company.[8] More stone would soon be headed to Kansas, for in early June 1913 the Turkey Creek Stone, Clay & Gypsum Company was awarded the contract to supply sandstone of a pinkish tint for the new post office in Ottawa, Kansas. W. S. Fallis of Ottawa was a stockholder in the Colorado-Kansas Railway.[9]

FIGURE 13.2. *Loading stone at the sawmill, November 11, 1912. Photo by John W. Floyd. Courtesy of Pueblo County Historical Society.*

Mining, too, was labor intensive, and the men suffered from a variety of ailments, such as emphysema, which contributed to their early deaths.[10] The access tunnels were horizontal, though later mines used the open-pit method for accessing the clay. No headframes capped the skyline, as they did in most Colorado mining towns. The mines utilized the room and pillar system, where miners opened up rooms in the clay seams between layers of sandstone, then supported the roof with pine timber pillars.[11] A narrow-gauge mine car railroad track system connected the mines both internally and externally. Burros would pull the ore carts around inside the mines and out to the loading platform and kilns.[12] A clay-loading chute stood alongside and above the railroad spur to the mines up Dry Creek Cañon. Miners filled the chute from their ore carts, and when the chute held enough for a carload, they dumped the clay into waiting gondolas for transport to Pueblo and beyond. Kilns for processing the calcined clay stood next to the chutes.[13]

FIGURE 13.3. *Inside the stone sawmill, November 11, 1912. Photo by John W. Floyd. Courtesy of Pueblo County Historical Society.*

The U. S. Zinc Company first mined clay on Turkey Creek in 1906 but abandoned its mine in 1912 when the Turkey Creek Stone, Clay & Gypsum Company bought the property and began mining. The company soon leased out their claims to Pueblo Clay Products, who took over mining operations.[14] Pueblo Clay Products built beehive kilns and tower kilns at the mines to produce calcined clay. The clay, both raw and calcined, was purchased by refractory manufacturers in Pueblo and Cañon City, such as Standard Firebrick Company and Colorado Fuel & Iron; other manufacturers of both iron and zinc products across the United States, from the East Coast, to Blackwell, Missouri; and even to a firebrick maker in Coahuila, Mexico.[15] Calcined clay accounted for 25 percent of sales. From 1945 to 1949, the Turkey Creek District produced an average of 24,000 tons of clay per year. Pueblo Clay Products estimated that about 40 percent of their production of raw clay was flint clay. By 1950, Pueblo Clay Products had purchased a plant in Pueblo to process their fifty to sixty tons of crushed, calcined clay per day. Standard Fire Brick

FIGURE 13.4. *Unnamed crew inside the stone sawmill, November 11, 1912. Photo by John W. Floyd. Courtesy of Pueblo City-County Library District.*

FIGURE 13.5. *Colorado-Kansas tracks to the quarries, 1936. Colorado Railroad Museum Collection.*

FIGURE 13.6. *Stone City, looking southwest from Booth Mountain, 1936. Colorado Railroad Museum Collection.*

FIGURE 13.7. *Quarrying stone at Stone City, July 1, 1908. Author's collection.*

FIGURE 13.8. *Quarries at Stone City, circa 1908. Courtesy of Pueblo City-County Library District.*

Company, of Pueblo, and the Laclede Christy Company, of Colorado, were two other companies involved in the mining and production of clays. Both Standard Fire Brick Company and Laclede used their own clay production in manufacturing refractory products. The Nellie Helen, an independent mine owned and operated by Arthur Wands and his Colorado Fire Clay Company, just south of Stone City, sold most of its production to the Denver Fire Clay Company, though some was sold to Freeman Fire Brick Company, in Cañon City. Wands, who started the Nellie Helen Mine in 1927, once operated a kiln at his mine but later shipped only raw clay.[16] The Nellie Helen was an underground mine in the early years though later became a pit mine.[17]

Lee Oldham, Arthur Wand's daughter, recalled, "I watched them drill holes in the face of the clay underground then later load the holes with dynamite, and blast the clay loose. It was loaded in mine cars and rode out to the tipple where it was dumped through a chute to the truck below. Since the

FIGURE 13.9. *Quarries at Stone City, circa 1908. Courtesy of Pueblo City-County Library District.*

mine was on an incline, the empty cars were then pulled back into place with donkeys."[18]

Wands constructed a pot kiln, with four fireboxes that were fired round the clock for several days, once the kiln was loaded with raw clay:

> The end result was calcine, or clay with all the moisture cooked out of it. After the calcine was cool enough to haul, it was put in railroad cars at Myrtle and shipped to Pueblo, then on to Denver . . . Irma MacDaniel took care of the railroad business and Dad would have to go to the store where the only telephone was located and order fresh cars and have the loaded ones pulled away. Later the pot kiln was replaced by a continuous kiln, a large, round tube, which rotated by the use of gears. The clay was fed in at one end, and it was so designed that by the time it came out of the other, it was cooked to the desired dryness. It was fired at about 2200 degrees and entered the kiln and gray clay and exited as pink and white calcine. After the government took the

FIGURE 13.10. *Stone blocks in a quarry, July 1908. Courtesy of Pueblo County Historical Society.*

property in 1965, the kiln was moved to the flats on Stone City Road and was fired by natural gas. After the railroad had ceased to run between Stone City and Pueblo the calcine or clay was hauled to the Colorado Fire Clay's (Dad's) loading dock at the end of 29th street in Pueblo where it was loaded onto railroad cars.[19]

The Colorado-Kansas Railway operated to Stone City daily throughout the 1910s and 1920s, hauling carloads of stone and clay. Colorado-Kansas No. 1 kept busy for the first few years, but it was already twenty-four years old when purchased from the Colorado Midland, and heavy use by both railroads took its toll. No. 1 turned out to be unreliable in less than a decade.[20] Needing some major repairs, the locomotive spent part of the year of 1920 out of service, forcing the railroad to lease another one, probably from the Santa Fe. The company spent $314 on repairs for No. 1 in 1921, probably from

FIGURE 13.11. *Clay mines at Stone City, in Dry Creek Cañon, December 31, 1912. Photo by John W. Floyd. Courtesy of Pueblo City-County Library District.*

FIGURE 13.12. *Looking east to Dry Creek Cañon, 1936. Kilns and clay loading chutes in the background. Colorado Railroad Museum Collection.*

flood damage, but it remained out of service the entire year, the next year, and on into 1923. A leased locomotive remained on the property during this time, keeping the freight and passengers moving. The railroad, perhaps unwisely, decided to spend nearly $5,000 in repairs on its only locomotive,

FIGURE 13.13. *Display of the Standard Fire Brick Company, which used Turkey Creek clay, circa 1913. Photo by John W. Floyd. Courtesy of Pueblo County Historical Society.*

almost as much as the original $7000 purchase price.[21] In 1922, The Interstate Commerce Commission settled with the Colorado-Kansas Railway for government control of the nation's railroads during World War I, offering the company $2,115.99 for the period of government control. $1,500 went toward paying down the repairs on the railway's locomotive.[22]

In the harshest blow, the locomotive again broke down in 1924, forcing the railroad to lease a locomotive for the next sixteen years. In a bit of creative accounting, No.1 remained on the books until 1930, apparently to keep accruing depreciation. The Interstate Commerce Commission, which required the nation's railroads to make annual reports, finally caught on to its "improper accounting performed in 1927 for a locomotive retired in 1923" and forced it to retire the locomotive from the books and scrap it. The scrap value for No. 1 was $3840.[23] At least as early as 1935, the Colorado-Kansas leased a Class C-28 2-8-0 locomotive from the Denver & Rio Grande Western, usually No. 672 or 674.[24] When the railroad scrapped No. 1, they placed the tender on blocks north of Stone City and reused it as a water tank.

The Colorado-Kansas Railway purchased older, secondhand rolling stock from a railroad back east, and it arrived in the spring of 1912.[25] Its freight equipment originally consisted of five 34-foot boxcars numbered 200 to 204; eight 35-foot flat cars, numbered 501 to 506, and 509 to 510; and two 35-foot gondolas, number 507 and 508. All the equipment had wooden bodies and underframes and rode on arch-bar trucks with cast wheels. The sole passenger car was 45-foot combination coach and baggage car No. 1, and it, too, had a wooden body and underframe but rode on wood trucks with cast wheels.[26] The freight equipment slowly wore out, and the railroad retired and scrapped all of it in 1930, except for boxcar No. 510, which became the railroad's caboose and tool car.[27] Even it was retired in 1945.[28] Far from being wasteful, the railroad did recycle some of the boxcars into storage sheds.[29]

The railroad ran a mixed train daily, meaning the train carried both passengers and freight. This system was good for the company and the employees, as it meant only an out-and-back run, while the train crew received pay based on wage rates for freight service, which was potentially more lucrative than passenger service wage rates.[30] The Colorado-Kansas Railway employed thirty-four men in 1914. Twenty trackmen make up the majority of the employees, with a single engineman, fireman, conductor, station agent and section foreman for each of those positions. Most employees worked 313 days that year. As for wages, the engineman earned $1,500 a year, or $4.80 per day, on par with other railroads in the state both larger and smaller, though not as high as the largest lines. The fireman and section foreman both earned $900, or $2.88 per day, while the conductor earned $1,030, or $3.30 per day. The lowest-paid employees were the trackmen, in charge of maintaining the line, who earned an average of $1.65 per day.[31]

In later years, the railroad employed anywhere from ten to seventeen people a year. until after 1930, when the figure dropped considerably, though employment reached a peak of twenty-six after the 1921 flood. The majority of the men worked as section hands, maintaining the railroad; however, the railroad laid off most of them by the Depression. Both the Pueblo and Stone City depots had station agents. Two clerks kept the paperwork moving, and an engineer, fireman, conductor, and occasional brakeman kept the train moving.[32]

Most of the officers of the company received no compensation. By 1913, J. F. Springfield was president of the company, and Charles E. Sutton was vice-president; Sutton would remain in that position until 1932. Neither ever received a salary from the company. General Manager Robert K. Potter received compensation, and occasionally the secretary-treasurer did as well. Potter remained as general manager until 1932.[33]

When A. B. Hulit offered stock for sale in the original Kansas-Colorado Railroad, he listed what he felt were "conservative" figures for revenue to entice investors in his project. These proposed revenue figures are incredibly optimistic when compared to actual statistics from the railroad, but it must be remembered that he based his estimates on the entire Western Division, from Pueblo to Cañon City, including several branch lines. Turkey Creek stone, of course, was to be the largest revenue producer, followed by limestone, coal, fireclay, cement and cement products, silica, iron ore, gypsum, firewood, ties, timber, and ganister. Commercial freight and passengers make up the remainder of his list.[34]

Looking at the years 1916 through 1919, when these figures were broken down in the annual reports, we can get an estimate of average traffic. Since the railroad never reached the coalfields of Florence and Cañon City, those figures are far lower than Hulit's original estimates, and the same goes for cement and related products. Lumping Turkey Creek stone together with the fireclay and ganister, the main products hauled by the railroad, originally gave A. B. Hulit an estimate of 530 tons to be hauled daily. In reality, all mineral products hauled during that time average out to just over sixty-four tons per day. Similarly, Hulit estimated commercial freight (essentially, manufactured goods) to be sixty tons daily. The actual figures were just over four tons hauled each day. Estimates for hauling timber were thirty tons per day but in fact worked out to less than a single ton each day.

With construction of the Pueblo City Hall underway, business was booming in 1917. City hall proved to be a difficult proposition for the Turkey Creek quarries, as the contractor complained variously that he could not get large enough blocks of stone from the quarries, that the colors were mismatched as the quarry company operated different parts of the quarries to supply the necessary stone, and that the some of the stone was too friable, or weak to use. In the end, only some Turkey Creek sandstone was used for city hall, with the rest being limestone from Bedford, Indiana.[35]

With planning and groundbreaking already underway, controversy as to the siting of the new city hall and auditorium arose in early February 1917. The Colorado-Kansas wanted the site moved twenty feet further north, to accommodate a sixty-foot strip of land for the four-track subway the railway still planned to build as Pueblo's central rail terminal.[36] After several days of back and forth through the advisory committee, the city commissioners eventually approved the change.[37] The subway was never built.

The Turkey Creek Stone, Clay & Gypsum Company operated three clay mines in 1917. Horses hauled the clay 1,500 feet to the kilns of the Pueblo Clay Products Company, where workers produced about forty tons of clay a day. Between the mines and kilns, twenty-five men were employed.[38]

Passenger service never really developed for the railroad. The railroad carried a record 3,449 passengers between Pueblo and Stone City in 1914, but five years later the number was only 936. By 1921, only 188 passengers rode the train. After that, the numbers are almost inconsequential. Only two paying passengers rode in 1925, ten in 1926, and then the number remains in single digits after that until 1931, when the railroad effectively ended passenger service between Pueblo and Stone City.[39] The Colorado-Kansas retired its only passenger car and placed it on blocks in Stone City, where the company rented it out at a residence.[40] While an increase in automobile ownership certainly contributed to the decline of the railroad's passenger revenues, bus service between Pueblo and Stone City started up in 1925, which probably offered more convenient service, if not cheaper fares.[41] During the early years, however, holiday excursions to Stone City were always popular, both with the several hundred excursionists who rode up from Pueblo and for the residents of Stone City. On these special occasions, the entire population turned out at the depot to welcome the excursion train.[42]

Despite the company's best efforts, the Colorado-Kansas Railway spent most of its life in red ink. Net railway operating income, or operating revenues after operating expenses have been deducted, only ran into positive numbers in four years prior to 1932. The year 1914 saw a net operating income of $2,053, and 1918 saw $1,519, while 1923 had a whopping $11,353. The year 1927 only offered up $295, the most meager of figures. Most years, the deficits ran $7,000 or less. In 1917, for instance, the railroad was only $82 in the hole. However, 1931 saw the hole grow to $26,025. The financial picture becomes mighty bleak when looking at the railroad's net income. Total net income is figured by subtracting the total interest charges on the bond mortgage from the net operating income for the year. With this calculation performed, the railroad's deficits ballooned to between $20,000 and $30,000 every year, a disheartening figure for any business executive.[43] Still, the railroad carried on about its business, always hoping there would be some new source of revenue coming its way in the near future. In addition, a common business practice might have aided the railroad. Besides Robert K. Potter, the owners and directors of the railroad—J. F. Springfield, J. R. Greenlees, and Charles E. Sutton—were the same owners and directors of the quarry company, essentially making the railroad a subsidiary of the Turkey Creek Stone, Clay & Gypsum Company.[44] Profits from the quarry company most likely allowed the railroad to continue running at a loss.

Building construction methods and materials changed during the first decades of the twentieth century, dooming the Stone City quarries and sawmill to obsolescence. Concrete and steel supplanted building stone as the preferred materials for construction, making it ever more difficult for the quarry company's owners to find a market for their stone. The last building to use Turkey Creek stone was the post office at Manhattan, Kansas, in 1930.[45] At the onset of the Great Depression, the tax base for municipal building projects, which typically used large quantities of building stone, disappeared.[46] The quarries and sawmill closed, never to reopen.[47] The explosion of sound from the quarries as dynamite fractured the stone, and the ringing of diamond saws as their blades cut and shaped the decorative stone, faded into silence, with only the rusting metal of the guy derricks cables and sawmill structures left to creak in the wind.

Following the closing of the quarries, the Turkey Creek Stone, Clay & Gypsum Company went defunct in 1932. With the exception of Robert K. Potter, the same owners—J. F. Springfield, J. R. Greenlees, and Charles E. Sutton—replaced it with another company they founded: Pueblo Quarries, Incorporated.[48] The name suggests that the owners expected the quarries to reopen when the economy improved. Since the quarries were no longer viable, the company instead turned their focus to clay. In a sense, the clay business flourished at the expense of the quarries. Fireclay, used in firebricks, was in great demand for the furnaces of steel mills, which turned out a product that helped put the quarries out of business.

Just as the Turkey Creek Stone, Clay & Gypsum Company had done, the new company continued to lease the mines to Pueblo Clay Products and the other companies, receiving royalties in return on the mining operations. The royalties from the clay mines and the clay-freighting business were not enough to help keep afloat their subsidiary, the Colorado-Kansas Railway. With no money available, the railroad could not meet the first payment on its bond, and, on July 1, 1931, a court order placed the railroad in receivership.[49] At the start of receivership, a legal secretary for the railroad's longtime attorney, J. T. McCorkle, held the company's assets as trustee for the railroad.[50] That secretary, Miss Irma MacDaniel, would go on to become the railroad's manager by 1940, possibly the first woman in the history of the United States to attain that position. Her management helped keep the railroad operating for nearly two more decades.[51]

PART IV
Silk Stockings and Steel Rails

14

My Friend Irma

A woman executive running a railroad in a Colorado setting might sound at first like the character of Dagny Taggart in Ayn Rand's famous novel *Atlas Shrugged*. Both Rand and Irma MacDaniel lived in the same era, and it is always possible, though highly improbable, that they crossed paths at some point, inspiring the novelist to posit a female business executive running a railroad. While the comparison ends there, the question remains, in such a male-dominated industry, how did a woman come to run a railroad? The answer to that lies in another question, so, to paraphrase the opening line of Rand's novel, "Who is Irma MacDaniel?"

Of all of the men discussed to this point, none of them have as ground-breaking an achievement as Irma MacDaniel. Her longevity with the railroad is a testament to her role as an unsung hero in this story. Irma MacDaniel had an indirect association with the Colorado-Kansas Railway almost from its inception but did not officially work for the company until around the time it entered receivership in 1931. Twenty years earlier, however, she had set a course that would propel her into management, business operations, and

DOI: 10.5876/9781646421282.c014

FIGURE 14.1. *Irma MacDaniel's senior photo, circa 1911, the only photo of her known to exist. Photo courtesy of Centennial High School Museum.*

even corporate ownership (something she would achieve as early as 1925). Even so, a position with the Colorado-Kansas Railway still lay years in her future. It is necessary to move backward in the chronology of the railroad in order to examine Irma MacDaniel's life, to see what choices she made in pursuing a career, and to find out how she first came to be associated with the railroad during its receivership period.

Irma MacDaniel came into the world on August 8, 1893, along with a twin sister, Elsa, born to James and Anna MacDaniel of Pueblo, Colorado. James was a real estate "operator," and probably kept the family comfortably in the middle class until his death in 1903.[1] Following his death, Irma MacDaniel's mother supported the girls working as a dressmaker.[2] Upon graduation from Centennial High School in 1911, MacDaniel took an extension course

FIGURE 14.2. *American Business College, August 1912. Irma MacDaniel attended here in 1912. Photo courtesy of Pueblo County Historical Society.*

from the University of Colorado at the high school. In 1912, she attended the American Business College at Pueblo, receiving training as a stenographer. This was not an unusual move for a young woman fresh out of high school. Postsecondary education was on the rise for women, with more than 140,000 attending colleges and universities in 1910.[3]

Still, it was a tough time for a woman to find a job, even in a prosperous city such as Pueblo. The Colorado Bureau of Labor Statistics bears this out, listing the applications for employment that were filled by females in 1913 and 1914, and these were primarily domestic-type service jobs: chambermaids, cooks, cleaning, dishwashers, houseworkers, housekeepers, kitchen girls, pantry girls, nurses, silver girls, and waitresses. Women submitted 3,173 applications for these jobs, and 2,611 were hired. The only nondomestic job was that of clerk, for which ninety-eight women applied. Only thirty-one landed employment.[4]

Despite the odds, a job awaited MacDaniel upon her leaving the business college, working as a stenographer for James T. McCorkle. This hire occurred about the time the Colorado-Kansas Railway was really getting started, so she had an association with the railroad from near the beginning, though as a secretary for the railroad's law firm. Both MacDaniel and McCorkle attended the First Presbyterian Church in Pueblo, and it is likely she knew him through church prior to her accepting a position with his firm.[5] McCorkle, along with his brother, was an attorney for the Colorado-Kansas Railway and MacDaniel worked as a secretary for McCorkle for twenty-three years. Through her work with McCorkle's firm over the course of the first twelve years, MacDaniel must have made a good impression on the railroad's owners as someone with a head for business. In 1925, they would welcome her into the fold of corporate life as a business partner in another railroad venture, though not yet as a manager. MacDaniel would not assume that role until 1940. As historian Angel Kwolek-Folland points out, "Few college women went on to become business executives in major male-controlled corporations," and railroads were certainly dominated by male executives.[6] Irma MacDaniel would become one of those few.

There were other female railroad executives, to be sure. Gertrude Hickman Thompson, chairman of the board of the Magma Arizona Railroad; Lucy Rogers Walsh, president of the Rock Island Southern; and Phoebe E. Clark, president of the Tennessee, Kentucky and Northern—all were female executives over railroads much larger than the Colorado-Kansas. All of these women inherited their positions following their husbands' deaths, and they were well versed in the railroads they ran. Contemporaries to MacDaniel, their stories were highlighted in in the May 1936 issue of *Baltimore and Ohio Magazine*, which had published an annual edition dedicated to women for eight years. Among smaller roads there were other women railway executives, as the magazine pointed out, including Mrs. D. R. Loworn, president of the Bowdon Railroad, Georgia; Mrs. A. D. Clark, president of the Jefferson and Northwestern Railway in Jefferson, Texas; Miss Marie Cronin, president of the Bartlett Western Railway, Texas; and Mrs. Virginia Persons, president of the Talbotton Railway, Georgia.[7] Irma MacDaniel certainly was not alone, but she was one of the female pioneers in the industry. She, too, moved into her position almost by default, as did these other women, though it was not through her husband's passing.

Traditional women's roles—such as teachers, librarians, nurses, and social workers—were well established.[8] The few businesses where women could hold an independent, entrepreneurial role were still scarce. Insurance and banking both hired women in record numbers for their public-service abilities.[9] Women, too, began selling real estate as well as life insurance as the numbers of women who were consuming these services grew. It made perfect sense that women could more easily sell to other women.[10] By 1930, they made up 8 percent of those agents.[11] It is not surprising, then, that MacDaniel entered both the insurance and real estate industries.

Women did not usually enter management positions, because corporations looked for workers who not only had the necessary college and business skills but also were committed to their work over the course of their lifetime. Marriage and the business of raising a family precluded this path for most women.[12] Whether by choice or by happenstance, MacDaniel never married. This freedom served to further her career, offering her an upward mobility and allowing her to involve herself in many different business ventures.

In 1925, several of the principal owners of the Colorado-Kansas Railway joined to build a new railroad in Pueblo, this one essentially designed to supplement the trackage washed out in the 1921 flood. The idea was to offer a direct connection from the Colorado-Kansas to the Missouri Pacific, Colorado & Southern, and Denver & Rio Grande Western railroads, extending all the way south to Southern Junction near the Colorado Fuel & Iron steel mill. The Pueblo Terminal Railway, as they named it, would also service businesses and industries around the area through which they built. Whether as an investment for her money or perhaps for some expertise she might bring to the venture, stenographer Irma MacDaniel moved forward into the corporate world when she joined Charles Sutton, J. T. McCorkle, C. E. Curran, and Robert K. Potter in forming the new corporation. J. F. Springfield was not a shareholder but served as a director for the new railroad. The partners capitalized the company for $500,000, divided into 5,000 shares with a par value of $100 each. How the shareholders divided the shares is unknown.[13]

The Pueblo Terminal Railway—like its associated railroad, the Colorado-Kansas—had aspirations bigger than reality would allow. The Colorado-Kansas Railway rebuilt most of its flood-damaged trackage in 1925, replacing the ties while reusing most of the old rails. With a direct connection to the Colorado-Kansas, the Pueblo Terminal Railway Company built nearly a half-mile of spurs that served industries around West Third and West Fourth Streets and Elizabeth Avenue in Pueblo, such as Navy Gas & Supply Co.

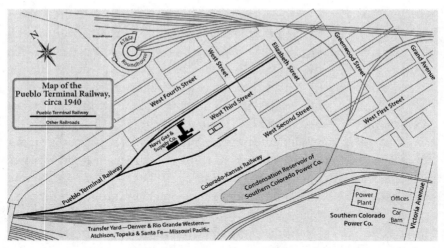

FIGURE 14.3. *Map of the Pueblo Terminal Railway, circa 1940. Drawn by the author, based on an engineering drawing courtesy of History Colorado–Denver.*

Not owning any rolling stock, the terminal railway entered into an arrangement with the parent road wherein the Colorado-Kansas would operate the new railroad while paying 25 percent of its switching revenue to the Pueblo Terminal Railway.[14] This arrangement lasted until 1931, when the Colorado-Kansas lapsed in its payments to the Pueblo Terminal Railway and instead opted to maintain the track as payment.[15] The Pueblo Terminal Railway also took out an option on a portion of the Colorado-Kansas right-of-way in 1926 but forfeited it the next year.[16]

Opportunities for women in business declined during the Depression, but Irma MacDaniel was one of the lucky ones, not only to hold onto her job but to improve her professional situation as well.[17] She maintained her titled position as stenographer with McCorkle, but in 1931 she solidified her position within the Colorado-Kansas Railway by accepting a promotion to an officer in the company, serving as secretary.[18] MacDaniel continued working for James T. McCorkle as secretary until his sudden death from a heart attack on January 29, 1936. Her title of secretary only extended to the railroad's board of directors, even though she probably helped their company out with clerical work. After McCorkle's death, she remained employed, accepting the position as a clerical secretary for the railroad.[19]

Meanwhile, MacDaniel continued developing business opportunities for herself. In 1933, she joined with James T. McCorkle and L. E. Langdon to found Sterling Securities, Incorporated, whose purpose was to "buy, own, hold, acquire real, personal, or mixed property, securities, and evidences of indebtedness, stocks bonds, debentures, and notes."[20] Besides her owner-ship in the company, MacDaniel maintained the books for the company and presumably operated it after McCorkle's death. Along with maintaining the accounts of the railroad, Pueblo Quarries, Inc., and the Welton Land and Water Company, she "won wide recognition for her ability and leadership." By the 1940s, she also operated a general insurance agency.[21] Irma MacDaniel was, by all accounts, a very busy person.

The Colorado-Kansas Railway entered receivership on July 1, 1931, to avoid bankruptcy and liquidation. For reasons now unknown but most likely due to the faith and trust placed in MacDaniel by the railroad's owners, she took on the position of trustee for the railroad until the suit for the foreclosure of trust deed in August 1931.[22] A year later, L. D. Riker of Oklahoma City, acting as agent for J. F. Springfield and Robert K. Johnston, purchased the railroad at a receiver's sale on September 30, 1932, for $14,603. The railroad, however, was subject to a lien for unpaid back taxes of $43,134.25, which the railroad owed to the county of Pueblo and the Pueblo Conservancy District. The Pueblo Conservancy District was a municipal organization formed after the 1921 flood to build and maintain flood protection facilities in Pueblo. Springfield and Johnston settled the lien for $10,000.[23] Their goal was to save the property by operating and maintaining it, thereby avoiding the "necessity of abandonment."[24]

The court appointed Ward S. Arnold as receiver for the railroad in 1931, and he operated the railway for Springfield and Johnston.[25] In 1933, Arnold offered a bookkeeping position, for both the quarries and railroad, to his nephew Raymond W. Arnold, a position that quickly expanded into a jack-of-all trades position. Arnold worked as superintendent of maintenance of way, superin-tendent of bridges and buildings, superintendent of the quarries, telephone lineman, water system ditch digger for Stone City, and power line mainte-nance man. For this, he earned $60 a month during the Great Depression.[26]

Irma MacDaniel undoubtedly had to show both Ward and Raymond Arnold the operations of the railroad, having been affiliated with it the longest. J. F. Springfield and Robert K. Johnston both still lived out of state,

Springfield in Austin, Texas, and Johnston in Oklahoma City. MacDaniel, then, was the most experienced person in the office in Pueblo. Springfield and Johnston were assistants to the receiver in 1932, but by 1933, Raymond Arnold and Irma MacDaniel claimed those positions. MacDaniel remained as secretary for the company.[27] Ward Arnold died in October 1935, leaving a power vacuum at the top.[28] Judge Voorhees of the District Court of Colorado then appointed Springfield and Johnston as co-receivers. Raymond Arnold's title switched to auditor, while MacDaniel remained as secretary.[29] Raymond Arnold and Irma MacDaniel struck up a friendship that lasted the rest of her life. Together, they ran the railroad from 1935 to May 1940, when Raymond Arnold left Pueblo to accept a job in Illinois.[30] MacDaniel continued the clerical work for the railroad while Arnold was technically the manager, but she gained valuable operations experience working side by side with him in the office.

15

The Depression Years

The Depression had a profound negative effect on revenue for the railroad, which Ward Arnold, and later, Raymond Arnold and Irma MacDaniel, tried to correct during the receivership. From an operating loss of $26,025 in 1931, the railroad dropped their losses to a *total* of $2,084 over the next seven years. Partly, this was due to a continuing increase of freight tonnage and revenue over those years, but the biggest factor was a drastic reduction in maintenance expenditures, which Ward Arnold kept to the bare minimum to allow the railroad to function. The majority of maintenance expenditures were labor costs, so at the start of the Depression the company laid off many of the employees who performed maintenance-of-way work. For the rest of the railroad's existence, the employees would perform multiple jobs, with the same four men used in train service as well as maintenance-of-way. The railroad divided its time and pay between the two positions, with the men receiving maintenance-of-way pay for that work, and train service pay for those hours.[1]

Switching for a couple of customers in Pueblo continued to provide revenue, and the clay-hauling business remained stable, despite the Depression.

DOI: 10.5876/9781646421282.c015

Engines of industry continued to need clay for firebricks, and so the railroad ran a train out to Stone City two or three times a week, whenever enough business had accumulated to furnish a light trainload.[2] Some weeks, though, not a single train ran to Stone City. The railroad would deliver an occasional carload of coal to the kilns and hay for the mules and burros used in the mines. Most of the traffic continued to be carloads of clay hauled from Stone City to Pueblo and beyond.[3] Without a mail contract or having to offer passenger service, the railroad did not need to maintain a regular schedule.[4]

A change in Colorado foreclosure law prompted Springfield and Johnston to issue a foreclosure deed by April 18, 1938. Moving quickly, they organized the Colorado Railroad, Incorporated, in 1938 to purchase the assets of the Colorado-Kansas Railway. John Q. Dier, an attorney who was acting as trustee for the railroad, purchased the deed of trust.[5] Upon approval by the Interstate Commerce Commission (ICC) on June 10, 1938, Springfield and Johnston's Colorado Railroad, Inc., acquired the old Colorado-Kansas Railway.[6] The receivership was at an end. Springfield again assumed the presidency, while Johnston acted as vice-president. Irma MacDaniel served as secretary-treasurer. The company issued 2,500 no-par-value shares of stock, of which 753 went to Springfield, 753 to Johnston, 496 to Sterling Securities, Inc., and 495 to Ward Arnold's widow, Catherine. MacDaniel received one share of stock, as did Raymond Arnold and L. N. McCorkle.[7]

After Raymond Arnold left for Illinois, Irma MacDaniel was the only person left in the office who knew how to run the railroad. Some speculation is necessary as to how MacDaniel inherited the manager's position, for the records have nothing to say on the matter. While it is always possible that Springfield and Johnston considered hiring someone else to manage the company (meaning, someone male), MacDaniel was in the perfect position to either ask for the job or, if Springfield and Johnston were paying attention, to offer the job to her. She had years of on-the-job-training and knew the operations of the company inside and out. By taking a manager's salary, which she received with her promotion, the company would actually save money by not having to pay her a clerical salary and hiring someone else as manager. For whatever the reason, MacDaniel's ascendancy to manager of the Colorado Railroad, Inc., in 1940 was a case where circumstances placed her in the right place at the right time and wherein she was the person best suited for the job, regardless of her sex. MacDaniel managed the day-to-day operations of the railroad for the next seventeen years but would occasionally seek out Arnold's advice when big, corporate decisions needed to be made, such as selling off railroad property.

Alfred D. Chandler Jr. defines modern business enterprises as having "many distinct operation units" and being "managed by a hierarchy of salaried executives."[8] Stocks were spread throughout many holders, who did not normally manage their firms. Instead, they "hired and promoted managers with little or no stock ownership in the company."[9] Chandler is speaking of big industries and businesses, such as the railroad and steel industries. In fact, large railroads led the way in establishing the ideas for managing modern business enterprises, and it is only natural that those ideas for management would find their way down to the smaller railroads.[10] Although the Colorado Railroad, Inc., was merely a small railroad in the greater transportation network of America, these "visible hand" modern business concepts show up between the absentee ownership of Springfield and Johnston and the salaried executive Irma MacDaniel, who managed their "multi-divisional" operating units, the railroad, and the quarries. Despite the fact that MacDaniel owned one share of stock, along with a portion of the Sterling Securities shares of the railroad, she served chiefly in the capacity of management. She controlled the daily operations, but when it came to making major decisions that would affect the entire company, she joined the other stockholders in voting on the company's future.

With clerical work, women needed to be quick, efficient, and accurate, while those women employed as secretaries also needed to be personable. Men, who mainly occupied the manager and executive positions, needed to be rational, ambitious, thorough, and ready to lead.[11] While there is no doubt MacDaniel was quick, efficient, accurate, and personable after her years as a secretary for McCorkle, she also possessed the managerial traits and brought them to her job as manager of the railroad. Of these traits, the one that stands out in MacDaniel's case is ambition. Clearly, she had ambition, due to the amount of work she took on. The company recognized her within the railroad industry for her managerial status with the Colorado Railroad, Inc. An edition of the industry publication *The Pocket List of Railroad Officials* from 1951 listed her as "Secretary-Treasurer" of the railroad, as well as Officer in Charge of Purchasing Supplies, "Officer in Charge of Mechanical Work," and "Officer in Charge of Engineering Work."[12]

MacDaniel's management took many forms and covered several facets of the business. The paperwork was probably the most time consuming. MacDaniel needed to bill customers for their shipments of clay and for the switching the railroad performed for them. Additionally, since the Colorado Railroad, Inc., used the rolling stock from other railroads for hauling clay from Stone City, she also paid rent to those railroads for the use of their cars.[13] She dealt with the local, state, and federal governments, whether it was the War Production Board over the possible sale of scrap metal during World War II, or the annual reports the railroad was required to file with the ICC and the Colorado Public Utilities Commission.[14] She also had to handle land issues that affected the railroad, such as when a property owner wanted to expand a building, requiring the rerouting of the railroad's track.[15] More important, MacDaniel continued to find additional sources of revenue, for both the railroad and the quarries, such as selling off the unused equipment rusting away at the Stone City quarries or the sawmill.[16]

MacDaniel's management of the railroad involved far more than simply keeping the books, for operations are the core of every railroad. She would have to schedule the runs for the train, which involved coordinating between when customers requested a shipment and when loads were ready for pickup at the mines. She had to arrange for their delivery, whether to local customers, or setting loads out for interchange with the other railroads in Pueblo when they were for out-of-town customers. MacDaniel also arranged for the interchange of empty cars destined for Stone City, which her railroad crew could then pick up.

Maintenance was a priority, at least within a limited budget. MacDaniel ordered supplies to keep the railroad operating, such as parts for occasional repairs to keep the locomotive running.[17] She made sure her employees performed any necessary maintenance, both on the locomotive, and on the track, roadbed, buildings, bridges, and culverts. Crosstie replacement was a necessary maintenance expenditure for the railroad, as the untreated pine ties did not last very long. Replacements fell off during the Depression while Ward Arnold was trying to cut losses, but once freight revenues increased after 1942, MacDaniel kept the replacement program going strong.[18] Indeed, the maintenance budget for the railroad increased from $1,677 in 1939 to $13,093 by 1945. Still, the railroad's physical plant continued to deteriorate. The same rails remained in place from 1911 and 1912 until the very end. Ballast, which helped water to drain from the roadbed as well as kept the track from shifting, was practically nonexistent. Only two miles of light cinders ballasted the roadbed for the first two miles out of Pueblo, and beyond that, the bare dirt of the grade lay exposed to the weather.[19] As a result, the track was rough and continued to worsen over the years without massive maintenance-of-way work on the rails and grade. The train traveled at slow speeds, but minor derailments still frequently occurred. The railroad never reported any major accidents.[20]

Part of MacDaniel's management involved renting houses to the people of Stone City, as well as maintaining the water and telephone system. Here, MacDaniel's empathy served her well. Mrs. Tacy Grant, the postmaster at Stone City, wrote to MacDaniel in a panic on October 1, 1951, having lost a check from Mrs. Eva Dorfer, probably for rent on a house in Stone City. Grant admitted the same thing had happened the year before. She felt awful for the loss, writing MacDaniel, "I thank you for your patience and kindness to me—I wish to resign. I will miss you. If I owe the company anything I will pay it. I am worried!!"[21] MacDaniel wrote back:

> Please do not worry about misplacing the check of Mrs. Dorfer's, that is something that happens to us all every day in our work—misplace some piece of paper or part of a file. Hurts me to think you would worry about it so, please do not, and please do not resign, let's just go on as we have in the past, you let me know what happens in Stone City and receive the payments which come to you if it is not too much strain on you.
>
> I am enclosing a check to you for this year to date, adding for the check which you lost, as it should not be your loss.
>
> Perhaps in the future you could just clip the check to your check book or put them in an envelope in your check book and in this way it should not get away from you.[22]

Sometime after electricity arrived at the houses at Stone City, MacDaniel decided that the residents should be billed for what electricity they used. She hired Harold "Bud" Moore from Johnson Electric to install meters on all of the houses. When the time came to read the meters, MacDaniel was dismayed to find them smashed to pieces and chalked the idea up to a lost cause.[23]

Between all of MacDaniel's businesses, her office was a busy place. She hired office workers—her "girls," as she referred to them—to help her juggle the work of multiple companies. At times, she had only one regular office worker, but usually she had at least two, and sometimes more. Dorothy Patch worked for MacDaniel for many years as her most consistent employee. As if she were following in MacDaniel's footsteps, she attended the American Business College in Pueblo after graduating from Centennial High School. Her first job was as secretary and bookkeeper for a Pueblo law firm before coming to work for MacDaniel. Unlike MacDaniel, however, Patch married twice, though her only children were two stepsons from her second marriage.[24]

Turnover in MacDaniel's office was somewhat frequent, owing perhaps to the nature of the work and the age of her employees, though MacDaniel herself might have been a taskmaster. She surely was thorough in her work, had a fixed way that things should run, and would have stayed on top of those who did not perform to expectations. Her state of mind probably varied from calm to frustrated, at times, as this note to Raymond Arnold indicated: "Hope all is well in your world Ray, am very tired myself, have worked so hard, have two girls all the time, but even so with the Morey deal, Loving Dairy, and such never have a second, and am too tired, but when this season is over hope to relax some. Do write Ray—tell Riley I enjoyed his valentine very much, was cute as could be and nice of him to think of just *me*?? Best of wishes with Love, Irma."[25]

In fact, Arnold had to hear about her employees on many occasions: "Awfully busy, had three girls working today trying to catch up—busy season and far behind," she wrote in 1947.[26] The next year, she wrote, "Am getting along okay, have a Jr. College girl who comes down each day and works Saturday am. Helps a lot with the routine accounts, etc. Dorothy is still working too—I do not work much nights any more, at the office anyway—take some work home now and then to do—but work long hours in the office, until six every night, and start around 7 at home as you know with all the Railroad calls."[27]

By 1951, good help seemed hard to come by. Two employees worked for her, but she seemed to need more: "Pueblo has a great shortage of stenographers, the Ordnance and CF&I taking them all, I have Dorothy still and Lucile a married woman, who has one boy, he is sick with cold now, so she took some farm voucher records home to run etc. Best I can do—life is not what we want but what we get."[28] Turnover, as usual, caused its share of headaches: "My college girl left today and have to start a new girl October first, so will make a difficult fall, with two new girls in the office, hope I am lucky with my new ones. Not an easy office to work in as you well know for an untrained mind at least."[29]

Even after the railroad was long gone, she still managed Pueblo Quarries, Inc., and her workload had not let up. In one particular instance in 1963, she revealed that a woman, if married, needs a husband with a good job, to perform at her best:

> Have mediocre help in the office, girl expecting a baby in December, so with four small children now, no finances, since her husband is trying to sell real estate, being a stranger and a novice, she is fatigued all of the time—just drags at every thing she does, and was so spoiled with my quick college girls etc. Celia is working today, has worked for me for nine years, when she has time, is married and has four children too, but her husband has an excellent position at the CF&I and they are buying a lovely new home, she can do anything beautifully.[30]

Even though she worked as a successful businesswoman, MacDaniel still adhered to older ideals of women in the workplace and notions of manhood tied to a good job.

In 1971, MacDaniel fell in her bathroom and cut her head. While she convalesced, she wrote to Arnold: "Have no help, the girl I had stayed a part of January and I was paying her $385 a month too, but left before I got back. I just came in this week, so have no help yet."[31]

In running not just the railroad but also her whole office, MacDaniel developed a manager's instincts. As part of her taking on the role of management, she developed a manager's outlook toward organized labor, though it probably did not affect her directly on the railroad. Her crew was small, typically two to four men, and she could come to know them like family, far easier than managers on larger railroads or other industries could. The clay miners at Stone City could cause problems: "Just at present I hear the miners are on a strike at Stone City for more pay for clay . . . [A]s they have hit a heavy rock formation, know the mine is not well mined," she wrote to Ray. The miners, however, were supervised by Pueblo Clay Products, the company that leased the clay mines from Pueblo Quarries, Inc., decades before, so she did not have to deal with the strikers directly.[32] Still, she had a definite management mindset: "The election is decidedly Democratic, which means little to me except indirectly, but then we will see how the world goes, hoping for the best, but am afraid it will give labor more power and look for more difficulty with organized labor."[33]

MacDaniel received very little help in running the railroad from Springfield and Johnston and was probably quite happy with things in that regard, but when her bosses were around, she felt like any other paid employee around them, writing, "Mr. Springfield stayed for almost three weeks, and while I tried to be nice about it, needless to say I was exhausted, I did not eat with them much, as I ate with Frank every night, but noons they came and I could not get rid of them, then they napped in the afternoon and arrived between 4 and 5 and just took possession of the corner office and 'commandeered' my time etc. was very difficult for me, kept me from accomplishing anything with them, or without them really truly—made me very nervous."[34]

Springfield and Johnston stayed away far more often than they came around, though. There was little for them to do that MacDaniel could not handle. In fact, they were absent so much that MacDaniel sometimes had to hold the annual board of directors meetings on her own: "Mr. Springfield sent his proxy in for the meeting, also Mr. Johnston, with a nice letters [sic] saying he thot [sic] he might sell out, but guess he will not since no one writes him, and then your Mother sent her[s] in so, so silently the meeting met—Mr. Springfield wrote an air mail letter to hold the meeting open as matters might come up which could be acted on in the meeting, so it is held open—was from last year at his request for that matter."[35]

Even the quarry company owners paid her little attention, for she wrote Ray, "Never hear a word from Mr. Sutton, nor Mr. Greenlees, both old and broken I imagine, not being prosperous, would add to their age no doubt."[36] Carl Springfield, one of the two trustees of his father's estate (the other being one Mr. O'Conner), discovered just how little his father had done, and praised MacDaniel for her management: "Personally, I have but very little knowledge of either the Railroad or the Quarry, but after talking with Mr. Johnston and Mr. O'Conner, it would appear that Miss MacDaniel has done a wonderful job looking after both these properties and it would appear that she had not had much assistance and guidance from the owners of either the Railroad or the Quarry."[37]

Johnston, too, praised MacDaniel to Raymond Arnold, writing, "Irma gets up at 5:00 o'clock and is down to the office working by 6:00. She is keeping the records on the quarry, the McCorkle Estate, the railroad and something else; also making out income taxes for about 200 accounts. How she does it all with only two girls in the office I do not see. If she would break down in health, I don't know who would run the railroad."[38]

One can only hope that praise of this sort or another made its way back to MacDaniel. Their respective ages and their distance from Pueblo might have had something to do with it, but whatever the reason, both the railroad and quarry owners were apparently comfortable with the manner in which MacDaniel was handling the companies. They felt they did not need to supervise her and were content to just sit back and let the quarry company royalty checks roll in. In 1946, MacDaniel was listed as the officer of record for the Colorado Railroad, Inc., with the federal government.[39]

Irma MacDaniel earned a decent salary during her years as a manager. She earned an annual salary of $1,980 in 1942, and a raise in 1943 brought it up to $2,010. She dipped back down to $1,990 in 1944, but from 1945 to 1952, she earned $2,400 per year.[40] For comparison, the U.S. Census Bureau reports that the mean, or average, income for white men in 1948 was $2,851 while women only earned $1,345.[41] The harsh reality of the fading railroad business hurt her, though. She took a cut in pay in 1953 to $1,800 and no salary in 1954 and 1955 in an attempt to save money for the company. The final two years of operation, MacDaniel earned $800 and $1,200, respectively.[42] These income figures do not reflect what she earned from her other businesses.

The nature of the job must have been wearing on her, with no other professionals of her stature in the office with whom to talk. Even office gossip had to take place long distance. MacDaniel's friendship with Raymond Arnold gave her someone to confide in about the crazy business in which she worked. He knew the owners and had worked closely with her for seven years before moving away, so he knew the ins and outs of the business and what to expect. Occasionally, Raymond Arnold would return to Pueblo to help with matters, as MacDaniel wrote to him, "The time you spent this summer passed all too short, and we accomplished less than I had hoped, naturally, but then that is always true."[43] For the most part, though, MacDaniel was on her own. At times, hints of isolation or even loneliness, along with a resigned weariness, crept into her letters to Arnold: "Mrs. McCorkle just called to tell me of her new dinner dress etc. but time flies and time for me to close up for Saturday afternoon Ray, thought would not wait as long as you did, felt as though I had dropped into a cave . . . [hearing] nothing from anyone—but soon thought well I can carry on.—at least."[44] She signed her letters to him, even those that were mostly business, "Love, Irma." She confided in Ray about her health, and always inquired about his wife and their sons, showing concern when they were ill.[45] In a way, they were her family as well.

Little information is available about MacDaniel's private life outside of the office. She enjoyed her home and her garden, which she cultivated "with great skill and taste."[46] She lived in the same neighborhood most of her life. She continued to live with her mother, and together they moved into a newly constructed house in 1940 at 310 West Fourteenth Street.[47] Her mother died in 1946, but MacDaniel called the place home until her own death in 1971.[48]

After working six days a week, Sundays at the First Presbyterian Church probably offered MacDaniel the most social time. She joined the church when she was thirteen years old, but had likely attended from a very young age. Some sort of transgression resulted in the church officially suspending her membership in 1933; the church did not record the nature of the infraction. A suspension meant that she was still a Presbyterian, but she could no longer partake in communion. MacDaniel never had her membership reinstated, even though she continued to attend the church the rest of her life.[49] Whatever wrong she had allegedly committed was not enough to make her leave the church and the friends she had there. Professionally, she belonged to the Pueblo Chamber of Commerce and, socially, to the Pueblo Country Club, both of which befitted her status as a business executive.[50]

In 1948, MacDaniel may have dated Frank Zavislan, a prominent agriculture leader in the region, or at least was very good friends with him.[51] Zavislan purchased Robert K. Potter's former Turkey Creek Ranch in 1946. With ten miles of Colorado Railroad, Inc., tracks crossing his property, he would have had to deal with MacDaniel during the purchase. Nine years her junior, yet long unmarried like herself, Zavislan might have just been a kindred spirit to whom she felt a connection. He finally married in 1954, but it was not to MacDaniel.[52]

16

The Colorado Railroad, Inc.

As business and operations on the Colorado Railroad, Inc., began to increase prior to World War II, the company decided it was time to modernize its motive power, while cutting operating costs at the same time. It had rented a steam locomotive from the Denver & Rio Grande Western for many years, but in 1940, they purchased a fifty-ton gas-electric locomotive. The locomotive originally came from the Fox & Illinois Union Railroad, an electric interurban line where it served as box motor No. 7, essentially an electrically powered boxcar. After the Fox & Illinois Union ended interurban operations in 1931, it modified the locomotive with two 150-horsepower Buda gasoline engines to power the four General Electric traction motors that propelled the car, the same basic technological idea as used in diesel-electric locomotives. A farmers' cooperative in Illinois used the locomotive to switch its grain elevators until 1938. From there, the locomotive went to a scrap dealer, who sold it to the Colorado Railroad, Inc., for $3,910. The locomotive became the Colorado Railroad, Inc.'s No. 1 and served the railroad for the next seventeen years. As diesel-electrics were doing with other railroads, the

DOI: 10.5876/9781646421282.c016

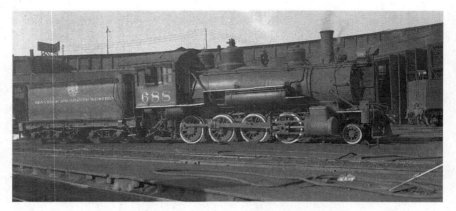

FIGURE 16.1. *D&RGW Class C-28 2-8-0 locomotive No. 688, September 16, 1939. This is the same class of locomotive that the Colorado-Kansas Railway rented. Photo courtesy of Denver Public Library, Western History Collection, OP-9377.*

FIGURE 16.2. *HMX No. 1, prior to delivery to Colorado Railroad, Inc., July 8, 1941. Photo by Robert W. Richardson, courtesy of Denver Public Library, Western History Collection, RR-1232.*

new locomotive proved to be substantially cheaper to operate than a steam locomotive. The company also saved money by not having to pay to rent a locomotive. When delivered, it came painted red with yellow ends, to which the Colorado Railroad, Inc., added bright yellow paint swooping down to

FIGURE 16.3. *Colorado Railroad, Inc., No. 1 on the wye at Stone City, October 1947. Photo Albert Knicklebine. Author's collection.*

FIGURE 16.4. *Another view of Colorado Railroad, Inc., No. 1 on the wye at Stone City, October 1947. Photo Albert Knicklebine, Author's collection.*

the center of the car at an angle from both ends.[1] To house the new locomotive, the railroad tore down the old corrugated iron engine house in 1943 and built a modern engine house out of cinder blocks.[2]

Business for clay boomed during World War II, with freight revenues peaking in 1942.[3] Even after the war, demand for clay far exceeded production from the mines.[4] The Colorado Railroad, Inc., was busy and about to get

FIGURE 16.5. *The Colorado Railroad, Inc.'s only caboose, July 8, 1941, purchased for $331 from the Atchison, Topeka and Santa Fe Railroad in 1937 and retired in 1945. Photo by Robert W. Richardson, courtesy of Denver Public Library, Western History Collection, RR-1231.*

FIGURE 16.6. *Engine house for the Colorado Railroad, Inc., 2005. Constructed in 1943 to replace a corrugated iron engine house of similar size and shape originally built on this site in 1911. Photo by the author.*

busier. In 1946 Chicago Freight Car & Parts opened a shop on West Twenty-Ninth Street and quickly became the railroad's chief revenue-producing customer. The Illinois company was less than twenty years old, but an opportunity had presented itself after the war, which necessitated building in far-off Pueblo, Colorado.

Fred H. Sasser started his own company, Central West Refrigerator Despatch, in Chicago, leasing cars to a local railroad for hauling fresh dairy and produce and selling reconditioned railcar parts. The parts business was big enough that Sasser shortly started a second company, Chicago Freight Car & Parts. This new company would maintain and recondition his own railcars and those of other customers as well as handle the parts business. Sasser kept the company going throughout the Great Depression and World War II, but big changes were soon to come, thanks to Robert Sasser, Fred's only child. Robert graduated from Purdue in 1939 with a degree in mechanical engineering, after which he went to work for his father. Once war broke out, he received the commission of major in the US Army, having gone through the Reserve Officers' Training Corps program while at Purdue. The army wasted no time in making Robert part of their Transportation Corps. Upon Robert Sasser's return from the service in 1946, he realized there were hundreds of surplus US Army troop sleepers leftover from the war, most of them no more than two or three years old. This insight compelled him to purchase the sleepers at bargain prices from the War Asset Administration. Chicago Freight Car & Parts ripped them down to the bare walls and converted them into head-end express, refrigerated, and baggage cars. Robert then formed a new company, Chicago Freight Car Leasing, which would take the newly converted cars and lease them to railroads throughout North America and Mexico.[5]

The Department of the Interior was rehabilitating the Alaska Railroad at the time, desperate for rolling stock, including diesel-electric locomotives, tank cars, and refrigerated cars.[6] Chicago Freight Car would convert these troop cars to be leased to the Alaska Railroad, but the task was more than its Chicago facility could handle. To deal with the growing backlog the company opened up an additional shop in Pueblo, but it was not enough, so the following year it opened a third, larger facility in Auburn, Washington. Washington was better situated logistically to ship cars to Alaska, but the Pueblo shop kept busy over the next several years converting troop sleepers into refrigerated cars. After completion of the Alaska Railroad order, the Railway Express Agency (REA) came calling. Chicago Freight Car converted hundreds more sleepers into refrigerated boxcars for the REA and then for the Mexican railway system.[7] In 1948 the Pueblo shop worked on an order of 100 kitchen cars, turning out one car per day. In contrast, the new Auburn shop was converting 390 troops sleepers at the rate of two per day.[8] Serviced solely by the Colorado Railroad, Inc., Chicago Freight Car & Parts Company kept the railroad busy switching cars into and out of its plant. The railroad used any unnecessary trackage, such as the old main line to Victoria Avenue, as storage for the freight car rebuild plant, receiving revenue for that storage.[9]

By the end of the 1940s, major changes were taking place for the Santa Fe Railway in Pueblo. The railroad planned to tear out its old railyards and main line through the center of town, which had caused motorists headaches for well over a half-century, and relocate to a new, modern gravity-fed hump classification yard next to the Denver & Rio Grande Western's large freight yard. This new yard, however, would be right in the middle of the Colorado Railroad's right-of-way. Selling off any portion of the railroad involved much consultation with the other shareholders, as there were many things to discuss. How much land did the Santa Fe intend to take? How much revenue would the railroad lose without that switching? Was the Santa Fe offering a fair price?

J. A. Noble, chief engineer of the Santa Fe Railway, discussed the situation with MacDaniel in the fall of 1948. The Santa Fe would need to take 53.72 acres from the Colorado Railroad, Inc., and the Pueblo Terminal Railway, and was willing to pay $45,000 for the land and an additional $14,000 for the trackage that the railroad would have to abandon. The Santa Fe also offered to switch the industries normally switched by the Colorado Railroad, Inc., for one dollar per car, as well as maintaining its trackage and billing the company for the task. The Santa Fe did not want the Colorado Railroad, Inc.'s, locomotive to use its yards.[10]

Raymond Arnold did not think that the price the Santa Fe was offering was adequate. Under the Santa Fe's proposal, the Colorado Railroad, Inc., would lose revenue from switching three different businesses. The railroad would retain one spur to the North Side Water Works from the west line of the city limits, but the Santa Fe would maintain it at the Colorado Railroad's expense, which MacDaniel felt to be "prohibitive, due to their costly maintenance."[11] Additionally, MacDaniel felt that, even though the railroad would receive

FIGURE 16.7. *Pueblo plant of the Chicago Freight Car & Parts Company, 1947. The Colorado Railroad, Inc.'s, main line to Stone City runs along the left of the facility. Photo courtesy of Sasser Family Holdings.*

$1.00 per car switched, the business would be practically none, though she does not make clear why this would be the case.[12]

The railroad would also lose the original Colorado-Kansas right-of-way to Victoria Avenue, which represented storage tracks for cars destined for Chicago Freight Car & Parts Company for repair or dismantling.[13] MacDaniel did not feel this would be a problem, as rumors were around that Chicago Freight Car & Parts would be moving out to the former Pueblo Air Base and no longer be serviced by the Colorado Railroad, Inc. If this happened, she felt abandonment was the next logical step for the railroad. MacDaniel also thought that the Santa Fe's offer on the land was not as high as it should be, for it was offering the same price for the railroad right-of-way as for land without trackage, while the right-of-way the Santa Fe wanted to buy would be used for a main line into Pueblo under the Fourth Street Bridge.[14]

Charles Sutton, one of the original investors in the Colorado-Kansas Railway and a longtime shareholder in the Pueblo Terminal Railway, informed MacDaniel that he would handle the Terminal Railway property but had done nothing up to that point on the matter. MacDaniel had left the matter up to him, but the Santa Fe grew impatient. She confided to Springfield that "it reflected on my integrity to handle the matter this way contacting no one, and just waiting," to which Springfield replied that he had someone in Houston who would buy both the railroad and the Terminal property. Springfield had used this same story before, and MacDaniel's frustration with the whole mess had to be mounting.[15]

The Pueblo Terminal Railway; Colorado Railroad, Inc.; and Irma MacDaniel, trustee for the defunct Colorado-Kansas Railway, were all named, along with many others, in a July 25, 1949, condemnation suit by the Atchison, Topeka & Santa Fe Railway to acquire the land for their new railyard.[16]

In the end, the Colorado Railroad, Inc., and Pueblo Terminal Railway ended up getting $57,000 from the Santa Fe for the land and the junk value of the rails, which the two companies agreed to split fifty-fifty.[17] After expenses, the Colorado Railroad, Inc., received $21,544. The railroad disposed of 1.335 miles of track, while the Pueblo Terminal Railway sold its .49 miles of track. That left the Colorado Railroad, Inc., with 20.971 miles of single track owned and operated, plus 1.694 miles of yard tracks, for a total of 22.665 miles of railroad.[18]

Throughout the 1950s, the railroad continued to run one to three times a week to Stone City for clay. In the late 1940s, though, Pueblo County had improved the road to Stone City, and so more of the clay began to move by truck.[19] To top it off, a flood in the summer of 1951 washed out the center support of the Booth Gulch trestle, effectively ending rail service into Stone City.[20] When MacDaniel considered it unpractical to rebuild the bridge, Bill Thomas, who operated the mines under lease for Pueblo Clay Products, Inc., wanted to haul the empty and loaded railroad cars across the bridge with winches and cables. MacDaniel nixed this idea as too hazardous. The Spring Cañon Mine, which opened to the south of Stone City, had no rail service, and while the railroad considered rerouting the main line over to the new mine, MacDaniel again did not consider it cost-effective, as the Spring Cañon Mine used trucks to haul out its shipments. Construction of an unloading dock at Twenty-ninth Street in Pueblo allowed the transfer of clay from train

FIGURE 16.8. *Irving Place Yard and Santa Fe Railway connection, circa 1950. The engine house is the long white building in the middle of the right side of the photo. Courtesy of Pueblo City-County Library District.*

to trucks for shipment to brick kilns in Pueblo.[21] Pueblo Clay Products, Inc., shipped clay to its destination in Pueblo in three separate movements, first, by trucking clay from the mines to the loading dock at Myrtle on the railroad, then hauling it by rail to Pueblo, and, finally, transferring it to truck again in Pueblo for the journey to its final destination. Pueblo Clay Products wised up to the fact that by trucking the clay directly from the mine to its final destination, the company could eliminate altogether two of the movements.[22] Subsequently, the railroad lost business. Only Arthur Wands continued to use the railroad for clay shipping from his privately owned mine.[23] The railroad still switched four or five days a week for Chicago Freight Car.[24] With the reduced workload for the railroad, the number of employees in train service dropped to two. Longtime employee Ray Johnson operated the train as engineer, and Harold L. Demeree acted as switchman.[25] "Johnson was probably the only person in the state that knew how to operate that locomotive," recalled Harold "Bud" Moore, the longtime electrician who serviced the locomotive.[26]

The World War II and postwar boom years represented the best years in
the railroad's history in terms of revenue and are due, in large part, to the
national economy. However, balancing income and expenses is a function
of management, and here the figures support MacDaniel's successful management of a shaky enterprise. The average yearly combined freight and
switching revenue from 1913 to 1939 was $16,563, compared to $24,235 during
MacDaniel's first decade of management. During the earlier period, the average annual loss was $3,340, while during MacDaniel's first decade the average
annual loss was merely $618. She should be given credit for helping to keep
the railroad functioning as long as it did. A decline would soon set in, though.
From peak revenues of $31,439 in 1948, they had dropped to $14,992 by 1952,
and bottomed out at $8,868 in 1956. This severe drop in revenue mirrors the
increasing movement of clay by trucks instead of the railroad, and the loss
of switching after the Santa Fe took over the line south of the Irving Place
yards.[27] With declining revenues and no new customers coming on line, the
end of the railroad was near.

17

End of the Line

The end of the railroad could be seen coming a long time before it happened, and one gentleman in particular offered several times to take the company off of the owners' hands. Guy B. Treat, an acquaintance of Robert K. Johnston's from Oklahoma City, had an interest in buying out the railroad and quarries for over a decade. In November 1947, MacDaniel wrote to Raymond Arnold:

> Friday Bob Johnston's Mr. Treat blew into Pueblo unannounced, to buy the Railroad, and Quarry HE SAID.
>
> Seems he had seen Mr. Springfield some month ago, and he half acquiesced that he would sell—so he asked a lot of questions some of which I answered, and some of which I did not know the answers to.
>
> Mr. Springfield did not advise me he had been to see him, Mr. Treat told me—he (Treat) is a typical promoter type, and I honestly think it is just a plan to get in control to handle the Santa Fe Grade crossing matter etc. I picked up much he asked and said, he was not so cute, and I frankly told him I was an employee and had no instructions to furnish the information he asked to anyone, particularly pertaining to the Quarry.[1]

DOI: 10.5876/9781646421282.c017

Johnston pursued the matter with Arnold, introducing him to Treat, who had had an association with the Oklahoma Street Railway Company since 1911. Springfield's health had deteriorated by this time, and both majority stockholders had lost interest in the railroad: "I seldom get out to Pueblo. The property has more or less been drifting along as in the past. I think this is a good time to get in cash position. We have not made much more than accounting expenses during all these boom times."[2]

The many owners of the quarries were not interested in selling at the time, as the clay mines were still producing, and Treat only wanted both the railway and the quarries together.[3] Ownership of the quarries was murky at best, as no stock had ever been issued, no officers or directors selected, and no stockholders' meeting ever held.[4]

Guy Treat remained interested in the quarries and the railroad over the years, continuing to pursue them for purchase as a pair. In 1949, Robert Johnston again approached Raymond Arnold about selling his share of the quarries. "I am for liquidating it," Johnston wrote, "as in the boomtime we have made no money."[5] Finally, in January 1956, the rusty wheels of progress began to turn in Treat's favor. Springfield had died the previous year, and his estate wished to sell their share of the stock in the Colorado Railroad, Inc., Robert Johnston agreed to sell his shares as well.[6]

MacDaniel suspected that they should see how much they could get for "pulling and selling the rail, and then trying to sell off the real estate," knowing the owners could get more money by scrapping the railroad themselves than by selling it to Treat and letting him handle the abandonment. The railroad by this time had sold the depot property on Victoria Avenue. Perhaps MacDaniel did not press hard enough on the notion, or else the owners just wanted to wash their hands of the railroad and be done with it, but her idea for scrapping the railroad on their own was evidently dismissed. MacDaniel might have felt like washing her hands of the whole deal as well, for she had taken no pay for over two years; as she expressed it, she felt "they are indebted to me."[7] The railroad also owed MacDaniel for three years' office rent.[8] Her income from the railroad was only supplemental to her other businesses, but it still had to gall her.

Several loose ends needed to be tied up prior to abandonment, notably, who would service the railroad's customers. Chicago Freight Car & Parts planned on expanding its facility, and MacDaniel felt that enterprise would be the most capable of handling its own switching, saving money in the process, even with the purchase of trackage from the Santa Fe connection to their shops. Chicago Freight Car would also obtain revenue switching for the industries at the County Shops across the street. In her opinion, Chicago Freight Car should have the first opportunity to purchase the required stretch of track.[9]

At their 1956 annual meeting, the board approved the sale of the railroad.[10] The quarries were still not for sale, but Guy Treat decided to purchase the railroad in any case.[11] MacDaniel suspected that Johnston, Springfield estate trustee O'Connor, and Treat were trying to go behind her back, holding secret meetings during the stockholders' meetings while in Pueblo, perhaps to make a little money on the sale. Maybe feeling MacDaniel could be a threat, Johnston had told her she would not have time to look after the sale. Confiding in Arnold, she responded, "Odd, I have had time all these years with all of the headaches etc. but now I would not, they are not even half clever, Mr. Johnston was definitely going to see that no one talked with me without him present, but actually, since the plan must be presented in detail, we will not approve unless it suits us, and it does not suit me to pay Treat, if they want to they can as I see it now."[12]

Upon returning home to Illinois, Raymond Arnold paid a visit to the Chicago Freight Car & Parts Company's headquarters to break the news of the pending sale. The freight car company made it clear that it did not want to get into the switching business but hoped the Santa Fe would build a connecting track and take over for the Colorado Railroad, Inc. The Santa Fe had mentioned the possibility several years earlier during its purchase of property from the railroad. If this happened, Arnold expected no opposition to the abandonment.[13]

By June, Treat had purchased the shares of stock owned by the Springfield estate, Robert Johnston, and Raymond Arnold. The price was $25 per share. Having sold his shares, Arnold resigned his position as a director of the Colorado Railroad, Inc.[14] After the sale, Treat inquired of Arnold about the future prospects for the railroad, based on the number of companies using the railroad's services, the percentage of tonnage handled by rail as opposed to that hauled by trucks, and the likelihood for development of future sources of revenue. Arnold replied that the railroad hauled very little clay for Pueblo Quarries, Inc., and any future tonnage, such as from the Spring Cañon Mine, would require relocation of the railroad at Stone City. Treat seemed to be considering keeping the railroad open, rather than abandoning it.[15]

Treat filed for abandonment of the railroad with the Interstate Commerce Commission on October 23, 1956. As proof of necessity for abandonment, the statement of income and expenses showed a net loss, after all business expenses were subtracted from revenues, of nearly $17,000 over the last five and a half years. Since the railroad offered no passenger service, the general public would not be affected by the removal of the railroad. The improvement of highways and roads in the area had caused a shift in the haulage of clay from the railroad to trucks, so the mines would be little affected as well. Only the Chicago Freight Car & Parts Company would be seriously affected, but Treat suggested that an extension of track by the Santa Fe would solve that problem. He estimated the salvage value of rails at just over $225,000, nearly double what he paid for the railroad.[16]

The Santa Fe apparently did not want to build a new track to Chicago Freight Car & Parts or take over the Colorado Railroad's trackage, for the sole opposition to the abandonment did come from Chicago Freight Car. This opposition did not seem to matter, though because on Monday, May 6, 1957, the Interstate Commerce Commission authorized the abandonment permit, subject to the condition that the railroad sell the line, entire or in portion, to anyone offering the fair market salvage value within the next thirty-five days. The stipulation was intended to help the Chicago Freight Car & Parts Company resume its business, should a buyer be found.[17]

No savior stepped forward, and the Colorado Public Utilities Commission also granted permission to abandon the line twenty-one days from June 24. By June 29, Guy Treat had sold the railroad to Commercial Metals of Dallas, Texas, a very large scrap dealer. As MacDaniel suspected, Treat was only looking for a quick profit. With the money he made from the deal, Treat sailed for Europe with his wife, and she expected Robert Johnston, as part of the deal, would soon go to Africa or South America to celebrate.[18]

A woman drove the first spike on the Colorado-Kansas Railway, so it was somehow fitting that a woman presided over its demise. In late July, MacDaniel contracted with Gottula Trucking and Transportation, Inc., of Pueblo, to dismantle the railroad and load the scrap metal on cars to be shipped to Commercial Metals.[19] Knowing the end was near, the Chicago Freight Car & Parts Company decided to close its Pueblo facility and transfer

FIGURE 17.1. *Stone City depot, October 1947. Photo by Albert Knicklebine. Author's collection.*

their forty employees to Chicago.[20] Scrapping of the line started in mid-August, but the railroad kept operating as usual until the very end.[21] Gottula finished removing the last of the rails on November 12, and the long-suffering former Colorado-Kansas Railway was gone.[22] For having scrapped the railroad, Commercial Metals made $171,537.92.[23]

The disposition of the Colorado Railroad, Inc., reflected a principle of reusing and recycling whatever was possible. Many of the rails and other hardware found a new home in Mexico, and whatever metal was left was melted down and put to other uses. Frank Zavislan bought 3,000 crossties and other timbers from the railroad for reuse as corrals. Other ties went to shore up coal mines in the area, while the culverts were removed for use on county roads.[24] Zavislan also purchased the small Stone City depot, to repurpose on his ranch, for $500.[25] It now resides, currently vacant, in nearby Penrose, Colorado, though it has served as a place of business, most recently as a beauty shop.

Like the exposed vertebrae of some giant prehistoric beast, decaying crossties stretch across sections of sunbaked prairie, littered in between with blackened cinders. Homes cover portions of the grade, from burrow

FIGURE 17.2. *Stone City depot at Penrose, Colorado, in 2020. Photograph by the author.*

entrances of black-tailed prairie dogs, to the ranch-style houses of Pueblo West. Along Highway 50, the only horses to traverse the grade are no longer iron. Although the railyard is long gone, the cinder-block engine house is still in existence and has been used as a garage or storage unit for years.

Locomotive No. 1, the gas-motor, was the last piece of the Colorado Railroad, Inc., remaining at the end, having been used to haul away the scrap metal on the line.[26] MacDaniel made an arrangement with the Denver & Rio Grande Western to store the locomotive on the latter's property until it could be sold, paying one dollar per month for the service.[27] Pressured by Commercial Metals to sell it, she diligently shopped the locomotive around the region, hoping to find a buyer.[28] Irma MacDaniel had tendered her resignation as secretary-treasurer of the Colorado Railroad, Inc., on May 24, 1958, but still acted as agent for the locomotive transaction.[29] She offered it to the San Luis Southern Railroad, a shortline operating out of Fort Garland in the San Luis Valley, for $4,000, and later to Robert W. Richardson, founder of the Colorado Railroad Museum.[30] According to Richardson, "The price quoted was no bargain for the locomotive."[31] MacDaniel was all business in her dealings with him, looking to get rid of the locomotive and nothing else. Richardson hoped to acquire the company's records for his growing

FIGURE 17.3. *Colorado Railroad Inc., No. 1 awaiting her fate in the D&RGW Round-house in Pueblo, 1958. Photo by Robert W. Richardson. Courtesy of Denver Public Library, Western History Collection, RR-1230.*

collection, but she was not encouraging in her answer. Declining to purchase the locomotive, Robert W. Richardson walked away empty handed.[32] Nearly seven months after it was last used to dismantle the railroad, the locomotive was sold to Bud Moore of Johnson Electric, for $800. Moore worked for Johnson Electric for fifty-seven years and had performed all of the electrical repairs on the locomotive during its life on the Colorado Railroad, Inc., so he knew it intimately. The locomotive sat in the Speken Iron & Metal scrapyard in Pueblo for a year while Moore worked on restoring the locomotive before selling off the generators. One went to New Mexico for $1,200, and the other to Salt Lake City for $2,000. Other valuable equipment was the next to go, until finally, Speken Iron & Metal purchased the empty car body for $800, recouping Moore's original investment.[33]

Reflecting back upon the Colorado Railroad, Inc., MacDaniel told one reporter, "It was a nice railroad. Everything seemed just to glide along. Sure, we had the same problems as a major railroad, only on a smaller scale. And we never had much turnover in personnel, either. About the same crew remained with us for more than 18 years."[34]

Although she no longer worked for the railroad, Irma MacDaniel continued to maintain the books and affairs for Pueblo Quarries, Inc. This job lasted until 1966, when the US government took over the land encompassing Stone City, the old quarries, and the working clay mines for the expansion of Fort Carson for training purposes.[35] At a preliminary meeting in 1964, MacDaniel recalled seeing some of the town's residents: "Just as I was leaving I noticed Mr. Wands, Mrs. Wands, and there [sic] two children at a distance, I did not talk to anyone at all—but saw several sad and broken hearted people who were to lose homes of a life time."[36] A way of life for many families was ending.

The US Army at Fort Carson, to the north of the Stone City area, began encroaching on the land around Stone City as early as June 1, 1962. The Fifth Infantry Mechanized Division had begun training on land owned by Arthur Wands and other ranchers below the Teller Dam. The army made a deal with the locals for the use of their land, though instead of compensation for usage, they were only to be compensated for any damages incurred by maneuvers. The army agreed that Stone City, its homes, and the Teller Reservoir would be off limits for army training. Lee Oldham recalled that some damages were incurred, because her father, Arthur Wands, was paid for them one year. A cow owned by the family was accidentally shot, for which the family received $132 in compensatory damages. Locals even acted as participants in one mock battle, civilians that helped to hide "friendly" troops from the "enemy."[37]

The army, however, was not content with the agreed-upon use of the private land. At a public landowners' meeting, held on Friday, November 20, 1964, Colonel Harold J. St. Clair explained to the crowd that the army needed up to an additional 76,000 acres and had already begun contacting landowners about selling. Their property would be appraised and offers made to the owners. If they refused to sell, condemnation proceedings would take place in federal court under the power of eminent domain. About thirty families would be affected by the expansion of Fort Carson.[38]

Besides the land, there was the question of clay, still being mined at Stone City. G. W. Jensen represented the biggest company concerned, as president of the Denver Fire Clay Company. He told Colonel St. Clair that his company had mineral rights to clay deposits worth $8 million. Colorado Fuel & Iron was one of their biggest customers. Arthur Wands had operated a clay mine in the area for nearly forty years, and Denver Fire Clay was one of his biggest customers.[39]

The army hoped that all proceedings would be wrapped up and payment made by June 30, 1965, though one family reported not being paid until 1973.[40] In the end, the army ended up buying or seizing the land it needed. Arthur Wands lost 6,401 acres, the third-largest individual acquisition. Frank Zavislan lost 2,940 acres. Other landowners lost as little as eleven acres, on up to hundreds, as well as thousands, of acres. Most folks could not afford to replace the same amount of land for what the government paid them and ended up buying smaller and more scattered parcels. Wands had to sell his profitable herd of cattle, no longer having the land to graze them. As for the fireclay, Wands and the government settled on terms that would allow him to mine from 400 acres for three months out of the year, from November 1 through January 31.[41] His company, the Colorado Fire Clay Company, continued to sell to Denver Fire Clay's operations in Cañon City.[42] As of 2017, the clay mine is still in limited operation.[43]

Through the power of eminent domain, the federal government forced the remaining residents, some of whom still mined clay, to leave their homes.[44] As if they were campaigning against enemy forces, US Army bulldozers leveled the buildings in the area, removing almost all traces of Stone City and effectively wiping it off the map.[45] Only the railroad grade and a few scattered foundations remain today. Stone City joined the list of storied Colorado ghost towns.

In her final years, MacDaniel became an insurance agent for the Home Insurance Company, maintaining an office in the Thatcher Building, from where she had long run the railroad.[46] A fall she suffered on April 14, 1971, caused an illness from which she never recovered. She passed away at Parkview Hospital in Pueblo on May 3, 1971, at the age of seventy-seven and is buried in Pueblo's Mountain View Cemetery next to her parents and twin sister. Her obituary listed her as a "veteran insuror" and made a mere mention that she was a secretary for the Colorado-Kansas Railway.[47] For a woman who moved up in the business world and achieved a unique level of power at a time when women were relegated to becoming real estate or insurance agents, it seems poignantly incongruous that she came to that position.

Irma MacDaniel was a pioneering businesswoman, who moved into a masculine corporate world when few women were allowed entrance. She stood toe to toe in the world of men, countering their business traits and pragmatism with her own. She proved her worth to her male business associates, who welcomed her as a partner as early as 1925. Not only did she manage a railroad (albeit, a small one), and keep it operating as long as possible when the market was turning against it, but she concurrently and successfully carried on multiple business ventures, running her own little business empire. This is a truly remarkable feat considering the reduction of women in the workforce after World War II at precisely the time MacDaniel's empire was flourishing.

Was she an overachiever? Perhaps, but Irma MacDaniel lived her life as she saw fit, with a vigorous work ethic. For nearly sixty years, she pursued business opportunities where she could find them, never accepting society's domesticated role for women. For that, she is one of the pioneers for women in business.

18

The Frontier Stabilized

Success from Failure

Far from being closed in 1890, the frontier in the early twentieth century was just opening up to new economic and industrial prospects. Venture upon venture, always ambitious in nature, were proposed and attempted, rife with promise and opportunity. Large-scale enterprises that could cater to industries and individuals alike offered the best use of the landscape and its resources. The harsh physical and economic realities were often overlooked by those men with the dynamic energy to succeed in a region where success was typically limited to a smaller human scale, such as that of the yeoman farmer. In their visions, industry, technology, science, and capital—all were able to overcome any limitations the physical landscape placed upon their schemes. "Dream big, scheme big" could easily have been the unofficial motto of the era.

Within a single county (two if we include Custer County), numerous attempts at large-scale enterprises failed to take root between the 1890s and 1910. John J. Burns tried to give it a go with both Custer City and his electrified railroad from Pueblo to Beulah and the Wet Mountain Valley. A. B.

DOI: 10.5876/9781646421282.c018

Hulit campaigned hard for the electrified Kansas-Colorado Railroad and Power Company in his endeavor to serve the Arkansas River Valley communities of Garden City, Pueblo, Cañon City, and all points in between. John C. Teller—timber cutter, rancher, irrigation company owner, and land developer—fought for nearly three decades to bring water and people to the empty prairies west of Pueblo. Geo. H. Paul, arriving in Pueblo as the purported savior of the Teller project, crashed and burned in spectacular fashion.

Others found success out of their mélange of businesses. Robert K. Potter—rancher, reservoir starter, and quarry owner—made effective use of his clay and stone holdings, at least while the market could support building stone. J. F. Springfield, R. C. Johnson, and Charles Sutton brought new life to the failed Kansas-Colorado Railroad by adapting it into a more modest and manageable shortline railroad. Gone were the exuberant days of dream big, scheme big. In the frontier of the early twentieth century, modest and manageable would prove to be the successful answer to development restraints, whether limited by landscape or capital. By remaining modest, the Colorado-Kansas Railway could eke out a prolonged existence across the prairies and hills of northwest Pueblo County for nearly half a century.

Financially, the Colorado-Kansas Railway was a failure, running deficits most of its existence. It did nothing to enhance the agriculture of the area, despite efforts to do so. It was not a large employer, though the stone quarries and clay mines the railroad served generally kept a number of men working. Founded as part of a grand vision for environmental and economic change along the Arkansas River Valley, it left little impression. And yet, through the business decisions, or adaptations, made by the railroad, a story of failure recedes and instead emerges as a story of economic survival, if not success.

The overall theme of the story of the Colorado-Kansas Railroad, and shortlines in general, is adaptability. Adaptability in a business sense means not only making decisions in response to changing economic or political issues, but making the *right* decisions in order to remain an economically viable enterprise. Some businesses may seem almost prescient in anticipating the coming changes in the marketplace and then making the correct decisions. These companies may be large enough, innovative enough, or maintain enough of a virtual stranglehold on the market, to coerce those changes into happening. For most businesses, however, particularly small ones, marginal ones, adaptability means making reactive, rather than proactive, decisions, and almost always out of economic necessity.

Indeed, economic necessity forced the owners of the Colorado-Kansas Railway to change its source of locomotion from electricity to steam power, as wells as limiting the length of its tracks to what it could actually afford to build. This might seem like a step backward, moving from a grand dream of an electric interurban railroad and power plants, to a very small shortline with one steam locomotive, but the decision enabled the railroad to function in a time of diminishing capital investment and competition from much larger railroads.

In hindsight, the decision to quarry and haul building stone might seem shortsighted, for someone should have foreseen the declining market share of the product. Consider, though, that there was still an immediate demand for the stone, which made it seem commercially viable to the company. Too, the demand continued for nearly twenty years, despite changing construction technology. It would, perhaps, be a bad business decision *not* to pursue this market as long as the owners could.

Adapting to the marketplace by developing new sources of revenue when the old ones diminish is paramount to any business. The railroad encouraged development along its line, working to meet the needs of the businesses. The Baker Steam Motor Car & Manufacturing Company and the Geo. H. Paul Orchard Company both tried to build large businesses on the outskirts of Pueblo, and both failed miserably. The internal combustion engine overtook Baker's steam-powered cars, and Paul's prospects dried up along with his fruit trees, a victim of the unmet demands placed upon the Teller and Paul projects by the landscape. If it anticipated great profits serving these industries, the railroad soon found itself alone on the prairie. Only the Chicago Freight Car & Parts Company in later years met with any success. The decision to help develop new businesses and industries, regardless of whether they failed or succeeded, was the correct one.

Promoting Irma MacDaniel to a managerial position is the one decision the railroad made that appeared to portend a future business trend. Her management of the railroad from 1940 to 1957 clearly indicates adaptability on the part of the owners, who hired MacDaniel to run the railroad regardless of sex. While it is certain that other people could have managed the company just as well as MacDaniel did, the owners' decision to hire her did, in fact, save them money, for MacDaniel essentially performed two jobs for the price of one, and her management kept losses down to a minimum. MacDaniel's efficiency in business extended the life of the Colorado Railroad, Inc., another decade. The railroad was fighting a losing battle against the trucking industry, but her management kept the losses lower than ever. Time was running out for the railroad, though, and so was its ability and will to adapt. With the owners dying or eager to sell out, the "nice railroad" met its demise. Irma MacDaniel presided over its funeral, diligently managing the abandonment with the same efficiency with which she oversaw its operations in its postwar heyday. Even though the railroad eventually went out of business, the adaptive decision to hire Irma MacDaniel was, undoubtedly, the correct one for the company, and a boon to MacDaniel's career.

Within the theme of adaptability, three remarkable stories emerge that tie this railroad to a larger historical fabric. First, the railroad stands as an example of political and economic reform at the local level and is probably representative of hundreds, if not thousands, of such tales from the early twentieth century. Second, it is a story of connections, from the landscape to the railroad, to the towns they served and the people who lived in them, and from the local shortline railroad to the national rail network where the transfer of raw materials and finished products took place. Third, this short-line stands as a testament to the work of a pioneer businesswoman who not only managed the railroad, but also ran her own local business empire in the years following World War II.

The first study of adaptability sheds light on a much larger issue in American history, showing how a shortline railroad played a small part in Progressive Era reform and how the builders persevered through both political and economic adversity. Looking at this particular shortline railroad involves the reader in local politics and economics. Large, transcontinental railroads affected economies wherever they built, and they added greatly to the national economy, but the local effects are seldom examined.

Progressive Reform was not a unified movement, even though it occurred nationwide. Instead, reform played out across the country in local dramas such that experienced by the Colorado-Kansas Railway. This particular episode provides greater insight into the people involved in the reform battles. On one level, such as that viewed by the reform-minded newspapers in Pueblo, the battle for the Colorado-Kansas franchise was all about political freedom from the tyranny of local bosses and about giving control of local politics back to the people. This is the justification for which Progressive Reform is well known, but it is neither the only one, nor the most important one.

Newspapers, politicians, and activists raised the moral questions and asked for moral answers, but the driving force behind local reform was purely economic. To the Colorado-Kansas Railway and other businesses counting on its success, reform was about the economic freedom to pursue and conduct business without local constraints. Political bosses wielded great economic power, and when Boss Vail viewed the upstart railroad as an economic threat to the monopoly of the traction and power company, he fought back, and lost. The cost to Vail was the loss of power for his political machine, but the loss to the railroad was perhaps greater, for it could no longer seriously consider building beyond the Pueblo to Stone City line. It had won a political battle for the reformers but had lost the economic ability to extend its railroad into more profitable regions. The railroad's marginality, hidden in plain sight during its enthusiastic, formative stages, became set in stone with the loss of whatever economic momentum it might have had to that point. Instead of a large business enterprise, the Colorado-Kansas Railway would become a struggling small business, indicative of thousands across the country fighting to survive in an era of increasing economic strangulation. These enterprises needed the political and economic reform to move beyond marginality. This story is significant in that it shows the motives and methods of the participants in the Progressive Era's struggles with reform; that the fighting took place, quite viciously, at the local level; and that, while political idealism gave voice to the fight, the war was really about economics.

A railroad is much more than a pair of iron or steel rails stretching across the countryside on a foundation of wooden crossties. The second study in shortline adaptability focused on the railroad and its connections to the landscape, to the metropolis and hinterlands, to the people, and to the nation. Like many shortline railroads, the Colorado-Kansas Railway functioned as the meeting place between an extractive region and the rest of the nation. Raw materials and finished goods travel on the line to and from connections with the larger railroads. Think of this as analogous to activity at the cellular level in the body, where interchanges vital to life take place. It is these national connections between hinterlands and metropolis where much of

FIGURE 18.1. *Abandoned grade of the Colorado-Kansas Railway, heading south to Pueblo, 2020. Photo by the author.*

the work of America is performed. Because of this significance, they are ripe for the study of business and economics at the local level.

The Colorado-Kansas Railway's owners conceived of the railroad as a means to develop the hinterlands around the metropolis of Pueblo and on down the Arkansas River Valley. Far from being an engine of economic change, however, the railroad did not profoundly change the landscape across the region. Changes in the landscape the railroad wrought were confined to Stone City, Pueblo, and the narrow right-of-way across the prairie. Not until a decade after the railroad's abandonment did the landscape experience greater change, and, even then, it took a burgeoning population to spread new homes and businesses across the prairie.

The significance here is that while metropolitan centers have a much more diversified economy, the towns that occupy the hinterlands generally rely on only one or two industries to survive. In the hinterlands, this existence on the economic margins was just as difficult for the people who lived there as it was for the businesses and industries that operated there. The railroad served as a vital, if sometimes fragile, economic lifeline to the hinterlands through the first half of the twentieth century.

The prism of the Colorado-Kansas Railway has shown how national trends affected industries at the local level, in some cases, places far removed from the big cities of the east, as in the case of the switch from building stone to concrete and steel. Because shortlines rely on perhaps one or two large customers and a host of smaller ones, they, like the small towns they serve, are highly susceptible to economic changes. This very marginality, while very much a liability for small enterprises, is also an exploitable asset. Shortlines need to remain flexible, readily adapting to changes in the marketplace in order to survive. Moreover, because of their size and their marginality, shortlines are able to make these changes with greater ease than are larger corporations.

The third study of adaptability centers on a woman. The life choices Irma MacDaniel made led her from business school to a first career as a stenographer with the railroad's law firm. Working for J. T. McCorkle gave her a strong foundation in business, for while still employed for him, she entered the world of corporate ownership with the founding of the Pueblo Terminal Railway. Later, after the death of her boss, she hired on with the Colorado-Kansas Railway, serving its owners in a clerical position. After the railroad finally left receivership, emerging as the Colorado Railroad, Inc., she entered into corporate management.

MacDaniel excelled at business, keeping several enterprises going at once. Not only did she own part of the Pueblo Terminal Railway and a small portion of the Colorado Railroad, Inc., she coowned Sterling Securities and operated an accounting office for other companies, including Pueblo Quarries, Inc., and the Welton Land and Water Company. Along with all this work, she also ran an insurance agency.

Over the course of her career, she progressed from the feminine role of stenographer, an acceptable position for women at the time, into the masculine dominion of the business world, managing not only the railroad and other related corporations, but her own enterprises as well. MacDaniel was a legitimate businesswoman, operating in and successfully bridging both masculine and feminine spheres of work.

Again, the railroad's marginality and subsequent flexibility enabled the managers to place MacDaniel in a position of power that was generally unavailable to women in the 1940s. While Irma MacDaniel moved into corporate life decades before it was open to most women, her story reveals a significant step in the acceptance of women in management. In the end, her career reflects on the men in her life as much as it does MacDaniel, men like J. T. McCorkle, J. F. Springfield, and Robert K. Johnston, who saw in MacDaniel someone reliable, hardworking, and ambitious and offered her a chance to join the men's club that was the corporate world of her day. They put aside (or, more likely, MacDaniel knocked down) their preconceived notions about gender roles in business and gave MacDaniel the opportunity to prove herself to them and the rest of the business community.

These stories all come from one shortline railroad, the Colorado-Kansas Railway. What appears, at first glance, to be an unremarkable little railroad, is actually a connecting link with the nation, and is inextricably interwoven into the very fabric of a rich American history. With shortline railroads on the rise again, the time has come to reevaluate their contributions to history. Shortline railroads still play an important role in the local, regional, and national economies. Lessons learned from the past will allow these shortlines to continue to exist as long as they can adapt to ever-changing markets. The question begs to be asked: With the multitude of shortlines, past and present, what stories are still waiting to be told?

Ultimately, the Colorado-Kansas Railway, among all of the abandoned workings of men, has one lasting legacy that transcends paper and ink, transcends fading memories, and transcends vanishing grades that stretch across the prairies. This legacy, in fact, is a strong one, strong as stone. Turkey Creek stone, in buildings all around the country, stands as a testament to the natural environment that created it, to the men who quarried and fashioned it, and, finally, to the little railroad that carried it: the Colorado-Kansas Railway.

FIGURE 18.2. *Abandoned grade at Appleton, heading west toward Stone City, 2020. Photo by the author.*

Appendix A

Colorado-Kansas Railway Historical Roster

Steam Locomotive No. 1

Wheel Arrangement	Drivers	Cylinders	Weight on Drivers	Total Weight	Tractive Effort	Boiler Pressure
4-6-0	60"	17" × 26"	93,500 LB.	117,000	17,031 LB.	160 PSI

1887	Built by Schenectady for the Colorado Midland, Builder no. 2437. Became CM no. 24.
1911	Purchased secondhand from the Colorado Midland for $7,000.
1920	Out of service part of the year.
1921–1926	Out of service.
1927	Sold for junk for $324.40 and scrapped. The tender was relocated to Stone City and served as a municipal water tank.

DOI: 10.5876/9781646421282.c019

Gasoline-Electric Motor No. 1

Length	Engines	Traction Motors	Control	Traction Brake	Brakes	Total Weight (lb.)	Trac- tive Effort (lb.)
50 ft.	(2) Buda JH6 gasoline engines, 150 hp	(2) 500-volt DC generators; (4) GE-73 motors, 70 hp; 500-volt DC control equipment	GE K-6 Controller; drives from either end	Westinghouse Traction Brake with A.M.M. Brake Equipment	M-22 Brake Valve; (2) Denver-Gardner Vertical Type Model A-A-A 1001 compres-sors	100,000, working order	23,300

1912	Built as an electric box-freight motor by McGuire-Cummings Car Co. for the Fox & Illinois Union Railroad, Motor no. 7.
1931	F&IU abandoned. Local farmer's co-op purchased for local service. Rebuilt into a gasoline-electric.
1938	Sold for salvage to Hyman-Michaels Company.
1940	Colorado Railroad, Inc., acquired Gas Motor No. 1 for $3,910.00.
1958	Sold to Bud Moore of Johnson Electric in Pueblo for $800 and scrapped.

Boxcars

Qty.	Description	Road Number	Inner Length	Inner Width	Inner Height	Outer Length	Outer Width	Cu. Ft.	Capacity, lb.
5	Boxcars	200–204	34'	8'	6', 7"	35'	8', 8"	1,790	60,000

1912	Purchased five boxcars, 200–204.
1920	Two of the boxcars, numbers unknown, were probably converted to station usage, one at Irving Place, and possibly the other at Stone City.
1929	Four of the five boxcars were retired. Dispositions unknown. The remaining boxcar was used as a tool car.
1938	The last remaining boxcar was retired. Disposition unknown.

Coal Gondolas

Qty.	Description	Road Number	Inner Length	Inner Width	Inner Height	Outer Length	Outer Width	Cu. Ft.	Capacity, lb.
10	Coal gondolas	507, 508	34'	8', 5"	3'	35'	9'	867	60,000

1912	Purchased ten coal gondolas, 501–510.
1913	Converted coal gondolas 501–506, 509, and 510 to flatcars.
1920	Coal gondolas 507 and 508 were converted to flatcars.

Flatcars

Qty.	Description	Road Number	Inner Length	Inner Width	Inner Height	Outer Length	Outer Width	Cu. Ft.	Capacity, lb.
10	Flatcars	501–510	35'	8', 5"					60,000

1913	Flatcars 501–506, 509, and 510 built from converted coal gondolas.
1920	507 and 508 built from converted coal gondolas.
1929	All flatcars retired. Disposition unknown.

Combination Baggage/Passenger Car

Qty.	Description	Road Number	Inner Length	Inner Width	Inner Height	Outer Length	Outer Width	Cu. Ft.	Capacity, lb.
1	Combination	101							

1912	Purchased Combination 101, probably secondhand.
1929	Combination 101 retired from passenger service and used as a caboose.
1931	Combination 101 retired and moved to Stone City and converted to housing during receivership.

Caboose

Qty	Description	Road Number	Inner Length	Inner Width	Inner Height	Outer Length	Outer Width	Cu. Ft.	Capacity, lb.
1	Caboose								

1937	Purchased secondhand side-door caboose from the Atchison, Topeka & Santa Fe Railroad for $331.
1945	Caboose retired. Disposition unknown.

Sources

Colorado-Kansas Railway. Report no. 3079, 1913–1932, 1938. Records of the Operating Division. Annual Reports of Railroads 1915–1961. Interstate Commerce Commission. RG 134. National Archives at College Park, College Park, MD.

Colorado-Kansas Railway. Report no. 3081, 1933–1937. Records of the Operating Division. Annual Reports of Railroads 1915–1961. Interstate Commerce Commission. RG 134. National Archives at College Park, College Park, MD.

Railway Equipment and Publication Company. *Official Railway Equipment Register* 28, no. 5 (October 1912): 251.

Railway Equipment and Publication Company. *Official Railway Equipment Register* 28, no. 9 (February 1913): 635.

Railway Equipment and Publication Company. *Official Railway Equipment Register* 28, no. 10 (March 1913): 635.

Stephens, Kent. "The Colorado Railroad." *New Mexico Railroader* 7 (October 1965; issued January 1966): 1–8.

Appendix B

Colorado-Kansas Railway Engineering
Notes from the ICC 1919 Valuation

Mile	
1	Victoria Avenue depot.
	Former blacksmith shop.
	Depot spur—415 ft.
	Buda-Harvey box switch stand.
	Crossing arms come down across Colorado-Kansas track to protect Santa Fe crossing.
	Sand Company spur—553 ft., High Paige switch stand.
2	3-rail 90-degree crossing.
	46-foot open-deck bridge.
	Crossing arms come down across Colorado-Kansas track to protect Santa Fe interchange.
	AT&SF transfer track–1285 feet, Buda-Harvey box #7A.
	2 road crossings just before engine house.
	Irving Place Yard.
	Engine house—16' × 70' × 16', corrugated iron walls.
	4 windows—3' × 5'.
	1 double door—12' × 16'.
	1 door—2½' × 7'.

DOI: 10.5876/9781646421282.c020

Mile	
2 (cont.)	Engine pit—3' × 30' × 3' deep.
	Coal Bin—33' × 9' × 4½'.
	Coal bin behind engine house to the south on the east side of track.
	Water hydrant.
	Water column with 5' × 5' × 4' wood pit, located south of coal bin.
	Tool house—12' × 24'.
	Engine House track—241 feet, Buda-Harvey switch Box #7A.
	Yard track—1,764 ft., High Paige switch stand.
	Yard Track—1,040 ft., Buda-Harvey switch box and High Paige switch stand.
	Dwelling rented to section hands.
	Road crossing beyond last yard switch.
3	Road crossing.
4	Road Crossing, just before bridge.
	150-ft. open-deck bridge over Dry Creek.
5	Cañon City Road highway crossing.
6	Farm road crossing.
9	Crossing just east of Appleton siding.
	Appleton.
	Spur—507 ft., High Paige switch stand.
	Loading crane along siding on south side.
	Pile trestle.
10	Road Crossing.
12	45-ft. open-deck bridge.
13	Road crossing.
	91-ft. open-deck bridge.
14	56-ft. open-deck bridge.
16	90-ft. open-deck bridge—Pumpkin Hollow.
17–18	173-ft. open-deck bridge—Turkey Creek.
	Road crossing just south of Turkey Creek passing siding.
	Turkey Creek.
	Passing siding—1,398-ft., High Paige switch stands.
19	59-ft. open-deck bridge.
20	Road crossing.
21	Road crossing right before Myrtle spur.
	Myrtle.
	Spur—278 ft., High Paige switch stand.

Mile	
22	98-ft. open-deck bridge—Booth Creek / Booth Gulch.
23	Stone City Depot.
	16', 4" × 32', 4".
	2 windows—4' × 6', boxed.
	1 door—4' × 8'.
	2 windows—3' × 2½", hinged.
	Wood platform—16' × 32' × 2'.
	Electric lighting.
	Water column, originally on west side of main line before being moved inside the wye.
	6 stone arch culverts.
	Stone sawmill.
	Mill spur—440 ft., High Paige switch stand.
	Mine track—1,036 ft., High Paige switch stand.
	Wye track—388½ feet, High Paige switch stand.
	Road crossing north of 2 arch culverts.
	Quarry spur—583 ft., High Paige switch stand.
	Quarry Spur—2,708 ft., High Paige switch stand.

Notes

Crossbucks: 2" × 10" × 5' boards painted white with black letters. Mounted on 8" × 8" × 16' posts. "Railroad" goes down from top right, and "Crossing" goes upward to the left. Center of crossbucks are mounted to the post 14" down from top.

Mileposts: 4' × 6' × 1' pine boards painted white with black letters and mounted on telephone poles.

Whistle posts: 3" × 10" × 10' fir posts. Tops are rounded with 3" radius. Planted 48" in ground to top of tie. Bottom 56" are painted red. W is 5" from top of post, and is 7" high, followed by 3" of blank space, and a 4" high X. Top 24" painted white with black letters. Top 64" may also be white.

Source

Interstate Commerce Commission. Engineering Report Notes. Colorado-Kansas Railway. Valuation Docket no. 81. Records of the Bureau of Valuation 1910–1974. Interstate Commerce Commission. RG 134. National Archives at College Park, College Park, MD.

Notes

Introduction

1. "Pueblo Opens Today Its Home-Built Railroad into State's Greatest Quarries," *Pueblo Leader* (CO), June 12, 1912; "Colorado-Kansas Is Formally Opened," *Pueblo Chieftain* (CO), June 13, 1912.

2. Richard White, *Railroaded: The Transcontinentals and the Making of Modern America* (New York: W.W. Norton & Company, Inc., 2011), xxi.

3. White, *Railroaded*, xxiv.

4. H. Roger Grant, *Twilight Rails: The Final Era of Railroad Building in the Midwest* (Minneapolis: University of Minnesota Press, 2010), 4.

5. White, *Railroaded*, xxiii.

6. Grant, *Twilight Rails*, 11–14.

7. White, *Railroaded*, 510.

8. White, *Railroaded*, xxiv–xxvi.

9. John F. Stover, *American Railroads*, 2nd ed. (Chicago: University of Chicago Press, 1997), 245–246.

10. Albro Martin, *Railroads Triumphant: The Growth, Rejection, and Rebirth of a Vital American Force* (New York: Oxford University Press, 1992), 311.

11. Stover, *American Railroads*, 250.

12. Association of American Railroads (AAR), "Freight Railroad Fact Sheets," *Railroad 101*, March 2021, accessed March 31, 2021, https://www.aar.org/wp-content/uploads/2020/08/AAR-Railroad-101-Freight-Railroads-Fact-Sheet.pdf.

13. Stover, *American Railroads*, 252.

14. Interstate Commerce Commission (ICC), *Seventy-First Annual Report on Transport Statistics in the United States for the Year Ended December 31, 1957* (Washington, DC: Government Printing Office, 1959), 1.

15. ICC, *Seventy-First Annual Report*, 3.

16. Stover, *American Railroads*, 252.

17. Association of American Railroads (AAR), "Freight Rail Resources," *Railroad 101*.

18. Martin, *Railroads Triumphant*, 384.

Chapter 1. Progressive Era Reform and "The Pueblo Road"

1. John Whiteclay Chambers II, *The Tyranny of Change: America in the Progressive Era, 1890–1920*, 2nd ed. (New York: St. Martin's Press, 1992), 141.

2. Steven J. Diner, *A Very Different Age: Americans of the Progressive Era* (New York: Hill and Wang, 1998), 205.

3. Chambers, *The Tyranny of Change*, 141, 156.

4. Chambers, *The Tyranny of Change*, 155–156.

5. Morris Cafky and John A. Haney, *Pueblo's Steel Town Trolleys* (Golden: Colorado Railroad Historical Foundation, 1999), 66.

6. McGraw Publishing Company, Inc., "Personal Mention," *Electric Railway Journal* 38, no. 2 (July 8, 1911): 98.

7. Chambers, *The Tyranny of Change*, 150.

8. "$25,000 Suit the First Result of 'Vail's Folly,'" *Pueblo Sun* (CO), June 3, 1910.

9. Masthead, *Pueblo Sun* (CO), November 11, 1908.

10. Masthead, *Pueblo Leader* (CO), February 13, 1913.

11. "Kansas-Colorado Railroad and Electric Transmission Companies," *Pueblo Chieftain* (CO), August 2, 1908.

12. "Narrow Gauge," *Burlington Weekly Hawk-Eye* (IA), March 23, 1876.

13. "The Native Limestone," *Topeka State Journal* (KS), July 11, 1889.

14. "Off for Mexico," *Topeka Daily Capital* (KS), September 18, 1895.

15. "Republican Silver League," *Saint Paul Globe* (MN), July 5, 1896.

16. "Trade with Mexico," *Des Moines Register* (IA), November 24, 1896.

17. Advertisement, *Kansas Farmer* (Topeka, KS), September 16, 1897.

18. "Is Quite Gigantic." *Salt Lake Tribune* (UT), December 12, 1897.

19. "The Choctaw Emigration," *El Paso Herald* (TX), February 9, 1898.

20. "A. B. Hulit Married," *Wichita Beacon* (KS), February 9, 1898.

21. "Charter Filed," *Wichita Beacon* (KS), April 9, 1898.

22. "Interesting Information," *Indian Sentinel* (Tahlequah, OK), April 15, 1898.

23. "National Reciprocity League Is Organized," *Chicago Tribune*, April 11, 1902.

24. "Goat Milk," *Cincinnati Enquirer* (OH), November 4, 1903.

25. "Hope for City Patients with Tuberculosis," *St. Louis Post-Dispatch* (MO), December 15, 1903.

26. "Goat's Milk for Infants," *Lebo Enterprise* (KS), August 11, 1904.

27. "Northern Electrical Manufacturing Company," *Madison Past and Present* (Madison: Wisconsin State Journal, 1902): 162–163.

28. Roy V. Scott, *Railroad Development Programs in the Twentieth Century* (Ames: Iowa State University Press, 1985): 80.

29. Scott, *Railroad Development Programs*, 21.

30. "Kansas-Colorado Railroad and Electric Transmission Companies," *Pueblo Chieftain* (CO), August 2, 1908.

31. "Kansas-Colorado Railroad and Electric Transmission Companies."

32. Alfred D. Chandler Jr., *The Visible Hand: The Managerial Revolution in American Business* (Cambridge: Belknap Press of Harvard University Press, 1977), 285–314.

33. John F. Stover, *American Railroads*, 2nd ed. (Chicago: University of Chicago Press, 1997), 133–166.

34. Edward T. Bollinger and Frederick Bauer, *The Moffat Road*, 2nd ed. (Chicago: Swallow Press, 1971), 232.

35. "Cheap Power to Make Pueblo A Manufacturing Center," *Pueblo Sun* (CO), April 24, 1908.

36. Chambers, *The Tyranny of Change*, 145.

37. James Earl Sherow, *Watering the Valley: Development along the High Plains Arkansas River, 1870–1950* (Lawrence: University Press of Kansas, 1990), 106.

38. Sherow, *Watering the Valley*, 119.

39. Brian S. Osborne, "The Kansas-Colorado Power and Railroad Project: A Multi-functional Plan for the Development of the Arkansas Valley," *Pioneer America* 6, no. 2 (1974): 25.

40. Sherow, *Watering the Valley*, 88.

41. "Gigantic Plans for Development Mean Millions for Arkansas Valley," *Pueblo Chieftain* (CO), April 19, 1908.

42. "Hulit Explains Mammoth Development Project for Arkansas Valley," *Pueblo Chieftain* (CO), April 24, 1908.

43. "New Arkansas Valley Road Inspected by Many Bankers," *Pueblo Chieftain* (CO), May 3, 1908.

44. "Enthusiasm Reigns at La Junta Meeting," *Pueblo Chieftain* (CO), May 15, 1908.

45. "Power and Railway Directors Organize," *Pueblo Chieftain* (CO), May 28, 1908.

46. "Pueblo Made Headquarters for Great Power Company," *Pueblo Chieftain* (CO), June 3, 1908.

47. "Interurban Papers Are Filed," *Pueblo Chieftain* (CO), June 13, 1908; Kansas-Colorado Railroad Company, Articles of Incorporation, record no. 160517, filed July 29, 1908, Pueblo County Recording Department, Pueblo, CO.

48. "Fifteen Million Dollar Proposition Doubted at First Now Becoming Reality," *Pueblo Chieftain* (CO), June 14, 1908.

Chapter 2. Construction and the Fight for the Franchise Begin

1. H. Roger Grant, *Twilight Rails: The Final Era of Railroad Building in the Midwest* (Minneapolis: University of Minnesota Press, 2010), 5.

2. H. Roger Grant, *Electric Interurbans and the American People* (Bloomington: Indiana University Press, 2016), 6.

3. George W. Hilton and John F. Due, *The Electric Interurban Railways in America* (Stanford, CA: Stanford University Press, 1960), vii.

4. Hilton and Due, *The Electric Interurban Railways in America*, 3.

5. Grant, *Electric Interurbans and the American People*, 41–49.

6. Grant, *Electric Interurbans and the American People*, 23.

7. Grant, *Twilight Rails*, 7.

8. McGraw Publishing Company, Inc., "Recent Incorporations," *Electric Railway Journal* 33, no. 8 (May 22, 1909): 352.

9. McGraw Publishing Company, Inc., "Track and Roadway," *Electric Railway Journal* 43, no. 9 (February 28, 1914): 502.

10. McGraw Publishing Company, Inc., "Recent Incorporations," *Electric Railway Journal* 38, no. 20 (November 11, 1911): 1045.

11. Street Railway Publishing Company, "Street Railway News," *Street Railway Journal* 7, no. 1 (January 1891): 41.

12. McGraw Publishing Company, Inc., "Recent Incorporations," *Electric Railway Journal* 38, no. 20 (November 11, 1911): 1046.

13. Street Railway Publishing Company, "Interurban Railroading at Cripple Creek," *Street Railway Journal* 14, no. 11 (November 1898): 701.

14. Street Railway Publishing Company, "Prospects for New Business," *Street Railway Journal* 14, no. 1 (January 1898): 46.

15. Blue Book Publishing Company, "O'er Canon and Crag to the Land of Gold via the Short Line," *Short Line Blue Book: A Handbook for Travelers* (April 1904):14.

16. Henry C. Spurr, ed., *Public Utilities Reports Containing Decisions of the Public Service Commissions, and of State and Federal Courts*, 1924A (Rochester, NY: Public Utilities Reports, 1924), 395.

17. McGraw Publishing Company, Inc., "News Notes," *Electric Railway Journal* 54, no. 8 (August 23, 1919): 408.

18. Spurr, *Public Utilities*, 395.

19. *Rapid Transit Railway: Pueblo and Beulah Valley*, n.p., n.d., ca. 1902.

20. Agreement among John J. Burns, Francis I. Meston, and W. A. Beatty, April 28, 1902, John J. Burns Papers, file 11, Stephen Hart Research Library, History Colorado–Denver.

21. Agreement between John J. Burns and W. A. Beatty, April 28, 1902, John J. Burns Papers, file 11, Stephen Hart Research Library, History Colorado–Denver.

22. J. Ed Rizer to John J. Burns, April 29, 1902, John J. Burns Papers, file 11, Stephen Hart Research Library, History Colorado–Denver.

23. "Construction," *Railway Age* 42, no. 18 (November 2, 1906): 558.

24. Articles of Incorporation, the Rapid Transit Company, May 17, 1902, John J. Burns Papers, file 11, Stephen Hart Research Library, History Colorado–Denver.

25. Memorandum of Agreement between John J. Burns, C. Henkle, H. R. Holbrook, and J. N. Carlile, August 1902, John J. Burns Papers, file 11, Stephen Hart Research Library, History Colorado–Denver.

26. W. A. Beatty to J. Ed Rizer, August 8, 1902, John J. Burns Papers, file 11, Stephen Hart Research Library, History Colorado–Denver.

27. Contract between George Peck and Business Men's Association of Pueblo, November 11, 1903, John J. Burns Papers, file 13, Stephen Hart Research Library, History Colorado–Denver.

28. W. A. Beatty to George Peck, March 25, 1903, John J. Burns Papers, file 13, Stephen Hart Research Library, History Colorado–Denver.

29. "First Furrow Turned on Beulah Road," *Denver Republic* (CO), September 28, 1903.

30. W. A. Beatty to George Peck, March 27, 1903, John J. Burns Papers, file 13, Stephen Hart Research Library, History Colorado–Denver.

31. W. A. Beatty to George Peck, February 17, 1903, John J. Burns Papers, file 13, Stephen Hart Research Library, History Colorado–Denver.

32. George Peck to John J. Burns, October 17, 1903, John J. Burns Papers, file 13, Stephen Hart Research Library, History Colorado–Denver.

33. Pueblo and Beulah Road, *Pueblo Chieftain* (CO), January 1, 1894.

34. James N Carlile, Audit, September 1, 1904. John J. Burns Papers, file 15, Stephen Hart Research Library, History Colorado–Denver.

35. George Peck to John J. Burns, February 15, 1905, John J. Burns Papers, file 16, Stephen Hart Research Library, History Colorado–Denver.

36. "Beulah Road," *Weekly Gazette* (Colorado Springs, CO), May 19, 1904.

37. George Peck to John J. Burns, March 22, 1904, John J. Burns Papers, file 16, Stephen Hart Research Library, History Colorado–Denver.

38. J. Ed Rizer to John J. Burns, April 4, 1906, John J. Burns Papers, file 16, Stephen Hart Research Library, History Colorado–Denver.

39. "Colorado," *San Francisco Chronicle*, December 11, 1903.

40. M. L. Moore to John J. Burns, April 16, 1903, John J. Burns Papers, file 12, Stephen Hart Research Library, History Colorado–Denver.

41. Memorandum of Agreement, John J. Burns representing Custer Mining and Realty Company and Charles W. Walters, March 31, 1902, John J. Burns Papers, file 12, Stephen Hart Research Library, History Colorado–Denver.

42. "Custer City," *Pueblo Chieftain* (CO), June 11, 1902.

43. "Custer City."

44. Robert L. Brown, *Ghost Towns of the Colorado Rockies* (Caldwell, ID: Caxton Press, 1968), 116.

45. "Custer City," *Pueblo Chieftain* (CO), June 11, 1902.

46. Elizabeth B. Custer to John J. Burns, May 9, 1902, John J. Burns Papers, file 12, Stephen Hart Research Library, History Colorado, Denver; William F. Cody to John J. Burns, April 12, 1902, John J. Burns Papers, file 12, Stephen Hart Research Library, History Colorado–Denver.

47. "Local News," *Wet Mountain Tribune* (Westcliffe, CO), January 31, 1903.

48. "Local Items," *Silver Cliff Rustler* (CO), April 22, 1903.

49. No headline, *Silver Cliff Rustler* (CO), March 22, 1905.

50. "Sheriff's Sale," *Silver Cliff Rustler* (CO), January 1, 1908.

51. "Buys a Whole City," *Silver Cliff Rustler* (CO), February 26, 1908.

52. "Notice," *Silver Cliff Rustler* (CO), December 2, 1908.

53. "Local and Personal," *Wet Mountain Tribune* (Westcliffe, CO), November 24, 1911.

54. "Alamosa Take Up Project for Air Line Railroad to Pueblo," *Pueblo Sun* (CO), September 16, 1909.

55. "Fifteen Million Dollar Proposition Doubted at First Now Becoming Reality," *Pueblo Chieftain* (CO), June 14, 1908.

56. "Officers Elected for Proposed Kansas-Colorado Railroad," *Pueblo Chieftain* (CO), June 19, 1908.

57. "Contracting Firms Have Confidence in Kansas-Colorado Railroad Project and Will Take $1,000,000 in Securities," *Pueblo Chieftain* (CO), June 21, 1908.

58. "Electric Line Will Be Great Aid in Development of Valley," *Pueblo Chieftain* (CO), July 25, 1908.

59. "Contracts for Building Great Electric System," *Pueblo Sun* (CO), August 1, 1908.

60. "Actual Work Is Started on Interurban Railway to Traverse the Valley," *Pueblo Chieftain* (CO), July 31, 1908.

61. Wilbur Fiske Stone, *History of Colorado*, vol. 3 (Chicago: S. J. Clarke Publishing Company, 1918), 532–534.

Chapter 3. Boss Fight

1. "New Electric Line Has Excellent Route," *Pueblo Chieftain* (CO), August 2, 1908.

2. "Electric Line Will Be Great Aid in Development of Valley," *Pueblo Chieftain* (CO), July 25, 1908.

3. *The Colorado-Kansas Railway Company, June 12, 1912* (Pueblo, CO: Franklin Press, 1912), 6.

4. Richard F. Carrillo, Christian J. Zier, and Andrea M. Barnes, *The Documentation of Stone City (5PE793): Historical Archaeology on the Fort Carson Military Reservation, Pueblo County, Colorado* (submitted to National Park Service–Rocky Mountain Regional Office, Branch of Interagency Archaeological Services, Denver, CO; and United States Army—Office of Environment, Energy and Natural Resources, Fort Carson, CO, Fort Collins, CO: Centennial Archaeology, Inc., July 1991), 25, 37.

5. *The Colorado-Kansas Railway Company, June 12, 1912*, 8.

6. Brian S. Osborne, "The Kansas-Colorado Power and Railroad Project: A Multi-functional Plan for the Development of the Arkansas Valley," *Pioneer America* 6, no. 2 (1974): 29; Raymond W. Arnold, "Memoirs of Raymond W. Arnold, Regarding the Colorado Kansas Railway" (unpublished manuscript, transcribed from a 1980 tape recording in 1992 by Jean Arnold Meier, Colorado-Kansas Railway Collection, Colorado Railroad Museum, Golden), 3.

7. Carrillo, Zier, and Barnes, *The Documentation of Stone City*, 25, 37.

8. "One Mile of Grading Is Completed," *Pueblo Sun* (CO), August 12, 1908.

9. "Rush Grading Work on Electric R. R.," *Pueblo Sun* (CO), August 24, 1908.

10. "Autoists Visit Line of New K.-C. Railway," *Pueblo Sun* (CO), October 1, 1908.

11. "Break Ground on Eastern Division," *Pueblo Sun* (CO), October 20, 1908.

12. "Engineer Arrives to Start Work on Three Power Plants," *Pueblo Chieftain* (CO), September 29, 1908.

13. "Railway Seeks to Condemn Portion of Right of Way," *Pueblo Chieftain* (CO), October 11, 1908.

14. "Condemn Land for Railway," *Pueblo Sun* (CO), October 23, 1908.

15. "Right of Way Deals Wound Up," *Pueblo Sun* (CO), November 6, 1908.

16. "Hard Work Gets K. C. Franchise," *Pueblo Sun* (CO), November 3, 1908.

17. "Hard Work Gets K. C. Franchise."

18. "Hard Work Gets K. C. Franchise."

19. "40 Teams at Work in City," *Pueblo Sun* (CO), November 4, 1908.

20. "Kansas-Colorado Buys Royal Gorge Interurban," *Pueblo Chieftain* (CO), October 31, 1908.

21. "Dream of Cripple Creek Road May Soon Be Reality," *Pueblo Sun* (CO), 22 June 1909.

22. "Graft Money Demanded by City Councilmen?," *Pueblo Sun* (CO), November 7, 1908.

23. "Graft Money Demanded."

24. "Graft Money Demanded."

25. "Immense Contract Is Signed," *Pueblo Sun* (CO), November 9, 1908.

26. "Ties and Rails Will Be the Next Thing," *Pueblo Sun* (CO), November 10, 1908.

27. "K.C. Puts in Order for Steel Rails," *Pueblo Sun*, November 12, 1908.

28. "Big Hotel Enterprise Backed by Railways," *Pueblo Sun* (CO), November 18, 1908; "Drawing of Proposed Hotel," *Pueblo Chieftain* (CO), January 1, 1909.

29. "Announce $6,000,000 Plan; City Gets New Terminals; Close All Grade Crossings," *Pueblo Leader* (CO), February 12, 1913; "Elevation of Proposed $6,000,000 Terminal at Intersection of Arkansas River and Union Ave.," *Pueblo Leader* (CO), February 13, 1913.

30. "K-C Ready to Meet Santa Fe on New Plan," *Pueblo Sun* (CO), January 17, 1910.

31. "Stock Goes Well," *Pueblo Sun* (CO), December 11, 1908.

32. "Begin Monday to Lay Steel Rails to the West," *Pueblo Sun* (CO), December 12, 1908.

33. "Lines of New Railway Located," *Pueblo Sun* (CO), December 23, 1908.

34. "Stock Goes Well," *Pueblo Sun* (CO), December 11, 1908.

35. Osborne, "The Kansas-Colorado Power and Railroad Project," 28.

36. "Knockers Fail to Stop Road," *Pueblo Sun* (CO), January 9, 1909.

37. Andrew J. Jalil, "A New History of Banking Panics in the United States, 1825–1929: Construction and Implications," *American Economic Journal: Macroeconomics* 7, no. 3 (July 2015): 295–330.

38. H. Roger Grant, *Twilight Rails: The Final Era of Railroad Building in the Midwest* (Minneapolis: University of Minnesota Press, 2010), 14.

39. "K. C. Affairs Being Straightened Up," *Pueblo Sun* (CO), February 5, 1909.

40. "Row Is on in Affairs of K. C. Railway," *Pueblo Sun* (CO), February 6, 1909.

41. "Creditors Making Settlement with K. C.," *Pueblo Sun* (CO), February 8, 1909.

42. "Anxious to Resume Work on K. C. Lines," *Pueblo Sun* (CO), February 9, 1909.

43. "Say Hulit Will Come Back in Game," *Pueblo Sun* (CO), February 10, 1909.

44. "Hulit Say Road Will Be Completed," *Pueblo Sun* (CO), February 18, 1909.

45. "Traction Co.'s Attempted Franchise Gobble Not Entirely Successful," *Pueblo Sun* (CO), February 19, 1909.

46. "Colorado Springs After K-C Road—How the Mossbacks Have Pounded Pueblo," *Pueblo Sun* (CO), June 1, 1910.

47. "Kansas Colorado Company Is Organized in Topeka," *Pueblo Sun* (CO), May 7, 1909.

48. *The National Cyclopaedia of American Biography*, vol. 44 (New York: James T. White and Company, 1962), 131–132.

49. "Kansas Colorado Company Is Organized in Topeka," *Pueblo Sun* (CO).

50. "Builders of K. C. Coming This Week," *Pueblo Sun* (CO), May 31, 1909.

51. "K. C. Busy with Job of Paying Off," *Pueblo Sun* (CO), June 28, 1909.

52. "Meeting Tonight on K. C. Project," *Pueblo Sun* (CO), July 15, 1909.

53. "K-C. Franchise, and Changes Proposed," *Pueblo Sun* (CO), July 19, 1909.

54. "Council Acts Favorably on K-C. and Carson Franchises," *Pueblo Sun* (CO), July 20, 1909.

55. "Franchise Given to New Railroad," *Pueblo Sun* (CO), August 3, 1909.

56. "New Road Ready to Pay Off $50,000 of Old Debts," *Pueblo Sun* (CO), August 4, 1909.

Chapter 4. Troubles Continue

1. "Paying of Debts of New Railroad," *Pueblo Sun* (CO), August 5, 1909.

2. "Activity on K. C. Project," *Pueblo Sun* (CO), September 9, 1909.

3. "General Co. Takes Hand in K-C Road," *Pueblo Sun* (CO), October 28, 1909.

4. "First Rails Laid on K-C Road," *Pueblo Sun* (CO), November 22, 1909.

5. "First Spike on Kansas-Colorado Railroad Driven," *Pueblo Chieftain* (CO), November 23, 1909.

6. "Fourth St. Bridge Will Be Raised," *Pueblo Sun* (CO), December 15, 1909.

7. "K-C Begins Work at Fourth Street Bridge," *Pueblo Sun* (CO), January 26, 1910.

8. "K-C Begins Work on River Levee," *Pueblo Sun* (CO), January 28, 1910.

9. "Declared City in Danger of Flood," *Pueblo Chieftain* (CO), January 12, 1912.

10. "Rails Placed in Center of City," *Pueblo Sun* (CO), February 24, 1910.

11. "First Lap Complete by Kansas-Colorado," *Evening Telegram* (Garden City, KS), March 2, 1910.

12. "First Train Passes over Kansas-Colorado Tracks," *Pueblo Chieftain* (CO), March 1, 1910.

13. "Short Rail Supply Halts the Work," *Pueblo Sun* (CO), March 17, 1910.

14. "Bond K-C For $3,000,000," *Pueblo Sun* (CO), March 24, 1910.

15. "K-C Franchise Comes Up for Discussion," *Pueblo Sun* (CO), April 29, 1910.

16. "More Time for K-C Favored by Citizens Mass Meeting," *Pueblo Sun* (CO), April 30, 1910.

17. "K-C Franchise Referred by the Council," *Pueblo Sun* (CO), May 10, 1910.

18. "Vail Hotel Bids May Be Held Up," *Pueblo Sun* (CO), May 11, 1910.

19. "Pueblo Sun Drives Vail to Cover," *Pueblo Sun* (CO), May 13, 1910.

20. "Councilmen Tour K-C Right-Of-Way," *Pueblo Sun* (CO), May 17, 1910.

21. "$25,000 Bond to Build Road," *Pueblo Sun* (CO), May 26, 1910.

22. "Hutchinson Man Says He Is Ready to Donate," *Evening Kansas-Republican* (Newton, KS), May 31, 1910.

23. "Boss Vail Wins Out in Fight to Drive Railroad Enterprise from the City," *Pueblo Sun* (CO), June 1, 1910.

24. "Boss Vail Wins Out in Fight."

25. "Boss Vail Wins Out in Fight."

26. "Charter Fight May Put Vail Out of Party," *Pueblo Sun* (CO), November 19, 1910.

27. "Traction Co. Takes Another Step in Valley Line Project," *Pueblo Sun* (CO), October 6, 1910.

28. "Clearing Away Vail Wreckage," *Pueblo Sun* (CO), October 15, 1910.

29. "Many Buyers for K-C Road," *Pueblo Sun* (CO), November 12, 1910.

30. "Kansas-Colorado Property Goes to Highest Bidder," *Pueblo Chieftain* (CO), November 29, 1910.

31. "'Back to the Farm' Jumps from Mere Words to Speedy Action When 31 States Fight to Get Immigrants onto the Soil," *Evansville Press* (IN), September 13, 1911.

32. "Charges Malice in Attack by Paper," *Inter Ocean* (Chicago, IL), August 26, 1912.

33. "A. B. Hulit, Promoter of Old K.-C. Road, Sees $5,000,000 Bubble Burst in Chicago," *Pueblo Leader* (CO), August 28, 1912.

34. "Hulit Bobs Up with New One," *Chicago Tribune*, January 2, 1914.

35. "A Tax on All Aliens," *Kingston Daily Freeman* (Kingston, NY), June 27, 1935.

36. Edward Pickard, "New Review of Current Events the World Over," *Current Local* (Van Buren, MO), December 13, 1934.

37. "Facts Puncture $5,000,000 Dream," *Chicago Tribune*, August 25, 1912.

38. Karen Mitchell, "Hulit, Lilian V.," *Pueblo County, Colorado, Roselawn Cemetery*, accessed 6 June 2017, http://www.kmitch.com/Pueblo/roseh.html.

Chapter 5. The Colorado-Kansas Railway

1. Interstate Commerce Commission, "Tentative Valuation Report," Valuation Docket no. 81, 7, Colorado-Kansas Railway, Records of the Bureau of Valuation 1910–1974, Interstate Commerce Commission, RG 134, National Archives at College Park, College Park, MD; Colorado-Kansas Railway Company, Articles of Incorporation, record no.180305, filed April 20, 1911, Pueblo County Recording Department, Pueblo, CO.

2. Colorado-Kansas Bond Issue, June 30, 1919, Charles E. Sutton Papers, Pueblo County Historical Society, Pueblo, CO.

3. "Colorado-Kansas Heads Purchase Pueblo Ranches," *Pueblo Chieftain* (CO), June 1, 1913.

4. B. L. Jefferson, Register, *Biennial Report of State Board of Land Commissioners of Colorado, 1909–1910* (Smith-Brooks Printing Co., State Printers, 1910), 71–98.

5. "Something New in Irrigation," *Topeka Daily Capital* (KS), January 12, 1911.

6. "Reclamation Notes," *Irrigation Age 28*, no. 1 (November 1912): 23–24.

7. "Andrew McClelland Replies to Chieftain," *Pueblo Chieftain* (CO), March 27, 1911.

8. "So the People May Be Advised," *Pueblo Chieftain* (CO), April 15, 1911.

9. "Excitement Follows in Council When Retiring Aldermen Give Away a Valuable Franchise," *Pueblo Chieftain* (CO), April 16, 1911.

10. "Colo.-Kansas Ordinance Vetoed by Mayor," *Pueblo Chieftain* (CO), April 18, 1911.

11. "City Clerk Mandamused by Railroad Promoters," *Pueblo Chieftain* (CO), April 22, 1911.

12. "Answer Is Filed by Clerk Duke," *Pueblo Chieftain* (CO), May 9, 1911.

13. "Duke Mandamus Hearing on Tuesday," *Pueblo Leader* (CO), July 1, 1911.

14. "Judge Rizer Orders City Clerk Duke to Publish Ordinance," *Pueblo Leader* (CO), July 19, 1911.

15. "Duke Leaves Suddenly with Out Notice," *Pueblo Leader* (CO), July 21, 1911.

16. "Legal Notices, Ordinance No. 839," *Pueblo Star-Journal* (CO), July 21, 1911.

17. "Claim Duke Did Not Run," *Pueblo Leader* (CO), July 22, 1911.

18. "Judge Rizer Orders City Clerk Duke to Publish Ordinance," *Pueblo Leader* (CO), July 19, 1911.

19. "Duke Leaves Suddenly with Out Notice."

20. "Claim Duke Did Not Run."

21. "Will Force City Clerk to Publish Initiative and Referendum Law," *Pueblo Leader* (CO), July 24, 1911.

22. "Duke Arrives at Close of Vacation," *Pueblo Leader* (CO), August 7, 1911.

23. "Colorado-Kansas Would Be in Operation Now but for Work of Vail; Et Al," *Pueblo Leader* (CO), July 22, 1911; "File Answer for New Road," *Pueblo Leader* (CO), August 11, 1911.

24. "File Answer for New Road."

25. The court documents have not come to light, but considering Rizer's propensity to rule in favor of the Colorado-Kansas Railway, and the fact that the railroad resumed construction at the end of November, it is evident the Colorado-Kansas Railway won their case.

26. "Want Railroad to Electrify Valley," *Pueblo Chieftain* (CO), March 30, 1913.

27. McGraw Publishing Company, Inc., "Franchises," *Electric Railway Journal*, 37, no. 25 (June 24, 1911): 1132.

28. "McGraw Publishing Company, Inc., Recent Incorporations," *Electric Railway Journal* 38, no. 23 (December 2, 1911): 1181.

29. McGraw Publishing Company, Inc., "Track and Roadway," *Electric Railway Journal* 46, no. 15 (October 9, 1915): 787.

30. Ralph C. Taylor, *Pueblo* (Pueblo, CO: Published for the Pueblo Board of Education, 1979), 72–73.

31. McGraw Publishing Company, Inc., "Personal Mention," *Electric Railway Journal* 38, no. 2 (July 8, 1911): 98.

32. "Tennesseans Marry in Colorado," *Tennessean* (Nashville, TN), August 27, 1916.

33. "C.-K. Road Buys Locomotive for Building Track," *Pueblo Leader* (CO), December 9, 1911.

34. "C.-K. Road Buys Locomotive," *Pueblo Leader* (CO).

35. Dan Abbott, *Colorado Midland: Daylight through the Divide* (Denver: Sundance Publications, 1989), 313.

36. Morris Cafky, *Colorado Midland* (Denver: World Press, 1965), 356.

37. Colorado-Kansas Railway, Report no. 3079, 1930, Records of the Operating Division, Annual Reports of Railroads 1915–1961, Interstate Commerce Commission, RG 134, National Archives at College Park, College Park, MD.

38. "Snow Storm Is Not Hindering Track Laying," *Pueblo Leader* (CO), December 19, 1911.

39. "New Railroad Is Now 6 Miles Long," *Pueblo Leader* (CO), January 11, 1912; "C.-K. Directors in Session Today," *Pueblo Leader* (CO), January 27, 1912.

40. Interstate Commerce Commission, "Stenographers' Minutes before the Interstate Commerce Commission," Application for Colorado Railroad, Inc., Finance Docket 11988, April 25, 1938, Case Files 1887–1955, Interstate Commerce Commission, RG 134, National Archives at College Park, College Park, MD, 9.

41. F. G. Kelley to Charles Sutton, March 29, 1912, Charles E. Sutton Papers, Pueblo County Historical Society, Pueblo, CO.

42. "New Railroad to Quarries Is Finished," *Pueblo Leader* (CO), April 16, 1912.

43. "First Shipment of Freight Here," *Pueblo Chieftain* (CO), April 26, 1912.

44. "Quarry Company Completes Switch," *Pueblo Chieftain* (CO), November 21, 1912.

45. "Home Industry Week Is Molding to Perfection," *Pueblo Chieftain* (CO), March 28, 1912.

46. "Automobile Parade Proves to Be Spectacular Feature," *Pueblo Chieftain* (CO), April 16, 1912.

47. Charles E. Sutton to managers, April 13, 1912, Charles E. Sutton Papers, Pueblo County Historical Society, Pueblo, CO.

48. "Industrial Pueblo Defies Storm and Thousands See Great Parade," *Pueblo Chieftain* (CO), April 19, 1912.

49. "Colorado-Kansas Is Formally Opened," *Pueblo Chieftain* (CO), June 12, 1912.

50. "Pueblo Opens Today Its Home-Built Road into the State's Greatest Quarries," *Pueblo Leader* (CO), June 12, 1912.

51. "The Colorado-Kansas Railroad," *Pueblo Star-Journal* (CO), June 13, 1912.

Chapter 6. Connecting Tracks

1. William Cronon, *Nature's Metropolis: Chicago and the Great West* (New York: W. W. Norton and Company, 1991), 263–269.

2. Kenneth E. Lewis, *The American Frontier: An Archaeological Study of Settlement Pattern and Process* (Orlando: Academic Press, Inc., 1984), 284.

3. Ralph C. Taylor, *Pueblo* (Pueblo, CO: Published for the Pueblo Board of Education, 1979), 6–9.

4. Richard F. Carrillo, Christian J. Zier, and Andrea M. Barnes, *The Documentation of Stone City (5PE793): Historical Archaeology on the Fort Carson Military Reservation, Pueblo County, Colorado* (submitted to National Park Service–Rocky Mountain Regional Office, Branch of Interagency Archaeological Services, Denver, CO and United States Army—Office of Environment, Energy and Natural Resources, Fort Carson, CO, Fort Collins, CO: Centennial Archaeology, Inc., July 1991), 23.

5. Taylor, *Pueblo*, 17–20.

6. "Colorado-Kansas Rails Are Ordered," *Pueblo Leader* (CO), December 1, 1911.

7. "Colorado-Kansas Ties on The Way," *Pueblo Leader* (CO), November 27, 1911; "C.-K. Material Is Beginning to Come," *Pueblo Leader* (CO), December 2, 1911.

8. Kent Stephens, "The Colorado Railroad," *New Mexico Railroader* 7 (October 1965; issued January 1966): 6.

9. "Raze Buildings to Begin Depot," *Pueblo Leader* (CO), December 7, 1912.

10. Wilbur Fiske Stone, *History of Colorado*, vol. 2 (S. J. Clarke Publishing Co.: Chicago, 1918), 510–511.

11. Interstate Commerce Commission, Engineering Report Notes, Colorado-Kansas Railway, Valuation Docket no. 81, Records of the Bureau of Valuation 1910–1974, Interstate Commerce Commission, RG 134, National Archives at College Park, College Park, MD.

12. "Stone City Gets Postoffice; 40 Families Aided," *Pueblo Leader* (CO), January 16, 1913.

13. Advertisement, "Stone City Lots," *Pueblo Chieftain* (CO), April 15, 1913.

14. Taylor, *Pueblo*, 6–8.

15. Taylor, *Pueblo*, 74.

16. Arthur Ridgway, *The Case for Train Number 3* (Denver: Rocky Mountain Railroad Club, 1956), 40.

17. Ridgway, *The Case for Train Number 3*, 31.

18. Colorado-Kansas Railway, Report no. 3079, 1925, Records of the Operating Division, Annual Reports of Railroads 1915–1961, Interstate Commerce Commission, RG 134, National Archives at College Park, College Park, MD.

19. Ridgway, *The Case for Train Number 3*, map inside back cover.

20. "Colorado Kansas Railroad Still Runs without Depot," *Pueblo Chieftain* (CO), August 21, 1921.

21. "Rebuild Colorado-Kansas R. R. Track to Victoria Ave.," *Pueblo Chieftain* (CO), April 11, 1925.

22. "Proposed Plan for Providing against Flood Hazard," *Pueblo Chieftain* (CO), July 10, 1921.

23. Taylor, *Pueblo*, 76.

24. Evan R. Ward, "Geo-environmental Disconnection and the Colorado River Delta: Technology, Culture, and the Political Ecology of Paradise," *Environment and History* 7, no. 2 (May 2001): 219–246.

25. Interstate Commerce Commission, Engineering Report Notes, Colorado-Kansas Railway, Valuation Docket no. 81, Records of the Bureau of Valuation 1910–1974, Interstate Commerce Commission, RG 134, National Archives at College Park, College Park, MD.

26. Raymond W. Arnold, "Memoirs of Raymond W. Arnold, Regarding the Colorado Kansas Railway" (unpublished manuscript, transcribed from a 1980 tape recording in 1992 by Jean Arnold Meier, Colorado-Kansas Railway Collection, Colorado Railroad Museum, Golden), 3.

27. Interstate Commerce Commission, "Stenographers' Minutes before the Interstate Commerce Commission," Application for Colorado Railroad, Inc., Finance Docket 11988, April 25, 1938, p. 18, Case Files 1887–1955, Interstate

Commerce Commission, RG 134, National Archives at College Park, College Park, MD.

28. Handwritten Per Diem spreadsheet of reporting marks and car numbers, January to April, June, and October 1923, Colorado-Kansas Railway company records, Colorado-Kansas Railway Collection, Colorado Railroad Museum, Golden.

29. Interstate Commerce Commission, "Engineering Report," Colorado-Kansas Railway, Valuation Docket no. 81, 12, Records of the Bureau of Valuation 1910–1974, Interstate Commerce Commission, RG 134, National Archives at College Park, College Park, MD.

30. Arnold, "Memoirs of Raymond W. Arnold," 3.

31. Colorado-Kansas Railway, Report no. 3081, 1933–1937; Colorado-Kansas Railway, Report no. 3079, 1938; Colorado Railroad, Inc., Report no. 3077, 1938–1943; all, Records of the Operating Division, Annual Reports of Railroads 1915–1961, Interstate Commerce Commission, RG 134, National Archives at College Park, College Park, MD.

32. Barbara P. Baker, *Steamy Dreamer: The Saga of Dr. Hartley O. Baker and the Baker Steam Motor Car* (Grand Junction, CO: Centennial Publications, 1996), 86, 162.

33. Baker, *Steamy Dreamer*, 150–151.

34. Carrillo, Zier, and Barnes, *The Documentation of Stone City*, 10.

35. Robert G. Bailey, *Description of the Ecoregions of the United States* (Washington, DC: United States Department of Agriculture, Forest Service, Miscellaneous Publication 1391, 1995), 71–72.

Chapter 7. Tales of the Teller Cousins

1. US Department of the Interior, Bureau of Land Management, "General Land Office Records, Land Patents," 1885–1892, accessed July 23, 2018, https://glorecords.blm.gov/results/default.aspx?searchCriteria=type=patent|st=CO|cty=101|ln=Teller|twp_nr=20|twp_dir=S|rng_nr=66|rng_dir=W|m=06|sp=true|sw=true|sadv=false.

2. Pueblo County Recorder, "Miscellaneous Record," book 49, record no. 19696, December 4, 1885, Pueblo County Recording Department, Pueblo, CO, 291–292.

3. Duane Smith, *Henry M. Teller: Colorado's Grand Old Man* (Boulder: University Press of Colorado, 2002), 105.

4. Pueblo County Recorder, "Miscellaneous Record," book 400, record No. 212424, November 30, 1915, Pueblo County Recording Department, Pueblo, CO, 243–245.

5. Pueblo County Recorder, "Miscellaneous Record," book 57, record No. 23946, September 10, 1887, Pueblo County Recording Department, Pueblo, CO, 114–116.

6. Pueblo County Recorder, "Miscellaneous Record," book 49, record no. 20319, March 29, 1886, Pueblo County Recording Department, Pueblo, CO, 431–432.

7. Pueblo County Recorder, "Land Deeds Reservoirs and Ditches," book 1B, March 29, 1886, Pueblo County Recording Department, Pueblo, CO, 159.

8. Pueblo County Recorder, "Miscellaneous Record," book 131, record no. 56718, March 12, 1892, Pueblo County Recording Department, Pueblo, CO, 350–352.

9. Pueblo County Recorder, "Miscellaneous Record," book 132, record no. 56720, March 12, 1892, Pueblo County Recording Department, Pueblo, CO, 241–244.

10. Pueblo County Recorder, "Miscellaneous Record," book 156, record no. 74054, April 4, 1895, Pueblo County Recording Department, Pueblo, CO, 217–221.

11. "Colorado State Capital Affairs," *Colorado Transcript* (Golden, CO), December 3, 1903.

12. *Sketches of Colorado in Four Volumes*, vol. 1, (Denver: Western Press Bureau Company, 1911), 96–97.

13. Holland Society of New York, "U.S., Dutch Reformed Church Records in Selected States, 1639–1989," Dutch Reformed Church Records from New Jersey, Archives of the Reformed Church in America, New Brunswick, New Jersey, *Schenectady Baptisms*, vol. 4, book 44, 501, n.d., *Ancestry.com*, https://www.ancestry.com/interactive/6961/42037_647350_0297-00091?pid=107766.

14. *Sketches of Colorado*, 96–97.

15. Canada East, Canada West, New Brunswick, and Nova Scotia, *Census of 1851*, Woodhouse, Norfolk County, Canada West (Ontario), Schedule A, Roll C-11741, Library and Archives Canada, Ottawa, Canada, digital image, *Ancestry.com*, https://www.ancestry.com/interactive/1061/e095-e002362161?pid=2211810.

16. US Bureau of the Census, *Ninth Census of the United States, 1870*, Erie County, Buffalo, New York, Buffalo Ward 8, sheet 384A, National Archives microfilm M593, Roll 934 (Washington, DC: National Archives and Records Administration, Records of the Bureau of the Census, RG 29, 1870), digital image, *Ancestry.com*, https://www.ancestry.com/interactive/7163/4274972_00781?pid=29672518.

17. US Bureau of the Census, *Tenth Census of the United States, 1880*, Bay County, Bay City, Michigan, Second Ward, Enumeration District 015, sheet 366A, National Archives microfilm T9, Roll 571 (Washington, DC: National Archives and Records Administration, Records of the Bureau of the Census, RG 29, 1880), digital image, *Ancestry.com*, https://www.ancestry.com/interactive/6742/4241653-00316?pid=314 19938; *Bay City Directory for 1883* (Detroit: R. L. Polk and Company, 1883), 311.

18. US Bureau of the Census, *Colorado State Census, 1885*, Pitkin County, Aspen, Colorado, Enumeration District 1, 13, National Archives microfilm M158, Roll 7 (Washington, DC: National Archives and Records Administration, Records of

the Bureau of the Census, RG 29, 1885), digital image, *Ancestry.com*, https://www
.ancestry.com/interactive/6837/cot158_7-0071.1?pid=153805.

19. "The Republican Primaries," *Rocky Mountain Sun* (Aspen, CO), September 11, 1886, 2.

20. *Corbett and Ballenger's Sixteenth Annual Denver City Directory* (Corbett and Ballenger: Denver, 1888), 870.

21. "New Road, Extensions, and Project," *Railway Age* 11, no. 43 (October 28, 1886): 601.

22. "Mining Notes," *Rocky Mountain Sun* (Aspen, CO), January 22, 1887, 2.

23. "North and South R. R.," *Deseret Evening News* (Salt Lake City, UT), October 23, 1897.

24. "Pueblo & Western," *Colorado Daily Chieftain* (Pueblo, CO), September 19, 1889.

25. No headline, *Silver Cliff Rustler* (CO), March 18, 1891.

26. A. B. McGaffey, *Biennial Report of the Secretary of State of Colorado for the Fiscal Years Ending November 30, 1895, and November 30, 1896* (Denver: Smith Brothers Printing Co.—State Printers, 1896), 53.

27. *Biographical and Reminiscent History of Richland, Clay and Marion Counties, Illinois* (Indianapolis: B. F. Bowen and Company, 1909), 192–193.

28. "Denver," *American Stationer* 37, no. 4 (January 24, 1895): 134.

29. *Biographical and Reminiscent History*, 193.

30. "The Old Aztec Placers," *Salt Lake Herald* (Salt Lake City, UT), November 6, 1897.

31. "News of the West," *Salt Lake Herald* (Salt Lake City, UT), August 6, 1898.

32. "Teller Secures a Verdict," *Omaha Daily Bee* (NE), November 25, 1899.

33. *The Federal Reporter*, vol. 106, *Cases Argued and Determined in the Circuit Courts of Appeals of the United States, March–April 1901* (St. Paul, MN: West Publishing Company, 1901), 447–451.

34. *Annual Report of the Attorney-General of the United States for the Year 1906* (Washington, DC: Government Printing Office, 1907), 65.

35. "Government Loses in the Teller Suit," *St. Louis Republic* (MO), December 3, 1901.

36. "Decision Affirmed," *Leavenworth Times* (Leavenworth, KS), December 31, 1901.

37. *Annual Report of the Attorney-General of the United States for the Year 1906*, 65.

38. "Spike and Rail," *Deseret Evening News* (Salt Lake City, UT), October 31, 1901.

39. "Will Arrest Teller," *Salt Lake Telegram* (Salt Lake City, UT), May 12, 1905; United States v. Teller, RG 21 US District Court of Wyoming, Entry 9 Criminal Case Files, 1890–1969, Box 10, Case file 284 US v Teller; United States v. Teller, RG

21 US District Court of Wyoming, Entry 9 Criminal Case Files, 1890–1969, Box 10, Case file 285 US v Teller.

40. *Congressional Record: Containing the Proceedings and Debates of the Sixtieth Congress, Second Session*, vol. 43, pt. 4 4 (Washington, DC: Government Printing Office, 1909), 3241.

41. "Is It the Standard Oil Co.?," *Colorado Weekly Chieftain* (Pueblo, CO), November 21, 1895.

42. Pueblo County Recorder, "Miscellaneous Record," book 400, record no. 212243, November 30, 1915, Pueblo County Recording Department, Pueblo, CO, 242–243.

43. "News Notes from Pueblo," *Weekly Gazette* (Colorado Springs, CO), May 15, 1901.

44. Pueblo County Recorder, "Miscellaneous Record," book 416, record no. 218565, June 12, 1916, Pueblo County Recording Department, Pueblo, CO, 66; Pueblo County Recorder, "Miscellaneous Record," book 539, record no. 299434, March 21, 1922, Pueblo County Recording Department, Pueblo, CO, 278.

45. Scrapbook Pliny Fisk Sharp, vol. 7, 53, "John C. Teller Dead," August 6, 1917, John J. Burns Papers, file 18, Stephen Hart Research Library, History Colorado–Denver.

46. "Washington News of Special Colorado Interest," *Weekly Gazette* (Colorado Springs, CO), February 19, 1903.

47. "Sells Many Acres," *Pueblo Chieftain* (CO), December 8, 1909.

48. Pueblo County Recorder, "Miscellaneous Record," book 269, record nos. 134542, 134543, December 7, 1904, Pueblo County Recording Department, Pueblo, CO, 556–562.

49. William Fullerton to John C. Teller and John J. Burns, September 1, 1908, John J. Burns Papers, file 18, Stephen Hart Research Library, History Colorado–Denver.

Chapter 8. Dam Troubles

1. J. W. Powell, *Twelfth Annual Report of the United State Geological Survey to the Secretary of the Interior: 1890–91, Part II: Irrigation* (Washington, DC: Government Printing Office), 1891, 9, 76.

2. Pueblo County Recorder, "Quit Claim Deeds," book 326, record no. 166530, June 11, 1909, Pueblo County Recording Department, Pueblo, CO, 315.

3. Pueblo County Recorder, "Land Deeds Reservoirs and Ditches," book 1B, record no. 155949, December 4, 1907, Pueblo County Recording Department, Pueblo, CO, 161.

4. Pueblo County Recorder, "Land Deeds Reservoirs and Ditches," book 1B, record nos. 162195, 164235, September 9, 1908, Pueblo County Recording Department, Pueblo, CO, 86.

5. Pueblo County Recorder, "Miscellaneous Record," book 320, record no. 165339, April 5, 1909, Pueblo County Recording Department, Pueblo, CO, 594–596.

6. Pueblo County Recorder, "Warranty Deed Record," book 338, record no. 161345, January 5, 1895, Pueblo County Recording Department, Pueblo, CO, 216.

7. Pueblo County Recorder, "Warranty Deed Record," book 348 record no. 165340, October 12, 1908, Pueblo County Recording Department, Pueblo, CO, 25.

8. Pueblo County Recorder, "Miscellaneous Record," book 400, record no. 212524, April 2, 1915, Pueblo County Recording Department, Pueblo, CO, 257–260.

9. John Olsen, Arkansas Valley Construction Company to Teller Reservoir & Irrigation Company, August 11, 1909, John J. Burns Papers, file 18, Stephen Hart Research Library, History Colorado—Denver.

10. Pueblo County Recorder, "Miscellaneous Record," book 342, record no. 165342, April 5, 1909, Pueblo County Recording Department, Pueblo, CO, 491–494.

11. Pueblo County Recorder, "Miscellaneous Record," book 400, record no. 212524, April 2, 1915, Pueblo County Recording Department, Pueblo, CO, 257–260.

12. "Plan Big Pleasure Resort along New Interurban Line," *Pueblo Chieftain* (CO), August 7, 1908.

13. "Will Irrigate Much Pueblo County Land," *Pueblo Chieftain* (CO), October 29, 1908.

14. John J. Burns to Richard S. Fuller, Messrs. Monson and Malcom, September 15, 1909, John J. Burns Papers, file 18; John J. Burns to John C. Teller, September 15, 1909, John J. Burns Papers, file 18; both, Stephen Hart Research Library, History Colorado–Denver.

15. Pueblo County Recorder, "Quit Claim Deeds," book 326, record no. 166530, June 11, 1909, Pueblo County Recording Department, Pueblo, CO, 315.

16. E. T. Wells, *Cases Argued and Determined in the Court of Appeals of Colorado at the April and September Terms A. D. 1913*, vol. 24 (Denver: Mills Publishing Co., 1913), 239–246.

17. John Olsen, Arkansas Valley Construction Company to Teller Reservoir & Irrigation Company, August 11, 1909, John J. Burns Papers, file 18, Stephen Hart Research Library, History Colorado–Denver.

18. E. T. Wells, *Cases Argued and Determined in the Court of Appeals of Colorado at the April and September Terms A. D. 1913*, 1913, 239–246.

19. *R.L. Polk & Co.'s Pueblo City Directory, 1899–1900*, vol. 2 (Pueblo: Chieftain Printers, 1900), 223; *R.L. Polk & Co.'s Pueblo City Directory, 1904–1905*, vol.7 (Pueblo: Chieftain Printers, 1900), 207; *Ballenger and Richards Thirty-Fifth Annual Denver City Directory for 1907* (Denver: Smith-Brooks Printing Co.), 496.

20. Teller Reservoir & Irrigation Company, Articles of Incorporation, record no. 197569, filed April 6, 1909, Pueblo County Recording Department, Pueblo, CO.

21. Pueblo County Recorder, "Warranty Deed Records," book 348, record no. 167712, August 17, 1909, Pueblo County Recording Department, Pueblo, CO, 284.

22. Turkey Creek Land & Cattle Company, Articles of Incorporation, record no. 171488, filed March 10, 1909, Pueblo County Recording Department, Pueblo, CO.

23. Pueblo County Recorder, "Miscellaneous Record," book 351, record no. 176457, October 28, 1910, Pueblo County Recording Department, Pueblo, CO, 582–583.

24. Pueblo County Recorder, "Miscellaneous Record," book 368, record no. 180349, April 19, 1911, Pueblo County Recording Department, Pueblo, CO, 340–343.

25. Pueblo County Recorder, "Miscellaneous Record," book 343, record no. 167713, August 24, 1909, Pueblo County Recording Department, Pueblo, CO, 193–220.

26. Alice Polk Hill, *Colorado Pioneers in Picture and Story* (Brock-Haffner Press: Denver, 1915), 504–505.

27. Pueblo County Recorder, "Miscellaneous Record," book 400, record no. 209786, November 24, 1914, Pueblo County Recording Department, Pueblo, CO, 174.

28. Pueblo County Recorder, "Miscellaneous Record," book 372, record no. 183835, September 22, 1911, Pueblo County Recording Department, Pueblo, CO, 5–6.

29. A. M. Welles, "Report on the Teller Reservoir and Irrigation Company's Property," August 10, 1909, John J. Burns Papers, file 18, Stephen Hart Research Library, History Colorado–Denver, 1–10.

30. T. W. Jaycox to parties interested in the Teller Reservoir & Irrigation Company, August 14, 1909, John J. Burns Papers, file 18, Stephen Hart Research Library, History Colorado–Denver.

31. A. M. Welles, "Report on the Teller Reservoir and Irrigation Company's Property," August 10, 1909, John J. Burns Papers, file 18, Stephen Hart Research Library, History Colorado–Denver, 9.

32. Charles W. Comstock, ed., *Fifteenth Biennial Report of the State Engineer for the Years 1909–10* (Smith-Denver: Brooks Printing Company, 1911), 118.

33. T. W. Jaycox to parties interested in the Teller Reservoir & Irrigation Company, August 14, 1909, John J. Burns Papers, file 18, Stephen Hart Research Library, History Colorado–Denver.

34. Pueblo County Recorder, "Miscellaneous Record," book 343, record no. 169165, November 11, 1909, Pueblo County Recording Department, Pueblo, CO, 300.

35. "Teller-Burns Project," *Pueblo Chieftain* (CO), May 9, 1909.

36. Vernon J. Rose to the Teller Reservoir & Irrigation Company, August 9, 1909, John J. Burns Papers, file 18, Stephen Hart Research Library, History Colorado–Denver.

37. "Eastern Men Buy Land after Viewing Water Project Near Pueblo," *Rocky Mountain News* (Denver), June 18, 1909, newspaper clipping, John J. Burns Papers, file 86, Stephen Hart Research Library, History Colorado–Denver.

38. Vernon J. Rose to the Teller Reservoir & Irrigation Company, August 9, 1909, John J. Burns Papers, file 18, Stephen Hart Research Library, History Colorado–Denver.

39. Henry M. Teller and Harper M. Orahood to John C. Teller, August 20, 1909, John J. Burns Papers, file 18, Stephen Hart Research Library, History Colorado–Denver.

40. "For Sale," *Indianapolis Star*, February 13, 1910.

41. *Pueblo Gardens* (Pueblo, CO: Teller Reservoir & Irrigation Company, 1910), Special Collections, Robert Hoag Rawlings Public Library, Pueblo City-County Library District, Pueblo, CO, 12.

42. *Pueblo Gardens*, 14.

43. *Pueblo Gardens*, 17.

44. "Reclamation Notes, Colorado," *Irrigation Age* 25, no. 8 (June 1910): 374.

45. John Olsen, Arkansas Valley Construction Company to Teller Reservoir & Irrigation Company, August 11, 1909, John J. Burns Papers, file 18, Stephen Hart Research Library, History Colorado–Denver.

46. Charles W. Comstock, ed., *Fifteenth Biennial Report of the State Engineer for the Years 1909–10*, 118–119.

47. "Cloudburst Washes Out Portion of Dam," *Pueblo Chieftain* (CO), July 13, 1910.

48. "Comparatively Small Part Teller Dam Is Destroyed," *Pueblo Chieftain* (CO), July 14, 1910.

49. "Reclamation Notes, Colorado," *Irrigation Age* 25, no. 3 (January 1910): 129; Pueblo County Recorder, "Miscellaneous Record," book 365, record no. 171744, January 18, 1910, Pueblo County Recording Department, Pueblo, CO, 13.

50. "Reclamation Notes, Colorado," *Irrigation Age* 26, no. 3 (January 1911): 744.

51. "Teller Dam and Reservoir on Turkey Creek Completed," *Pueblo Chieftain* (CO), April 10, 1911.

Chapter 9. Geo. H. Paul, Boy Wonder

1. Geo. H. Paul to Lyra Haisley Sparks, May 30, 1961, Lyra Haisley Sparks Papers, 1896–1963, Center for American History, University of Texas at Austin.

2. US Selective Service System, World War I Selective Service System Draft Registration Cards, 1917–1918, Washington County, Iowa, National Archives microfilm M1509 (Washington, DC: National Archives and Records Administration, RG 163), Ancestry.com, https://www.ancestry.com/interactive/6482/005250418_02096 ?pid=30031498; A. U. Mershon, Apples of Gold (Pueblo, CO: Geo. H. Paul Orchard Company, 1911), Special Collections, Robert Hoag Rawlings Public Library, Pueblo City-County Library District, Pueblo, CO, 2.

3. Mershon, Apples of Gold, 2.

4. Geo. H. Paul to Lyra Haisley Sparks, April 27, 1961, Lyra Haisley Sparks Papers, 1896–1963, Center for American History, University of Texas at Austin.

5. Geo. H. Paul to Lyra Haisley Sparks, May 4, 1961, Lyra Haisley Sparks Papers, 1896–1963, Center for American History, University of Texas at Austin.

6. "Iowa State News," Boyden Reporter (IA), February 27, 1913.

7. Geo. H. Paul to Lyra Haisley Sparks, October 8, 1961, Lyra Haisley Sparks Papers, 1896–1963, Center for American History, University of Texas at Austin.

8. Edna L. Jones to Brad Bowers, May 31, 2001, author's collection.

9. Geo. H. Paul to Lyra Haisley Sparks, June 16, 1961, Lyra Haisley Sparks Papers, 1896–1963, Center for American History, University of Texas at Austin.

10. Howard A. Burrell, History of Washington County, Iowa, From the First White Settlements to 1908, vol. 2 (Chicago: S. J. Clarke Publishing Company, 1909), 72–76.

11. Geo. H. Paul to Lyra Haisley Sparks, September 19, 1962, Lyra Haisley Sparks Papers, 1896–1963, Center for American History, University of Texas at Austin.

12. Geo. H. Paul to Lyra Haisley Sparks, June 12, 1961, Lyra Haisley Sparks Papers, 1896–1963, Center for American History, University of Texas at Austin.

13. Geo. H. Paul to Lyra Haisley Sparks, August 21, 1961, Lyra Haisley Sparks Papers, 1896–1963, Center for American History, University of Texas at Austin.

14. Geo. H. Paul to Lyra Haisley Sparks, May 5, 1961, Lyra Haisley Sparks Papers, 1896–1963, Center for American History, University of Texas at Austin.

15. Geo. H. Paul to Lyra Haisley Sparks, May 29, 1961, Lyra Haisley Sparks Papers, 1896–1963, Center for American History, University of Texas at Austin.

16. Geo. H. Paul to Lyra Haisley Sparks, May 11, 1961, Lyra Haisley Sparks Papers, 1896–1963, Center for American History, University of Texas at Austin.

17. Geo. H. Paul to Lyra Haisley Sparks, June 2, 1962, Lyra Haisley Sparks Papers, 1896–1963, Center for American History, University of Texas at Austin.

18. Geo. H. Paul to Lyra Haisley Sparks, May 5, 1961, Lyra Haisley Sparks Papers, 1896–1963, Center for American History, University of Texas at Austin.

19. Geo. H. Paul to Lyra Haisley Sparks, February 23, 1963, Lyra Haisley Sparks Papers, 1896–1963, Center for American History, University of Texas at Austin.

20. Geo. H. Paul to Lyra Haisley Sparks, June 23, 1962, Lyra Haisley Sparks Papers, 1896–1963, Center for American History, University of Texas at Austin.

21. Geo. H. Paul to Lyra Haisley Sparks, May 4, 1961, Lyra Haisley Sparks Papers, 1896–1963, Center for American History, University of Texas at Austin.

22. Geo. H. Paul to Lyra Haisley Sparks, May 5, 1961, Lyra Haisley Sparks Papers, 1896–1963, Center for American History, University of Texas at Austin.

23. Geo. H. Paul to Lyra Haisley Sparks, October 18, 1961, Lyra Haisley Sparks Papers, 1896–1963, Center for American History, University of Texas at Austin.

24. Geo. H. Paul to Lyra Haisley Sparks, May 5, 1961, Lyra Haisley Sparks Papers, 1896–1963, Center for American History, University of Texas at Austin.

25. Geo. H. Paul to Lyra Haisley Sparks, August 8, 1961, Lyra Haisley Sparks Papers, 1896–1963, Center for American History, University of Texas at Austin.

26. Geo. H. Paul to Lyra Haisley Sparks, May 11, 1961, Lyra Haisley Sparks Papers, 1896–1963, Center for American History, University of Texas at Austin.

27. Geo. H. Paul to Lyra Haisley Sparks, May 11, 1961, Lyra Haisley Sparks Papers, 1896–1963, Center for American History, University of Texas at Austin.

28. Keith Guthrie, Texas State Historical Association, Handbook of Texas Online, "Coleman-Fulton Pasture Company," uploaded on June 12, 2010, modified on July 19, 2016, http://www.tshaonline.org/handbook/online/articles/aqc02.

29. Geo. H. Paul to Lyra Haisley Sparks, May 4, 1961, Lyra Haisley Sparks Papers, 1896–1963, Center for American History, University of Texas at Austin.

30. Geo. H. Paul to Lyra Haisley Sparks, May 4, 1961, Lyra Haisley Sparks Papers, 1896–1963, Center for American History, University of Texas at Austin.

31. Geo. H. Paul to Lyra Haisley Sparks, July 4, 1961, Lyra Haisley Sparks Papers, 1896–1963, Center for American History, University of Texas at Austin.

32. Geo. H. Paul to Lyra Haisley Sparks, May 4, 1961, Lyra Haisley Sparks Papers, 1896–1963, Center for American History, University of Texas at Austin.

33. Geo. H. Paul to Lyra Haisley Sparks, October 21, 1961, Lyra Haisley Sparks Papers, 1896–1963, Center for American History, University of Texas at Austin.

34. Geo. H. Paul to Lyra Haisley Sparks, May 4, 1961, Lyra Haisley Sparks Papers, 1896–1963, Center for American History, University of Texas at Austin.

35. Geo. H. Paul to Lyra Haisley Sparks, May 4, 1961, Lyra Haisley Sparks Papers, 1896–1963, Center for American History, University of Texas at Austin.

36. Geo. H. Paul to Lyra Haisley Sparks, June 23, 1961, Lyra Haisley Sparks Papers, 1896–1963, Center for American History, University of Texas at Austin.

37. Geo. H. Paul to Lyra Haisley Sparks, June 12, 1961, Lyra Haisley Sparks Papers, 1896–1963, Center for American History, University of Texas at Austin.

38. Geo. H. Paul to Lyra Haisley Sparks, October 17, 1961, Lyra Haisley Sparks Papers, 1896–1963, Center for American History, University of Texas at Austin.

39. Geo. H. Paul to Lyra Haisley Sparks, June 30, 1961, Lyra Haisley Sparks Papers, 1896–1963, Center for American History, University of Texas at Austin.

40. Geo. H. Paul to Lyra Haisley Sparks, October 23, 1961, Lyra Haisley Sparks Papers, 1896–1963, Center for American History, University of Texas at Austin.

Chapter 10. "Land of Sunshine, Health, and Opportunity"

1. "Still They Come," *Alamosa Journal* (Alamosa, CO), February 3, 1911.

2. Charles S. Thomas to Mrs. John J. Burns, April 20, 1931, John J. Burns Papers, file 18, Stephen Hart Research Library, History Colorado–Denver.

3. "The Teller Reservoir System Sold," *Pueblo Chieftain* (CO), August 31, 1911, newspaper clipping, John J. Burns Papers, file 86, Stephen Hart Research Library, History Colorado–Denver.

4. "$800,000 Land Deal Means 2,000 New Families Here," *Pueblo Chieftain* (CO), September 1, 1911, newspaper clipping, John J. Burns Papers, file 86, Stephen Hart Research Library, History Colorado–Denver.

5. El Paso County Recorder, "Agreements of Sale," book 457, record no. 226983, November 13, 1915, El Paso County Recording Department, 223; E. T. Wells, Reporter, *Cases Argued and Determined in the Supreme Court of the State of Colorado at the Term of September A.D. 1917, January, April and September, A.D. 1918*, vol. 65 (Chicago: Callaghan and Company, 1920), 466–467; Geo. H. Paul Co. v. Shaw, 86 Kan. 136, 119 P. 546, 37 L.R.A.N.S. 1123, Am.Ann.Cas. 1913B, 956; "George H. Paul Loses Case," *Daily Times* (Davenport, IA), September 26, 1914.

6. "Iowa Men Will Improve 16,000 Colorado Acres," *Denver Post*, September 1, 1911, newspaper clipping, John J. Burns Papers, file 86, Stephen Hart Research Library, History Colorado–Denver.

7. "3,600 Acres Will Be Planted to Fruit," *Denver Post*, 3 September 1911, newspaper clipping, John J. Burns Papers, file 86, Stephen Hart Research Library, History Colorado—Denver.

8. Geo. H. Paul Orchard Company, Articles of Incorporation, record no. 184514, filed October 25, 1911, Pueblo County Recording Department, Pueblo, CO.

9. "10,000 Acres to Go in Fruits," *Pueblo Leader* (CO), November 7, 1911.

10. A. U. Mershon, *Apples of Gold* (Pueblo, CO: Geo. H. Paul Orchard Company, 1911), Special Collections, Robert Hoag Rawlings Public Library, Pueblo City-County Library District, Pueblo, CO, 35–36.

11. Mershon, *Apples of Gold*, front cover.

12. "Apples of Gold in Two Editions," *Pueblo Chieftain* (CO), February 16, 1912.

13. "Fine Exhibition of 'The King of Fruits,'" *Democratic Messenger* (Eureka, KS), February 8, 1912.

14. "Apple Orchard at Land Show," *Evening Star* (Independence, KS), February 23, 1912.

15. Advertisement, "The Geo. H. Paul Orchard Company," *Evening Kansan-Republican* (Newton, KS), March 14, 1912.

16. "100 Colonists Here in First Summer Excursion," *Pueblo Leader* (CO), March 20, 1912.

17. Ed Simonich, "Pueblo West, 1917," *Pueblo Lore* (January 1983): 6–7.

18. Helen Hardin, "Early History of Pueblo West," *Pueblo Lore* (November 1988): 5.

19. Mershon, *Apples of Gold*, 27.

20. "Huge Land Deal by Paul Company Is State Record," *Pueblo Chieftain* (CO), September 22, 1912.

21. "Syndicate Takes Charge of 4,000 Acres Fruit Land," *Montrose Daily Press* (CO), October 2, 1912.

22. Advertisement, *Evening Kansas-Republican* (Newton, KS), December 28, 1912.

23. "Orchard Company Has Finished Planting," *Pueblo Chieftain* (CO), June 3, 1913.

24. Hardin, "Early History of Pueblo West," 5.

25. Mershon, *Apples of Gold*, 34.

26. "Orchard Company Has Finished Planting."

27. Ed Simonich, "Pueblo West, 1917," *Pueblo Lore* (January 1983): 7.

28. "Southern Iowa Items," *Evening Times Republican* (Marshalltown, IA), August 20, 1917.

29. "Obituary," *Railway Age* 56, no. 13 (March 29, 1912): 290.

30. John C. Teller to Mrs. John J. Burns, March 20, 1913, John J. Burns Papers, file 19, Stephen Hart Research Library, History Colorado–Denver.

31. Pueblo County Recorder, "Miscellaneous Record," book 390, record no. 201307, October 20, 1913, Pueblo County Recording Department, Pueblo, CO, 100–102.

32. Pueblo County Recorder, "Miscellaneous Record," book 390, record no. 201307, October 20, 1913, Pueblo County Recording Department, Pueblo, CO, 100–102.

33. Geo. H. Paul to Lyra Haisley Sparks, March 14, 1962, Lyra Haisley Sparks Papers, 1896–1963, Center for American History, University of Texas at Austin.

34. Pueblo County Recorder, "Miscellaneous Record," book 400, record no. 209786, November 24, 1914, Pueblo County Recording Department, Pueblo, CO, 172–174.

35. Pueblo County Recorder, "Miscellaneous Record," book 400, record nos. 212704, 212705, April 9, 1915, Pueblo County Recording Department, Pueblo, CO, 265.

36. Geo. H. Paul to Lyra Haisley Sparks, September 22, 1961, Lyra Haisley Sparks Papers, 1896–1963, Center for American History, University of Texas at Austin.

37. Geo. H. Paul to Lyra Haisley Sparks, June 23, 1961, Lyra Haisley Sparks Papers, 1896–1963, Center for American History, University of Texas at Austin.

38. Mark Paul to Brad Bowers, January 22, 2018, author's collection; George O. Coalson, Texas State Historical Association, *Handbook of Texas Online*, "Paul, George H," accessed August 4, 2018, http://www.tshaonline.org/handbook/online/articles/fpa64.

39. "The Largest Wheat Field," *Pueblo Indicator* (CO), August 9, 1919.

40. "For Sale-Colorado Land," *Topeka Daily Capital* (KS), November 16, 1913.

41. Pueblo County Recorder, "Miscellaneous Record," book 400, record no. 212524, April 2, 1915, Pueblo County Recording Department, Pueblo, CO, 257–260.

42. Pueblo County Recorder, "Miscellaneous Record," book 421, record no. 227114, October 23, 1915, Pueblo County Recording Department, Pueblo, CO, 387–390.

43. Geo. H. Paul Orchard Company, Articles of Incorporation, record no. 184514, filed October 25, 1911, Pueblo County Recording Department, Pueblo, CO.

44. R. S. Morrison, *Morrison's Corporation Law: Colorado*, 4th ed. (Denver: W. H. Courtwright Publishing Co., 1922), 399.

45. Scrapbook Pliny Fisk Sharp, vol. 7, 53, "John C. Teller Dead," August 6, 1917, John J. Burns Papers, file 18, Stephen Hart Research Library, History Colorado—Denver.

46. Pueblo County Recorder, "Miscellaneous Record," book 435, record no. 234700, August 30, 1917, Pueblo County Recording Department, Pueblo, CO, 272–275.

47. Pueblo County Recorder, "Miscellaneous Record," book 445, record no. 235861, October 24, 1917, Pueblo County Recording Department, Pueblo, CO, 385–386.

48. Pueblo County Recorder, "Miscellaneous Record," book 481, record no. 259357, January 7, 1920, Pueblo County Recording Department, Pueblo, CO, 619–628.

49. Pueblo County Recorder, "Miscellaneous Record," book 523, record nos. 242480, 242481, March 31, 1921, Pueblo County Recording Department, Pueblo, CO, 185–187.

50. Pueblo County Recorder, "Miscellaneous Record," book 589, record nos. 335295, 335296, 335297, January 7, 1924, Pueblo County Recording Department,

Pueblo, CO, 72–76; Pueblo County Recorder, "Miscellaneous Récord," book 548, record no. 335298, January 7, 1924, Pueblo County Recording Department, Pueblo, CO, 558–559; Wilbur Fiske Stone, *History of Colorado*, vol. 4 (Chicago: S. J. Clarke Publishing Company, 1919), 302–303.

51. Red Rock Reservoir, Inc., Articles of Incorporation, record no. 334678, filed December 28, 1923, Pueblo County Recording Department, Pueblo, CO.

52. Pueblo County Recorder, "Miscellaneous Record," book 590, record no. 350334, August 7, 1924, Pueblo County Recording Department, Pueblo, CO, 363–364.

53. Pueblo West Metropolitan District. Pueblo West, Colorado, "History," n.d., accessed November 21, 2018, https://pueblowestmetro.com/322/History.

54. United States Bureau of the Census, "QuickFacts, Pueblo West CDP, Colorado," April 1, 2010, https://www.census.gov/quickfacts/fact/table/pueblowestcdp colorado/PST045217#qf-flag-X.

55. "Complete Colorado-Kansas Road within Three Weeks," *Pueblo Leader* (CO), March 29, 1912.

56. Interstate Commerce Commission, Engineering Survey Notebook, Colorado-Kansas Railway, Colorado-Kansas Railway company records, Colorado-Kansas Railway Collection, Colorado Railroad Museum, Golden.

57. "C.-K. Depots Have 6 Spanish Names," *Pueblo Leader*, 7 February 1912, 3.

58. Interstate Commerce Commission, Engineering Survey Notebook, Colorado-Kansas Railway, Colorado-Kansas Railway company records, Colorado-Kansas Railway Collection, Colorado Railroad Museum, Golden.

Chapter 11. Geology, Geography, and the Town

1. "C.-K. Depots Have 6 Spanish Names," *Pueblo Leader* (CO), February 7, 1912.

2. Raymond W. Arnold, "Memoirs of Raymond W. Arnold, Regarding the Colorado Kansas Railway" (unpublished manuscript, transcribed from a 1980 tape recording in 1992 by Jean Arnold Meier, Colorado-Kansas Railway Collection, Colorado Railroad Museum, Golden), 3.

3. "C.-K. Depots Have 6 Spanish Names."

4. Bill McKenzie, "Stone City Lies Buried Somewhere inside Ft. Carson," *Colorado Springs Sun Silhouette* (CO), September 3, 1972.

5. Richard F. Carrillo, Christian J. Zier, and Andrea M. Barnes, *The Documentation of Stone City (5PE793): Historical Archaeology on the Fort Carson Military Reservation, Pueblo County, Colorado* (submitted to National Park Service–Rocky Mountain Regional Office, Branch of Interagency Archaeological Services, Denver, CO; and United States Army—Office of Environment, Energy and Natural Resources, Fort

Carson, CO, Fort Collins, CO: Centennial Archaeology, Inc., July 1991), 10; Harry Hansen, ed., *Colorado: A Guide to the Highest State*, new rev. ed., American Guide Series (New York: Hastings House, 1970), 180; Interstate Commerce Commission, "Engineering Report," Colorado-Kansas Railway, Valuation Docket no. 81, p. 2, Records of the Bureau of Valuation 1910–1974, Interstate Commerce Commission, RG 134, National Archives at College Park, College Park, MD.

6. US Geological Survey, Stone City Quadrangle, Colorado, topographic map, 1:24,000, 7.5 minute Series (Reston, VA: Geological Survey, 1963, 1978).

7. Carrillo, Zier, and Barnes, *The Documentation of Stone City*, 12.

8. Tammy Stone, *The Prehistory of Colorado and Adjacent Areas* (Salt Lake City: University of Utah Press, 1999), 142–158.

9. "Complete Colorado-Kansas Road within Three Weeks," *Pueblo Leader* (CO), March 29, 1912.

10. Mrs. Tacy S. Grant, Postmaster, Stone City, CO, to the Colorado State Historical Society, Denver, CO, February 19, 1935, Special Collections, Robert Hoag Rawlings Public Library, Pueblo City-County Library District, Pueblo, CO.

11. Carrillo, Zier, and Barnes, *The Documentation of Stone City*, 11.

12. T. R. Henahen, *Thirteenth Biennial Report of the Bureau of Mines of the State of Colorado for the Years of 1913 and 1914* (Denver: Smith-Brooks Printing Company, State Printers, 1914), 145.

13. Henahen, *Thirteenth Biennial Report*, 145.

14. Carrillo, Zier, and Barnes, *The Documentation of Stone City*, 37.

15. Wilbur Fiske Stone, *History of Colorado*, vol. 3 (Chicago: S. J. Clarke Publishing Company, 1918), 532.

16. Advertisement, "The Turkey Creek Stone Co.," *Pueblo Chieftain* (CO), January 1, 1913.

17. "Snow Storm Is Not Hindering Track Laying," *Pueblo Leader* (CO), December 19, 1911.

18. Carrillo, Zier, and Barnes, *The Documentation of Stone City*, 37.

19. Advertisement, "The Turkey Creek Stone Co.," *Pueblo Chieftain* (CO), January 1, 1913.

20. "Pueblo Stone Will Be Used at Wichita," *Pueblo Leader* (CO), August 5, 1912.

21. "Government Is to Use Turkey Creek Product," *Pueblo Chieftain* (CO), June 6, 1913.

22. Wilbur Fiske Stone, *History of Colorado*, vol. 3 (Chicago: S. J. Clarke Publishing Company, 1918), 532.

23. "Turkey Creek Is to Furnish Rock in Utah Capitol," *Pueblo Chieftain* (CO), June 5, 1913; State of Utah, "Utah State Capitol Planning & Historic Structures report, vol. 2: Construction History of the State Capitol and Capitol Hill," accessed

April 1, 2021, https://utahstatecapitol.utah.gov/wp-content/uploads/02capitolcon structiondesign.pdf, 24.

24. "Turkey Creek Stone Finding Ready Use in All Markets," *Pueblo Chieftain* (CO), January 1, 1916.

25. "Colorado Kansas Railroad Still Runs without Depot," *Pueblo Chieftain* (CO), August 21, 1921.

26. Carrillo, Zier, and Barnes, *The Documentation of Stone City*, 46.

27. Carrillo, Zier, and Barnes, *The Documentation of Stone City*, 36.

28. Karl M. Waagé, *Refractory Clay Deposits of South Central Colorado*, Geological Survey Bulletin 993 (Washington, DC: United States Government Printing Office, 1953), 31–32.

29. Waagé, *Refractory Clay Deposits*, 35.

30. Waagé, *Refractory Clay Deposits*, 35–38.

31. Carrillo, Zier, and Barnes, *The Documentation of Stone City*, 39.

32. Carrillo, Zier, and Barnes, *The Documentation of Stone City*, 16.

33. Carrillo, Zier, and Barnes, *The Documentation of Stone City*, 267.

34. Kenneth E. Lewis, *The American Frontier: An Archaeological Study of Settlement Pattern and Process* (Orlando, FL: Academic Press, 1984), 284.

35. "Colorado-Kansas Land Co. Formed," *Pueblo Leader* (CO), March 21, 1912; Advertisement, "Stone City Lots," *Pueblo Chieftain* (CO), April 15, 1913.

36. "Colorado-Kansas Is Formally Opened," *Pueblo Chieftain* (CO), June 13, 1912.

37. Carrillo, Zier, and Barnes, *The Documentation of Stone City*, 5.

38. Carrillo, Zier, and Barnes, *The Documentation of Stone City*, 10.

39. Carrillo, Zier, and Barnes, *The Documentation of Stone City*, 90.

40. Arnold, "Memoirs of Raymond W. Arnold," 5; Jerry Waller, Hand-drawn map of Stone City, Waller Collection, Folder 93–29, Local History Center, Cañon City Public Library, Cañon City, CO.

41. Carrillo, Zier, and Barnes, *The Documentation of Stone City*, 32.

42. "Stone City Gets Postoffice; 40 Families Aided," *Pueblo Leader* (CO), January 16, 1913.

43. Interstate Commerce Commission, "Engineering Report," Colorado-Kansas Railway, Valuation Docket no. 81, 12, Records of the Bureau of Valuation 1910–1974, Interstate Commerce Commission, RG 134, National Archives at College Park, College Park, MD.

44. US Bureau of the Census, *Fourteenth Census of the United States, 1920*, Pueblo County, Colorado, Precinct 1, Enumeration District 190, sheets 1A–2B, National Archives microfilm T625, Roll 169 (Washington, DC: National Archives and Records Administration, Records of the Bureau of the Census, RG 29, 1920), digital image, *Ancestry.com*, https://www.ancestry.com/interactive/6061/4294439-01028.

45. US Bureau of the Census, *Fifteenth Census of the United States, 1930*, Pueblo County, Colorado, Precinct 101, Enumeration District 51–69, sheets 1A–2A, National Archives microfilm T626, Roll 250 (Washington, DC: National Archives and Records Administration, Records of the Bureau of the Census, RG 29, 1930), digital image, *Ancestry.com*, https://www.ancestry.com/interactive/6224/4532395_00097; Pueblo County Recorder, "Warranty Deed Record," book 455, record no. 244700, August 27, 1918, Pueblo County Recording Department, Pueblo, CO, 372.

46. Carrillo, Zier, and Barnes, *The Documentation of Stone City*, 35.

47. Shirley Louise Baker, "Shirley Louise Baker's Life in Stone City Colorado" (unpublished manuscript, n.d., author's collection), 2.

48. Baker, "Shirley Louise Baker's Life," 4.

49. Lee Oldham, "Bridging the Past" (unpublished manuscript, 2004), 10.

50. Carrillo, Zier, and Barnes, *The Documentation of Stone City*, 36.

51. Oldham, "Bridging the Past," 10.

52. Baker, "Shirley Louise Baker's Life," 4.

53. US Bureau of the Census, *Thirteenth Census of the United States, 1910*, Pueblo County, Colorado, Precinct 1, Enumeration District 0142, sheets 1A–4A, National Archives microfilm T624, Roll 124 (Washington, DC: National Archives and Records Administration, Records of the Bureau of the Census, RG 29, 1910), digital image, *Ancestry.com*, https://www.ancestry.com/interactive/7884/31111_4327327-00421.

54. Baker, "Shirley Louise Baker's Life," 4.

55. Baker, "Shirley Louise Baker's Life," 10–11.

56. Carrillo, Zier, and Barnes, *The Documentation of Stone City*, 78.

57. Baker, "Shirley Louise Baker's Life," 2; Waller, Hand-drawn map of Stone City. Shirley Baker remembers twenty-five to thirty houses, and the map drawn by former resident Jerry Waller shows twenty-three houses, not counting the passenger coach, which was used as a residence.

58. Lee Oldham, "Homeowners Didn't Abandon Stone City," *Denver Post* (CO), March 7, 2002.

59. Baker, "Shirley Louise Baker's Life," 12.

60. Baker, "Shirley Louise Baker's Life," 3.

61. Waller, Hand-drawn map of Stone City.

62. Carrillo, Zier, and Barnes, *The Documentation of Stone City*, 35–36.

Chapter 12. The People of Stone City

1. US Bureau of the Census, *Thirteenth Census of the United States, 1910*, Pueblo County, Colorado, Precinct 1, Enumeration District 0142, sheets 1A–4A, National Archives microfilm T624, Roll 124 (Washington, DC: National Archives and Records

Administration, Records of the Bureau of the Census, RG 29, 1910), digital image, *Ancestry.com*, https://www.ancestry.com/interactive/7884/31111_4327327-00421.

2. US Bureau of the Census, *Thirteenth Census of the United States, 1910.*

3. US Bureau of the Census, *Thirteenth Census of the United States, 1910.*

4. "Stone City Gets Postoffice: 40 Families Aided," *Pueblo Leader* (CO), January 16, 1913.

5. Richard F. Carrillo, Christian J. Zier, and Andrea M. Barnes, *The Documentation of Stone City (5PE793): Historical Archaeology on the Fort Carson Military Reservation, Pueblo County, Colorado* (submitted to National Park Service–Rocky Mountain Regional Office, Branch of Interagency Archaeological Services, Denver, CO; and United States Army—Office of Environment, Energy and Natural Resources, Fort Carson, CO, Fort Collins, CO: Centennial Archaeology, Inc., July 1991), 35–37.

6. Shirley Louise Baker, "Shirley Louise Baker's Life in Stone City Colorado" (unpublished manuscript, n.d., author's collection), 3.

7. US Bureau of the Census, *Fourteenth Census of the United States, 1920*, Pueblo County, Colorado, Precinct 1, Enumeration District 190, sheets 1A–2B, National Archives microfilm T625, Roll 169 (Washington, DC: National Archives and Records Administration, Records of the Bureau of the Census, RG 29, 1920), digital image, *Ancestry.com*, https://www.ancestry.com/interactive/6061/4294439-01028.

8. "Colorado-Kansas Raises Salaries: Men Are Needed," *Pueblo Chieftain* (CO), May 20, 1917.

9. US Bureau of the Census, *Fifteenth Census of the United States, 1930*, Pueblo County, Colorado, Precinct 101, Enumeration District 51–69, sheets 1A–2A, National Archives microfilm T626, Roll 250 (Washington, DC: National Archives and Records Administration, Records of the Bureau of the Census, RG 29, 1930), digital image, *Ancestry.com*, https://www.ancestry.com/interactive/6224/4532395_00097.

10. Carrillo, Zier, and Barnes, *The Documentation of Stone City*, 36.

11. Baker, "Shirley Louise Baker's Life," 1.

12. US Bureau of the Census, *Fifteenth Census of the United States, 1930*; US Bureau of the Census, *Sixteenth Census of the United States, 1940*, Pueblo County, Colorado, Precinct 101, Enumeration District 51–72, sheets 1A-2B, National Archives microfilm T627, Roll 477 (Washington, DC: National Archives and Records Administration, Records of the Bureau of the Census, RG 29, 1940), digital image, *Ancestry.com*, https://www.ancestry.com/interactive/2442/m-t0627-00477-00108.

13. US Bureau of the Census, *Thirteenth Census of the United States, 1910*; US Bureau of the Census. *Fourteenth Census of the United States, 1920.*

14. US Bureau of the Census, *Thirteenth Census of the United States, 1910.*

15. US Bureau of the Census, *Thirteenth Census of the United States, 1910*; US Bureau of the Census. *Fourteenth Census of the United States, 1920*; US Bureau of

the Census, *Fifteenth Census of the United States, 1930*; US Bureau of the Census, *Sixteenth Census of the United States, 1940*, all Pueblo County, Colorado, Precinct 101, Enumeration District 51–72, sheets 1A-2B, National Archives microfilm T627, Roll 477 (Washington, DC: National Archives and Records Administration, Records of the Bureau of the Census, RG 29, 1940), digital image, *Ancestry.com*, https://www .ancestry.com/interactive/2442/m-t0627-00477-00108.

16. US Bureau of the Census, *Thirteenth Census of the United States, 1910*.

17. US Bureau of the Census. *Fourteenth Census of the United States, 1920*.

18. US Bureau of the Census. *Fourteenth Census of the United States, 1920*; US Bureau of the Census, *Fifteenth Census of the United States, 1930*.

19. US Bureau of the Census, *Sixteenth Census of the United States, 1940*.

20. "Mexicans Held after Killing," *El Paso Herald* (TX), September 13, 1919.

21. Baker, "Shirley Louise Baker's Life," 2–9.

22. Lee Oldham, "Bridging the Past" (unpublished manuscript, 2004), 14.

23. Baker, "Shirley Louise Baker's Life," 2.

24. Baker, "Shirley Louise Baker's Life," 3.

25. Baker, "Shirley Louise Baker's Life," 10.

26. Oldham, "Bridging the Past," 4.

27. Baker, "Shirley Louise Baker's Life," 7–12.

28. Baker, "Shirley Louise Baker's Life," 9.

29. Erin Emery, "Memories Mined from Stone City," *Denver Post* (Denver, CO), January 21, 2002.

30. Baker, "Shirley Louise Baker's Life," 6.

31. Baker, "Shirley Louise Baker's Life," 5.

32. Carrillo, Zier, and Barnes, *The Documentation of Stone City*, 36.

33. "Pueblo-Stone City Railroad Flirting with Mothballs and Historical Ghosts," *Pueblo Chieftain*, May 8, 1957.

34. Carrillo, Zier, and Barnes, *The Documentation of Stone City*, 36–37.

Chapter 13. Quarrying and Clay Mining

1. "Pueblo Opens Today Its Home-Built Railroad into State's Greatest Quarries," *Pueblo Leader* (CO), June 12, 1912.

2. Richard F. Carrillo, Christian J. Zier, and Andrea M. Barnes, *The Documentation of Stone City (5PE793): Historical Archaeology on the Fort Carson Military Reservation, Pueblo County, Colorado* (submitted to National Park Service–Rocky Mountain Regional Office, Branch of Interagency Archaeological Services, Denver, CO; and United States Army—Office of Environment, Energy and Natural Resources, Fort Carson, CO, Fort Collins, CO: Centennial Archaeology, Inc., July 1991), 37.

3. T. R. Henahen, *Thirteenth Biennial Report of the Bureau of Mines of the State of Colorado for the Years of 1913 and 1914* (Denver: Smith-Brooks Printing Company, State Printers, 1914), 145.

4. Carrillo, Zier, and Barnes, *The Documentation of Stone City*, 35.

5. Carrillo, Zier, and Barnes, *The Documentation of Stone City*, 42.

6. Henahen, *Thirteenth Biennial Report*, 145.

7. "New Road Carries First Car of Stone into Pueblo," *Pueblo Leader* (CO), April 25, 1912.

8. "Close a Big Deal," *Lawrence Daily Journal-World* (KS), May 19, 1913.

9. "Let P. O. Stone Contract," *Evening Herald* (Ottawa, KS), June 2, 1913.

10. Shirley Louise Baker, "Shirley Louise Baker's Life in Stone City Colorado" (unpublished manuscript, n.d., author's collection), 6.

11. Karl M. Waagé, *Refractory Clay Deposits of South Central Colorado*, Geological Survey Bulletin 993 (Washington, DC: United States Government Printing Office, 1953), 59–60.

12. Carrillo, Zier, and Barnes, *The Documentation of Stone City*, 67.

13. Carrillo, Zier, and Barnes, *The Documentation of Stone City*, 46–47.

14. Waagé, *Refractory Clay Deposits*, 54–55.

15. Raymond W. Arnold, "Memoirs of Raymond W. Arnold, Regarding the Colorado Kansas Railway" (unpublished manuscript, transcribed from a 1980 tape recording in 1992 by Jean Arnold Meier, Colorado-Kansas Railway Collection, Colorado Railroad Museum, Golden), 4.

16. Waagé, *Refractory Clay Deposits*, 54–60.

17. Lee Oldham, "Bridging the Past" (unpublished manuscript, 2004), 3.

18. Oldham, "Bridging the Past," 3

19. Oldham, "Bridging the Past," 3.

20. Kent Stephens, "The Colorado Railroad," *New Mexico Railroader* 7 (October 1965; issued January 1966): 8.

21. Colorado-Kansas Railway, Report no. 3079, 1930, Records of the Operating Division, Annual Reports of Railroads 1915–1961, Interstate Commerce Commission, RG 134, National Archives at College Park, College Park, MD.

22. J. F. Springfield to Charles E. Sutton, January 2, 1922, Charles E. Sutton Papers, Pueblo County Historical Society, Pueblo, CO.

23. Colorado-Kansas Railway, Report no. 3079, 1930, Records of the Operating Division, Annual Reports of Railroads 1915–1961, Interstate Commerce Commission, RG 134, National Archives at College Park, College Park, MD.

24. Colorado-Kansas Railway, Report no. 3081, 1935–1937; Colorado-Kansas Railway, Report no. 3079, 1938; Colorado Railroad, Inc., Report no. 3077, 1938–1940; all, Records of the Operating Division, Annual Reports of Railroads 1915–1961,

Interstate Commerce Commission, RG 134, National Archives at College Park, College Park, MD; Arnold, "Memoirs of Raymond W. Arnold," 4; Interstate Commerce Commission, "Stenographers' Minutes before the Interstate Commerce Commission," Application for Colorado Railroad, Inc., Finance Docket 11988, April 25, 1938, Case Files 1887–1955, Interstate Commerce Commission, RG 134, National Archives at College Park, College Park, MD, 18.

25. "Complete Colorado-Kansas Road within Three Weeks," *Pueblo Leader* (CO), March 29, 1912.

26. Interstate Commerce Commission, "Engineering Report," Colorado-Kansas Railway, Valuation Docket no. 81, p. 15, Records of the Bureau of Valuation 1910–1974, Interstate Commerce Commission, RG 134, National Archives at College Park, College Park, MD.

27. Colorado-Kansas Railway, Report no. 3079, 1930, Records of the Operating Division, Annual Reports of Railroads 1915–1961, Interstate Commerce Commission, RG 134, National Archives at College Park, College Park, MD; Arnold, "Memoirs of Raymond W. Arnold," 4.

28. Colorado Railroad, Inc., Report no. 3077, 1945, Records of the Operating Division, Annual Reports of Railroads 1915–1961, Interstate Commerce Commission, RG 134, National Archives at College Park, College Park, MD.

29. Arnold, "Memoirs of Raymond W. Arnold," 3.

30. Colorado-Kansas Railway, Report no. 3079, 1920, Records of the Operating Division, Annual Reports of Railroads 1915–1961, Interstate Commerce Commission, RG 134, National Archives at College Park, College Park, MD.

31. James B. Pearce, *Fourteenth Biennial Report of the Bureau of Labor Statistics of the State of Colorado, 1913–1914* (Denver: Smith-Brooks Printing Company, State Printers, 1914), 218.

32. Colorado-Kansas Railway, Report no. 3079, 1915–1932, 1938; Colorado-Kansas Railway, Report no. 3081, 1933–1937; Colorado Railroad, Inc., Report no. 3077, 1938–1940; all, Records of the Operating Division, Annual Reports of Railroads 1915–1961, Interstate Commerce Commission, RG 134, National Archives at College Park, College Park, MD.

33. Colorado-Kansas Railway, Report no. 3079, 1913–1932, Records of the Operating Division, Annual Reports of Railroads 1915–1961, Interstate Commerce Commission, RG 134, National Archives at College Park, College Park, MD.

34. Advertisement, "Kansas-Colorado R. R. Co.," *Pueblo Chieftain* (CO), December 6, 1908.

35. Jeffrey DeHerrera, Adam Thomas, and Cheri Yost, *"Among the Elites of the Great West": Pueblo City Hall and Memorial Hall* (Denver: Historitecture, LLC., January 2014), 47–52.

36. "Vote against the Proposed Subway Recorded Yesterday," *Pueblo Chieftain* (CO), February 7, 1917.

37. "Provide Room for Subway: Council Votes Two to One," *Pueblo Chieftain* (CO), February 8, 1917.

38. Fred Carroll, *Fifteenth Biennial Report Issued by the Bureau of Mines of the State of Colorado for the Years 1917 and 1918* (Denver, Eames Brothers, State Printers, 1919), 58.

39. Colorado-Kansas Railway, Report no. 3079, 1914–1931, Records of the Operating Division, Annual Reports of Railroads 1915–1961, Interstate Commerce Commission, RG 134, National Archives at College Park, College Park, MD.

40. Colorado-Kansas Railway, Report no. 3079, 1930, Records of the Operating Division, Annual Reports of Railroads 1915–1961, Interstate Commerce Commission, RG 134, National Archives at College Park, College Park, MD; Arnold, "Memoirs of Raymond W. Arnold," 4.

41. Carrillo, Zier, and Barnes, *The Documentation of Stone City*, 36.

42. "Stone City Plans Entertainment for Sunday Visitors," *Pueblo Chieftain* (CO), September 6, 1917.

43. Colorado-Kansas Railway, Report no. 3079, 1914–1931, Records of the Operating Division, Annual Reports of Railroads 1915–1961, Interstate Commerce Commission, RG 134, National Archives at College Park, College Park, MD.

44. Interstate Commerce Commission, "Tentative Valuation Report," Valuation Docket no. 81, p. 1, Colorado-Kansas Railway, Records of the Bureau of Valuation 1910–1974, Interstate Commerce Commission, RG 134, National Archives at College Park, College Park, MD; V. J. Bloom for Walter F. Morrison, secretary of state, State of Colorado to C. V. Marmaduke, Attorney, Pueblo, CO, November 4, 1947, Colorado Railroad, Inc. Company records, 1938–1957, Colorado-Kansas Railway Collection, Colorado Railroad Museum, Golden.

45. "Pueblo-Stone City Railroad Flirting with Mothballs and Historical Ghosts," *Pueblo Chieftain* (CO), May 8, 1957.

46. Erin Emery, "Memories Mined from Stone City," *Denver Post* (CO), January 21, 2002.

47. Carrillo, Zier, and Barnes, *The Documentation of Stone City*, 27.

48. Pueblo Quarries, Incorporated, Articles of Incorporation, record no. 593163, filed October 26, 1930, Pueblo County Recorder, Pueblo, CO.

49. Colorado-Kansas Railway, Report no. 3079, 1931, Records of the Operating Division, Annual Reports of Railroads 1915–1961, Interstate Commerce Commission, RG 134, National Archives at College Park, College Park, MD.

50. Colorado Railroad, Incorporated, Articles of Incorporation, record no. 586332, filed March 3, 1938, Pueblo County Recorder, Pueblo, CO.

51. Alan Arnold, "Colorado & Kansas Line Was Small but Different," *Pueblo Chieftain* (CO), October14, 1958.

Chapter 14. My Friend Irma

1. LeRoy R. Hafen, ed., *Colorado and Its People: A Narrative and Topical History of the Centennial State*, vol. 3 (New York: Lewis Historical Publishing Company, 1948), 85; James MacDaniel, Headstone, Plot no. K-5, Mountain View Cemetery, Pueblo, CO.

2. *Pueblo City Directory* (Kansas City, MO: R. L. Polk, 1945), 205.

3. Angel Kwolek-Folland, *Incorporating Women: A History of Women and Business in the United States* (New York: Twayne Publishers, 1998; Palgrave, 2002), 99.

4. James B. Pearce, *Fourteenth Biennial Report of the Bureau of Labor Statistics of the State of Colorado, 1913–1914* (Denver: Smith-Brooks Printing Company, State Printers, 1914), 146–147.

5. "James T. M'Corkle Expires Suddenly at His Residence," *Pueblo Chieftain* (CO), January 30, 1936.

6. Kwolek-Folland, *Incorporating Women*, 99.

7. "Ace High among Women of the Rail," *Baltimore and Ohio Magazine* 22, no. 5 (May 1936): 84–86.

8. Kwolek-Folland, *Incorporating Women*, 106.

9. Kwolek-Folland, *Engendering Business*, 30.

10. Kwolek-Folland, *Incorporating Women*, 107.

11. Kwolek-Folland *Engendering Business*, 42.

12. Kwolek-Folland, *Incorporating Women*, 142.

13. Pueblo Terminal Railway Company, Articles of Incorporation, record no. 367171, filed April 21, 1925, Pueblo County Recording Department, Pueblo, CO.

14. Colorado-Kansas Railway, Report no. 3079, 1925, Records of the Operating Division, Annual Reports of Railroads 1915–1961, Interstate Commerce Commission, RG 134, National Archives at College Park, College Park, MD.

15. Colorado-Kansas Railway, Report no. 3079, 1931, Records of the Operating Division, Annual Reports of Railroads 1915–1961, Interstate Commerce Commission, RG 134, National Archives at College Park, College Park, MD.

16. Colorado-Kansas Railway, Report no. 3079, 1926–1927, Records of the Operating Division, Annual Reports of Railroads 1915–1961, Interstate Commerce Commission, RG 134, National Archives at College Park, College Park, MD.

17. Kwolek-Folland, *Incorporating Women*, 127.

18. Colorado-Kansas Railway, Report no. 3079, 1932, Records of the Operating Division, Annual Reports of Railroads 1915–1961, Interstate Commerce Commission, RG 134, National Archives at College Park, College Park, MD.

19. Hafen, *Colorado and Its People*, 85.

20. Sterling Securities, Inc., Articles of Incorporation, record no. 501482, filed January 31, 1933, Pueblo County Recording Department, Pueblo, CO.

21. Hafen, *Colorado and Its People*, 85.

22. Interstate Commerce Commission (ICC), "Stenographers' Minutes before the Interstate Commerce Commission," Application for Colorado Railroad, Inc., Finance Docket 11988, April 25, 1938, 6, Case Files 1887–1955, Interstate Commerce Commission, RG 134, National Archives at College Park, College Park, MD.

23. ICC, "Stenographers' Minutes," 9–11.

24. ICC, "Stenographers' Minutes," 24.

25. ICC, "Stenographers' Minutes," 6.

26. Raymond W. Arnold, "Memoirs of Raymond W. Arnold, Regarding the Colorado Kansas Railway" (unpublished manuscript, transcribed from a 1980 tape recording in 1992 by Jean Arnold Meier, Colorado-Kansas Railway Collection, Colorado Railroad Museum, Golden), 1.

27. Colorado-Kansas Railway, Report no. 3079, 1932; Colorado-Kansas Railway, Report no. 3081, 1933–1935; all, Records of the Operating Division, Annual Reports of Railroads 1915–1961, Interstate Commerce Commission, RG 134, National Archives at College Park, College Park, MD.

28. ICC, "Stenographers' Minutes," 6.

29. Colorado-Kansas Railway, Report no. 3081, 1936, Records of the Operating Division, Annual Reports of Railroads 1915–1961, Interstate Commerce Commission, RG 134, National Archives at College Park, College Park, MD.

30. Arnold, "Memoirs of Raymond W. Arnold," 1.

Chapter 15. The Depression Years

1. Colorado-Kansas Railway, Report no. 3079, 1931–1932, 1938; Colorado-Kansas Railway, Report no. 3081, 1933–1937; all, Records of the Operating Division, Annual Reports of Railroads 1915–1961, Interstate Commerce Commission, RG 134, National Archives at College Park, College Park, MD.

2. Interstate Commerce Commission (ICC), "Stenographers' Minutes before the Interstate Commerce Commission," Application for Colorado Railroad, Inc., Finance Docket 11988, April 25, 1938, Case Files 1887–1955, Interstate Commerce Commission, RG 134, National Archives at College Park, College Park, MD, 14–15.

3. Raymond W. Arnold, "Memoirs of Raymond W. Arnold, Regarding the Colorado Kansas Railway" (unpublished manuscript, transcribed from a 1980 tape recording in 1992 by Jean Arnold Meier, Colorado-Kansas Railway Collection, Colorado Railroad Museum, Golden), 4.

4. ICC, "Stenographers' Minutes," 14.

5. ICC, "Stenographers' Minutes," 3–5.

6. Interstate Commerce Commission, "Finance Docket 11988, Colorado Railroad, Incorporated, Acquisition and Stock," *Interstate Commerce Commission Reports: Decisions of the Interstate Commerce Commission of the United States*, vol. 228, Finance Reports, April–November 1938 (Washington, DC: United States Government Printing Office), 273–276.

7. Colorado Railroad, Inc., Report no. 3077, 1939, Records of the Operating Division, Annual Reports of Railroads 1915–1961, Interstate Commerce Commission, RG 134, National Archives at College Park, College Park, MD.

8. Alfred D. Chandler Jr., *The Visible Hand: The Managerial Revolution in American Business* (Cambridge: Belknap Press of Harvard University Press, 1977), 1.

9. Chandler, *The Visible Hand*, 415–416.

10. Chandler, *The Visible Hand*, 80.

11. Angel Kwolek-Folland, *Engendering Business: Men and Women in the Corporate Office, 1870–1930* (Baltimore: Johns Hopkins University Press, 1994), 71.

12. Railway Equipment & Publication Company, *The Pocket List of Railroad Officials* 57, no. 8, 3rd quarter, 1951 (New York: Railway Equipment & Publication Company, 1951), 459.

13. "Pueblo-Stone City Railroad Flirting with Mothballs and Historical Ghosts," *Pueblo Chieftain* (CO), May 8, 1957.

14. F. G. Jamison, War Production Board, Salvage Division to Irma MacDaniel, October 9, 1943, Pueblo Quarries, Inc., company records, Colorado-Kansas Railway Collection, Colorado Railroad Museum, Golden; Irma MacDaniel to W.H.S. Stevens, Interstate Commerce Commission, March 28, 1951, Colorado Railroad, Inc., company records, Colorado-Kansas Railway Collection, Colorado Railroad Museum, Golden.

15. Irma MacDaniel to Raymond W. Arnold, January 23, 1947, Colorado Railroad, Inc., company records, Colorado-Kansas Railway Collection, Colorado Railroad Museum, Golden.

16. Irma MacDaniel to Raymond W. Arnold, September 8, 1948, Pueblo Quarries, Inc., company records, Colorado-Kansas Railway Collection, Colorado Railroad Museum, Golden.

17. Irma MacDaniel to Raymond W. Arnold, February 24, 1947; Irma MacDaniel to Raymond W. Arnold, December 13, 1947; both, Colorado Railroad, Inc., company records, Colorado-Kansas Railway Collection, Colorado Railroad Museum, Golden.

18. Colorado-Kansas Railway, Report no. 3079, 1913–1932, 1938; Colorado-Kansas Railway, Report no. 3081, 1933–1937; Colorado Railroad, Inc., Report no. 3077,

1938–1954; all, Records of the Operating Division, Annual Reports of Railroads 1915–1961, Interstate Commerce Commission, RG 134, National Archives at College Park, College Park, MD.

19. Interstate Commerce Commission, "Engineering Report," Colorado-Kansas Railway, Valuation Docket no. 81, p. 2, Records of the Bureau of Valuation 1910–1974, Interstate Commerce Commission, RG 134, National Archives at College Park, College Park, MD.

20. Kent Stephens, "The Colorado Railroad," *New Mexico Railroader* 7 (October 1965; issued January 1966): 7; Arnold, "Memoirs of Raymond W. Arnold," 4.

21. Tacy S. Grant to Irma MacDaniel, October 1, 1951, Pueblo Quarries, Inc., company records, Colorado-Kansas Railway Collection, Colorado Railroad Museum, Golden.

22. Irma MacDaniel to Tacy S. Grant, October 3, 1951, Pueblo Quarries, Inc., company records, Colorado-Kansas Railway Collection, Colorado Railroad Museum, Golden.

23. Harold N. Moore, interviewed by the author, August 31, 2005, Pueblo, CO.

24. "Dorothy Patch Kimsey," *Pueblo Chieftain* (CO), November 18, 1998.

25. Irma MacDaniel to Raymond W. Arnold, February 24, 1947, Colorado Railroad, Inc., company records, Colorado-Kansas Railway Collection, Colorado Railroad Museum, Golden.

26. Irma MacDaniel to Raymond W. Arnold, February 24, 1947, Colorado Railroad, Inc., company records, Colorado-Kansas Railway Collection, Colorado Railroad Museum, Golden.

27. Irma MacDaniel to Raymond W. Arnold, November 9,1948, Colorado Railroad, Inc., company records, Colorado-Kansas Railway Collection, Colorado Railroad Museum, Golden.

28. Irma MacDaniel to Raymond W. Arnold, October 13, 1951, Colorado Railroad, Inc., company records, Colorado-Kansas Railway Collection, Colorado Railroad Museum, Golden.

29. Irma MacDaniel to Raymond W. Arnold, September 15, 1956, Colorado Railroad, Inc., company records, Colorado-Kansas Railway Collection, Colorado Railroad Museum, Golden.

30. Irma MacDaniel to Raymond W. Arnold, November 1, 1963, Pueblo Quarries, Inc., company records, Colorado-Kansas Railway Collection, Colorado Railroad Museum, Golden.

31. Irma MacDaniel to Raymond W. Arnold, January 19, 1971, Pueblo Quarries, Inc., company records, Colorado-Kansas Railway Collection, Colorado Railroad Museum, Golden.

32. Irma MacDaniel to Raymond W. Arnold, September 8, 1948, Pueblo Quarries, Inc., company records, Colorado-Kansas Railway Collection, Colorado Railroad Museum, Golden.

33. Irma MacDaniel to Raymond W. Arnold, November 9, 1948, Pueblo Quarries, Inc., company records, Colorado-Kansas Railway Collection, Colorado Railroad Museum, Golden.

34. Irma MacDaniel to Raymond W. Arnold, September 8, 1948, Colorado Railroad, Inc., company records, Colorado-Kansas Railway Collection, Colorado Railroad Museum, Golden.

35. Irma MacDaniel to Raymond W. Arnold, February 24, 1947, Pueblo Quarries, Inc., company records, Colorado-Kansas Railway Collection, Colorado Railroad Museum, Golden.

36. Irma MacDaniel to Raymond W. Arnold, February 24, 1947, Pueblo Quarries, Inc., company records, Colorado-Kansas Railway Collection, Colorado Railroad Museum, Golden.

37. Carl K. Springfield to Raymond W. Arnold, February 6, 1956, Pueblo Quarries, Inc., company records, Colorado-Kansas Railway Collection, Colorado Railroad Museum, Golden.

38. Robert K. Johnston to Raymond W. Arnold, March 19, 1951, Colorado Railroad, Inc., company records, Colorado-Kansas Railway Collection, Colorado Railroad Museum, Golden.

39. National Archives and Records Administration, "Title 49—Transportation and Railroads, Appendix B," *Federal Register* 11, no. 238 (December 7, 1946): 14168, https://cdn.loc.gov/service/ll/fedreg/fro11/fro11238/fro11238.pdf.

40. Colorado Railroad, Inc., Report no. 3077, 1942–1952, Records of the Operating Division, Annual Reports of Railroads 1915–1961, Interstate Commerce Commission, RG 134, National Archives at College Park, College Park, MD.

41. US Bureau of the Census, "Current Population Reports," Series P-60, No. 146, *Money Income of Households, Families, and Persons in the United States, 1983* (Washington, DC: US Government Printing Office, 1985), 122–124.

42. Colorado Railroad, Inc., Report no. 3077, 1953–1955; Colorado Railroad, Inc., Report no. 2215, 1956–1957; all, Records of the Operating Division, Annual Reports of Railroads 1915–1961, Interstate Commerce Commission, RG 134, National Archives at College Park, College Park, MD.

43. Irma MacDaniel to Raymond W. Arnold, September 8, 1948, Colorado Railroad, Inc., company records, Colorado-Kansas Railway Collection, Colorado Railroad Museum, Golden.

44. Irma MacDaniel to Raymond W. Arnold, October 13, 1951, Colorado Railroad, Inc., company records, Colorado-Kansas Railway Collection, Colorado Railroad

Museum, Golden. Irma always wrote "thought" as "thot," and "though" as "tho," perhaps a holdover from her stenographer days. I have corrected the spelling here for readability.

45. Irma MacDaniel to Raymond W. Arnold, October 13, 1951, Colorado Railroad, Inc., company records, Colorado-Kansas Railway Collection, Colorado Railroad Museum, Golden.

46. LeRoy R. Hafen, *Colorado and Its People: A Narrative and Topical History of the Centennial State*, vol. 3 (New York: Lewis Historical Publishing Company, 1948), 85.

47. *Pueblo City Directory* (Kansas City, MO: R. L. Polk, 1940), 218; *Pueblo City Directory* (Kansas City, MO: R. L. Polk, 1941), 226.

48. "Miss Irma MacDaniel, Veteran Insuror, Dies," *Pueblo Chieftain* (CO), May 4, 1971.

49. First Presbyterian Church, *Church Register*, no. 1357, Pueblo, CO, 1933.

50. "Miss Irma MacDaniel, Veteran Insuror, Dies," *Pueblo Chieftain* (CO), May 4, 1971.

51. Irma MacDaniel to Raymond W. Arnold, September 8, 1948, Colorado Railroad, Inc., company records, Colorado-Kansas Railway Collection, Colorado Railroad Museum, Golden.

52. "Frank J. Zavislan," *Pueblo Chieftain* (CO), December 27, 1986.

Chapter 16. The Colorado Railroad, Inc.

1. Kent Stephens, "The Colorado Railroad," *New Mexico Railroader* 7 (October 1965; issued January 1966): 6–8; Colorado Railroad, Inc., Report no. 3077, 1940, 1946, Records of the Operating Division, Annual Reports of Railroads 1915–1961, Interstate Commerce Commission, RG 134, National Archives at College Park, College Park, MD.

2. Colorado Railroad, Inc., Report no. 3077, 1941, Records of the Operating Division, Annual Reports of Railroads 1915–1961, Interstate Commerce Commission, RG 134, National Archives at College Park, College Park, MD.

3. Colorado Railroad, Inc., Report no. 3077, 1942, Records of the Operating Division, Annual Reports of Railroads 1915–1961, Interstate Commerce Commission, RG 134, National Archives at College Park, College Park, MD.

4. Irma MacDaniel to Raymond W. Arnold, February 24, 1947, Pueblo Quarries, Inc., company records, Colorado-Kansas Railway Collection, Colorado Railroad Museum, Golden.

5. Sasser Family Holdings, Inc., *This Is Our Story*, n.d., 32, accessed May 25, 2018, https://static1.squarespace.com/static/56c9e8217c65e44270c7c0a6/t/5b535fb12b6a 280bdeb93f52/1532190669666/Sasser+Book+compressed.pdf.

6. Simmons-Boardman Publishing Corporation, "Alaska Gets Troop Cars," *Railway Age* 121, no. 10 (September 7, 1946): 418.

7. Charles F. "Chick" Simpson to Brad Bowers, June 21, 2003, author's collection. Mr. Simpson was a retired vice-president of Chicago Freight Car Leasing, the current name of the former Chicago Freight Car & Parts Company, serving the company from 1948 to 1984.

8. David R. Watson, "Bring Shop to the Cars," *Modern Railroads* 3, no. 6 (June 1948), 47.

9. Irma MacDaniel to Raymond W. Arnold, December 13, 1947, Colorado Railroad, Inc., company records, Colorado-Kansas Railway Collection, Colorado Railroad Museum, Golden.

10. J. A. Noble, Atchison, Topeka & Santa Fe Railway to Irma MacDaniel, September 16, 1948, Colorado Railroad, Inc., company records, Colorado-Kansas Railway Collection, Colorado Railroad Museum, Golden.

11. Irma MacDaniel to Raymond W. Arnold, November 9, 1948, Colorado Railroad, Inc., company records, Colorado-Kansas Railway Collection, Colorado Railroad Museum, Golden.

12. MacDaniel to Arnold, November 9, 1948.

13. Raymond W. Arnold to Irma MacDaniel, October 12, 1948; Irma MacDaniel to Raymond W. Arnold, November 9, 1948; both, Colorado Railroad, Inc., company records, Colorado-Kansas Railway Collection, Colorado Railroad Museum, Golden.

14. Irma MacDaniel to Raymond W. Arnold, November 9, 1948, Colorado Railroad, Inc., company records, Colorado-Kansas Railway Collection, Colorado Railroad Museum, Golden.

15. MacDaniel to Arnold, November 9, 1948.

16. Summons, in the District Court in and or the County of Pueblo and State of Colorado Civil Action No. 32833 Div. A, Charles E. Sutton Papers, Collection of Pueblo County Historical Society.

17. Robert K. Johnston to Raymond W. Arnold, June 13, 1949, Colorado Railroad, Inc., company records, Colorado-Kansas Railway Collection, Colorado Railroad Museum, Golden.

18. Colorado Railroad, Inc., Report no. 3077, 1949, Records of the Operating Division, Annual Reports of Railroads 1915–1961, Interstate Commerce Commission, RG 134, National Archives at College Park, College Park, MD.

19. Raymond W. Arnold, "Memoirs of Raymond W. Arnold, Regarding the Colorado Kansas Railway" (unpublished manuscript, transcribed from a 1980 tape recording in 1992 by Jean Arnold Meier, Colorado-Kansas Railway Collection, Colorado Railroad Museum, Golden), 5.

20. Stephens, "The Colorado Railroad," 7; Irma MacDaniel to Raymond W. Arnold, August 25, 1951, Colorado Railroad, Inc., company records, Colorado-Kansas Railway Collection, Colorado Railroad Museum, Golden.

21. Bill McKenzie, "Stone City Lies Buried Somewhere inside Ft. Carson," *Colorado Springs Sun Silhouette* (CO), September 3, 1972.

22. "Pueblo-Stone City Railroad Flirting with Mothballs and Historical Ghosts," *Pueblo Chieftain* (CO), May 8, 1957.

23. Irma MacDaniel to Raymond W. Arnold, August 25, 1951, Colorado Railroad, Inc., company records, Colorado-Kansas Railway Collection, Colorado Railroad Museum, Golden.

24. Stephens, "The Colorado Railroad," 7.

25. Colorado Railroad, Inc., Paycheck stubs for Raymond Johnson and Harold L. Demeree, Colorado Railroad, Inc., company records, Colorado-Kansas Railway Collection, Colorado Railroad Museum, Golden.

26. Harold N. Moore, interviewed by the author, August 31, 2005, Pueblo, CO.

27. Colorado-Kansas Railway, Report no. 3079, 1913–1932, 1938; Colorado-Kansas Railway, Report no. 3081, 1933–1937; Colorado Railroad, Inc., Report no. 3077, 1938–1955; Colorado Railroad, Inc., Report no. 2215, 1956–1958; all, Records of the Operating Division, Annual Reports of Railroads 1915–1961, Interstate Commerce Commission, RG 134, National Archives at College Park, College Park, MD.

Chapter 17. End of the Line

1. Irma MacDaniel to Raymond W. Arnold, November 10, 1947, Colorado Railroad, Inc., company records, Colorado-Kansas Railway Collection, Colorado Railroad Museum, Golden.

2. Robert K. Johnston to Raymond W. Arnold, November 24, 1947, Colorado Railroad, Inc., company records, Colorado-Kansas Railway Collection, Colorado Railroad Museum, Golden.

3. Irma MacDaniel to Raymond W. Arnold, December 13, 1947, Pueblo Quarries, Inc., company records, Colorado-Kansas Railway Collection, Colorado Railroad Museum, Golden.

4. Carl K. Springfield to Raymond W. Arnold, February 6, 1956, Pueblo Quarries, Inc., company records, Colorado-Kansas Railway Collection, Colorado Railroad Museum, Golden.

5. Robert K. Johnston to Raymond W. Arnold, June 13, 1949, Colorado Railroad, Inc., company records, Colorado-Kansas Railway Collection, Colorado Railroad Museum, Golden.

6. Robert K. Johnston to Raymond W. Arnold, January 14, 1956, Colorado Railroad, Inc., company records, Colorado-Kansas Railway Collection, Colorado Railroad Museum, Golden.

7. Irma MacDaniel to Raymond W. Arnold, January 17, 1956, Colorado Railroad, Inc., company records, Colorado-Kansas Railway Collection, Colorado Railroad Museum, Golden.

8. Robert K. Johnston to Raymond W. Arnold, January 14, 1956, Colorado Railroad, Inc., company records, Colorado-Kansas Railway Collection, Colorado Railroad Museum, Golden.

9. Irma MacDaniel to Raymond W. Arnold, February 19, 1956, Colorado Railroad, Inc., company records, Colorado-Kansas Railway Collection, Colorado Railroad Museum, Golden.

10. Raymond W. Arnold to Irma MacDaniel, February 25, 1956, Colorado Railroad, Inc., company records, Colorado-Kansas Railway Collection, Colorado Railroad Museum, Golden.

11. Raymond W. Arnold to Irma MacDaniel, June 17, 1956, Colorado Railroad, Inc., company records, Colorado-Kansas Railway Collection, Colorado Railroad Museum, Golden.

12. Irma MacDaniel to Raymond W. Arnold, February 19, 1956, Colorado Railroad, Inc., company records, Colorado-Kansas Railway Collection, Colorado Railroad Museum, Golden.

13. Raymond W. Arnold to Irma MacDaniel, February 25, 1956, Colorado Railroad, Inc., company records, Colorado-Kansas Railway Collection, Colorado Railroad Museum, Golden.

14. Guy B. Treat to Raymond Arnold, March 15, 1956; Raymond W. Arnold to Irma MacDaniel, June 17, 1956; both, Colorado Railroad, Inc., company records, Colorado-Kansas Railway Collection, Colorado Railroad Museum, Golden.

15. Raymond W. Arnold to Irma MacDaniel, June 17, 1956, Colorado Railroad, Inc., company records, Colorado-Kansas Railway Collection, Colorado Railroad Museum, Golden.

16. Interstate Commerce Commission, "Return to Questionnaire," Colorado Railroad, Inc., Finance Docket 19540, 3–7, October 23, 1956, Colorado Railroad, Inc., company records, Colorado-Kansas Railway Collection, Colorado Railroad Museum, Golden.

17. "Colorado Railroad Line Abandonment Authorized," Pueblo Chieftain (CO), May 7, 1957.

18. Irma MacDaniel to Raymond W. Arnold, June 29, 1957, Colorado Railroad, Inc., company records, Colorado-Kansas Railway Collection, Colorado Railroad Museum, Golden.

19. Colorado Railroad, Inc., copy of agreement between Gottula Trucking and Transportation, Inc., and the Colorado Railroad, Inc., July 1957, Colorado Railroad, Inc., company records, Colorado-Kansas Railway Collection, Colorado Railroad Museum, Golden.

20. "Freight Car Firm to Discontinue Operations Here," *Pueblo Chieftain* (CO), August 2, 1957.

21. Irma MacDaniel to C. W. Emken, Bureau of Account, Cost Find and Valuation, Interstate Commerce Commission, Washington, DC, August 10, 1957, Colorado Railroad, Inc., company records, Colorado-Kansas Railway Collection, Colorado Railroad Museum, Golden.

22. Irma MacDaniel to Glen S. Turner, city manager, Pueblo City Hall, November 12, 1957, Colorado Railroad, Inc., company records, Colorado-Kansas Railway Collection, Colorado Railroad Museum, Golden.

23. Colorado Railroad, Inc., Report no. 2215, 1958, Records of the Operating Division, Annual Reports of Railroads 1915–1961, Interstate Commerce Commission, RG 134, National Archives at College Park, College Park, MD.

24. "Abandoned Rail Line Source of Timber at Zavislan Ranch," *Pueblo Chieftain* (CO), January 5, 1962.

25. Irma MacDaniel to B. M. Womack, Commercial Metals, March 1, 1958, Colorado Railroad, Inc., company records, Colorado-Kansas Railway Collection, Colorado Railroad Museum, Golden.

26. Irma MacDaniel to R. F. Concannon, Commercial Metals, December 26, 1957, Colorado Railroad, Inc., company records, Colorado-Kansas Railway Collection, Colorado Railroad Museum, Golden.

27. E. W. Waring, Denver & Rio Grande Western Railroad to Irma MacDaniel, November 11, 1957, Colorado Railroad, Inc., company records Colorado-Kansas Railway Collection, Colorado Railroad Museum, Golden.

28. B. M. Womack, Commercial Metals, to Irma MacDaniel, February 25, 1958, Colorado Railroad, Inc., company records, Colorado-Kansas Railway Collection, Colorado Railroad Museum, Golden.

29. Irma MacDaniel to the Colorado Railroad, Inc., May 24, 1958, Colorado Railroad, Inc., company records, Colorado-Kansas Railway Collection, Colorado Railroad Museum, Golden.

30. Irma MacDaniel to San Luis Southern Railroad, Fort Garland, CO, November 29, 1957; Irma MacDaniel to R. W. Richardson, April 24, 1958; both, Colorado Railroad, Inc., company records, Colorado-Kansas Railway Collection, Colorado Railroad Museum, Golden.

31. Robert W. Richardson to Brad Bowers, August 21, 2005, author's collection.

32. Robert W. Richardson to Brad Bowers, August 21, 2005.

33. Harold N. Moore, interviewed by the author, August 31, 2005, Pueblo, CO.

34. Alan Arnold, "Colorado & Kansas Line Was Small but Different," *Pueblo Chieftain* (CO), October 14, 1958.

35. Irma MacDaniel to Stockholders of Pueblo Quarries, Inc., draft of a letter, May 1966, Pueblo Quarries, Inc., company records, Colorado-Kansas Railway Collection, Colorado Railroad Museum, Golden.

36. Irma MacDaniel to Raymond W. Arnold, September 5, 1964, Pueblo Quarries, Inc., company records, Colorado-Kansas Railway Collection, Colorado Railroad Museum, Golden.

37. Lee Oldham, "Bridging the Past" (unpublished manuscript, 2004), 89.

38. Oldham, "Bridging the Past," 89–90.

39. Oldham, "Bridging the Past," 90.

40. Oldham, "Bridging the Past," 91.

41. Oldham, "Bridging the Past," 90–92.

42. Richard F. Carrillo, Christian J. Zier, and Andrea M. Barnes, *The Documentation of Stone City (5PE793): Historical Archaeology on the Fort Carson Military Reservation, Pueblo County, Colorado* (submitted to National Park Service–Rocky Mountain Regional Office, Branch of Interagency Archaeological Services, Denver, CO; and United States Army—Office of Environment, Energy and Natural Resources, Fort Carson, CO, Fort Collins, CO: Centennial Archaeology, Inc., July 1991), 39, 42.

43. US Army Garrison Fort Carson, Colorado, *Integrated Cultural Resources Management Plan for U.S. Army Garrison Fort Carson, Fort Carson, Fiscal Years 2017–2021*, 71. March 2017.

44. Lee Oldham, "Homeowners Didn't Abandon Stone City," *Denver Post* (CO), March 7, 2002.

45. Erin Emery, "Memories Mined from Stone City," *Denver Post* (CO), January 21, 2002.

46. Irma MacDaniel to Raymond W. Arnold, September 5, 1964, Pueblo Quarries, Inc., company records, Colorado-Kansas Railway Collection, Colorado Railroad Museum, Golden; "Miss Irma MacDaniel, Veteran Insuror, Dies," *Pueblo Chieftain* (CO), May 4, 1971.

47. "Miss Irma MacDaniel, Veteran Insuror, Dies," *Pueblo Chieftain* (CO), May 4, 1971.

Bibliography

Abbott, Dan. *Colorado Midland: Daylight through the Divide*. Denver: Sundance Publications, 1989.

Annual Report of the Attorney-General of the United States for the Year 1906. Washington, DC: Government Printing Office, 1907.

Arnold, Raymond W. "Memoirs of Raymond W. Arnold, Regarding the Colorado Kansas Railway." Unpublished manuscript. Transcribed from a 1980 tape recording in 1992 by Jean Arnold Meier. Colorado-Kansas Railway Collection, Colorado Railroad Museum, Golden.

Association of American Railroads. "Freight Railroad Fact Sheets." *Railroad 101*. March 2021. Accessed March 31, 2021. https://www.aar.org/wp-content/uploads/2020/08/AAR-Railroad-101-Freight-Railroads-Fact-Sheet.pdf.

Bailey, Robert G. *Description of the Ecoregions of the United States*. Washington, DC: United States Department of Agriculture, Forest Service, Miscellaneous Publication 1391, 1995.

Baker, Barbara P. *Steamy Dreamer: The Saga of Dr. Hartley O. Baker and the Baker Steam Motor Car*. Grand Junction, CO: Centennial Publications, 1996.

Baker, Shirley Louise. *Shirley Louise Baker's Life in Stone City Colorado*. Unpublished manuscript, n.d. Author's collection.

DOI: 10.5876/9781646421282.c021

Ballenger and Richards Thirty-Fifth Annual Denver City Directory for 1907. Denver: Smith-Brooks Printing, 1907.

Baltimore and Ohio Railroad. "Ace High among Women of the Rail." *Baltimore and Ohio Magazine* 22, no. 5 (May 1936): 84–86.

Bay City Directory for 1883. Detroit: R. L. Polk and Company, 1883.

Biographical and Reminiscent History of Richland, Clay and Marion Counties, Illinois. Indianapolis: B. F. Bowen and Company, 1909.

Blue Book Publishing Company. "O'er Canon and Crag to the Land of Gold Via the Short Line." *Short Line Blue Book: A Handbook for Travelers* (April 1904): 14.

Bollinger, Edward T., and Frederick Bauer. *The Moffat Road.* 2nd ed. Chicago: Swallow Press, 1971.

Bowers, Brad. "Prairie Dreams and Apple Schemes: Appleton and the George H. Paul Orchard Company." *Pueblo Lore* (September 2003): 1–5.

Brown, Robert L. *Ghost Towns of the Colorado Rockies.* Caldwell, ID: Caxton Press, 1968.

Burns, John J. Papers. Stephen Hart Research Library. History Colorado–Denver.

Burrell, Howard A. *History of Washington County, Iowa, From the First White Settlements to 1908.* Vol. 2. Chicago: S. J. Clarke Publishing, 1909.

Cafky, Morris. *Colorado Midland.* Denver: World Press, 1965.

Cafky, Morris, and John A. Haney. *Pueblo's Steel Town Trolleys.* Golden: Colorado Railroad Historical Foundation, 1999.

Canada East, Canada West, New Brunswick, and Nova Scotia. *Census of 1851.* Woodhouse, Norfolk County, Canada West (Ontario), Schedule A, Roll C-11741. Library and Archives Canada, Ottawa, Canada. Digital image, *Ancestry.com.* https://www.ancestry.com/interactive/1061/e095-e002362161?pid=2211810.

Carrillo, Richard F., Christian J. Zier, and Andrea M. Barnes. *The Documentation of Stone City (5PE793): Historical Archaeology on the Fort Carson Military Reservation, Pueblo County, Colorado.* Submitted to National Park Service—Rocky Mountain Regional Office, Branch of Interagency Archaeological Services, Denver, CO.; and United States Army—Office of Environment, Energy and Natural Resources, Fort Carson, CO. Fort Collins, CO: Centennial Archaeology, Inc., July 1991.

Carroll, Fred. *Fifteenth Biennial Report Issued by the Bureau of Mines of the State of Colorado for the Years 1917 and 1918.* Denver: Eames Brothers, State Printers, 1919.

Chambers, John Whiteclay, II. *The Tyranny of Change: America in the Progressive Era, 1890–1920.* 2nd ed. New York: St. Martin's Press, 1992.

Chandler, Alfred D., Jr. *The Visible Hand: The Managerial Revolution in American Business.* Cambridge: Belknap Press of Harvard University Press, 1977.

Coalson, George O. Texas State Historical Association. *Handbook of Texas Online.* "Paul, George H." n.d. Accessed August 4, 2018. http://www.tshaonline.org/handbook/online/articles/fpa64.

Colorado Railroad, Inc. Company records, 1938–1957. Colorado-Kansas Railway Collection, Colorado Railroad Museum, Golden.

Colorado Railroad, Inc. Report no. 2215, 1956–1958. Records of the Operating Division. Annual Reports of Railroads 1915–1961. Interstate Commerce Commission. Record Group 134. National Archives at College Park, College Park, MD.

Colorado Railroad, Inc. Report no. 3077, 1938–1955. Records of the Operating Division. Annual Reports of Railroads 1915–1961. Interstate Commerce Commission. RG 134. National Archives at College Park, College Park, MD.

Colorado-Kansas Railway. Company records. 1911–1938. Colorado-Kansas Railway Collection, Colorado Railroad Museum, Golden, CO.

Colorado-Kansas Railway. Report no. 3079, 1913–1932, 1938. Records of the Operating Division. Annual Reports of Railroads 1915–1961. Interstate Commerce Commission. RG 134. National Archives at College Park, College Park, MD.

Colorado-Kansas Railway. Report no. 3081, 1933–1937. Records of the Operating Division. Annual Reports of Railroads 1915–1961. Interstate Commerce Commission. Record Group 134. National Archives at College Park, College Park, MD.

Colorado-Kansas Railway Company, June 12, 1912, The. Pueblo, CO: Franklin Press, 1912.

Comstock, Charles W., ed. *Fifteenth Biennial Report of the State Engineer for the Years 1909–10.* Denver: Smith-Brooks Printing Company, 1911.

"Construction," *Railway Age* 42, no. 18 (November 2, 1906): 558.

Congressional Record: Containing the Proceedings and Debates of the Sixtieth Congress, Second Session. Vol. 43, pt. 4. Washington: Government Printing Office, 1909.

Corbett and Ballenger's Sixteenth Annual Denver City Directory. Denver: Corbett and Ballenger, 1888.

Cronon, William. *Nature's Metropolis: Chicago and the Great West.* New York: W. W. Norton and Company, 1991.

DeHerrera, Jeffrey, Adam Thomas, and Cheri Yost. *"Among the Elites of the Great West": Pueblo City Hall and Memorial Hall.* Denver: Historitecture, LLC, January 2014.

"Denver." *American Stationer* 37, no. 4 (January 24, 1895): 133–134.

Diner, Steven J. *A Very Different Age: Americans of the Progressive Era.* New York: Hill and Wang, 1998.

El Paso County Recorder. "Agreements of Sale." Book 457, record no. 226983. El Paso County Recorder's Office. November 13, 1915.

Federal Reporter, The. Vol. 106, *Cases Argued and Determined in the Circuit Courts of Appeals of the United States, March–April 1901.* St Paul: West Publishing Company, 1901.

First Presbyterian Church. *Church Register.* No. 1357. Pueblo, CO, 1933.

Grant, H. Roger. *Electric Interurbans and the American People.* Bloomington: Indiana University Press, 2016.

Grant, H. Roger. *Twilight Rails: The Final Era of Railroad Building in the Midwest.* Minneapolis: University of Minnesota Press, 2010.

Grant, Mrs. Tacy S., Postmaster, Stone City, CO, to the Colorado State Historical Society, Denver, CO, February 19, 1935. Special Collections, Robert Hoag Rawlings Public Library, Pueblo City-County Library District, Pueblo, CO.

Guthrie, Keith. Texas State Historical Association. Handbook of Texas Online. "Coleman-Fulton Pasture Company." Uploaded June 12, 2010. Modified July 19, 2016. http://www.tshaonline.org/handbook/online/articles/aqco2.

Hafen, LeRoy R. *Colorado and Its People: A Narrative and Topical History of the Centennial State.* Vols. 3–4. New York: Lewis Historical Publishing Company, 1948.

Hansen, Harry, ed. *Colorado: A Guide to the Highest State.* New rev. ed., American Guide Series. New York: Hastings House, 1970.

Hardin, Helen. "Early History of Pueblo West." *Pueblo Lore* (November 1988): 1–8.

Henahen, T. R. *Thirteenth Biennial Report of the Bureau of Mines of the State of Colorado for the Years of 1913 and 1914.* Denver: Smith-Brooks Printing Company, State Printers, 1914.

Hill, Alice Polk. *Colorado Pioneers in Picture and Story.* Denver: Brock-Haffner Press, 1915.

Hilton, George W., and John F. Due. *The Electric Interurban Railways in America.* Stanford, CA: Stanford University Press, 1960.

Holland Society of New York. "U.S., Dutch Reformed Church Records in Selected States, 1639–1989." Dutch Reformed Church Records from New Jersey. Archives of the Reformed Church in America, New Brunswick, NJ. *Schenectady Baptism.* Vol. 4, book 44, 501. N.d. *Ancestry.com.* https://www.ancestry.com/interactive/6961/42037_647350_0297-00091?pid=107766.

Interstate Commerce Commission. "Engineering Report." Colorado-Kansas Railway. Valuation Docket no. 81. Records of the Bureau of Valuation 1910–1974. Interstate Commerce Commission. RG 134. National Archives at College Park, College Park, MD.

Interstate Commerce Commission. Engineering Report Notes. Colorado-Kansas Railway. Valuation Docket no. 81. Records of the Bureau of Valuation 1910–1974. Interstate Commerce Commission. RG 134. National Archives at College Park, College Park, MD.

Interstate Commerce Commission. "Finance Docket 11988, Colorado Railroad, Incorporated, Acquisition and Stock." *Interstate Commerce Commission Reports: Decisions of the Interstate Commerce Commission of the United States,* vol. 228. Finance Reports, April–November 1938. Washington, DC: United States Government Printing Office, 273–276.

Interstate Commerce Commission. *Seventy-First Annual Report on Transport Statistics in the United States for the Year Ended December 31, 1957.* Washington, DC: Government Printing Office, 1959.

Interstate Commerce Commission. "Stenographers' Minutes before the Interstate Commerce Commission." Application for Colorado Railroad, Inc. Finance Docket 11988. April 25, 1938. Case Files 1887–1955. Interstate Commerce Commission. National Archives at College Park, College Park, MD.

Interstate Commerce Commission. "Tentative Valuation Report." Valuation Docket no. 81. Colorado-Kansas Railway. Records of the Bureau of Valuation 1910–1974. Interstate Commerce Commission. RG 134. National Archives at College Park, College Park, MD.

Jalil, Andrew J. "A New History of Banking Panics in the United States, 1825–1929: Construction and Implications." *American Economic Journal: Macroeconomics* 7, no. 3 (July 2015): 295–330.

Jefferson, B. L. *Biennial Report of State Board of Land Commissioners of Colorado, 1909–1910.* Denver: Smith-Brooks Printing Co., State Printers, 1910.

Kwolek-Folland, Angel. *Engendering Business: Men and Women in the Corporate Office, 1870–1930.* Baltimore: Johns Hopkins University Press, 1994.

Kwolek-Folland, Angel. *Incorporating Women: A History of Women and Business in the United States.* New York: Twayne Publishers, 1998; Palgrave, 2002.

Lewis, Kenneth E. *The American Frontier: An Archaeological Study of Settlement Pattern and Process.* Orlando, FL: Academic Press, 1984.

MacDaniel, James. Headstone. Plot no. K-5. Mountain View Cemetery, Pueblo, CO.

Martin, Albro. *Railroads Triumphant: The Growth, Rejection, and Rebirth of a Vital American Force.* New York: Oxford University Press, 1992.

McGaffey, A. B. *Biennial Report of the Secretary of State of Colorado for the Fiscal Years Ending November 30, 1895, and November 30, 1896.* Denver: Smith Brothers Printing Co.—State Printers, 1896.

McGraw Publishing Company, Inc. "Franchises." *Electric Railway Journal* 37, no. 25 (June 24, 1911): 1132.

McGraw Publishing Company, Inc. "News Notes." *Electric Railway Journal* 54, no. 8 (August 23, 1919): 408.

McGraw Publishing Company, Inc. "Personal Mention." *Electric Railway Journal* 38, no. 2 (July 8, 1911): 98.

McGraw Publishing Company, Inc. "Recent Incorporations." *Electric Railway Journal* 33, no. 8 (May 22, 1909): 352.

McGraw Publishing Company, Inc. "Recent Incorporations." *Electric Railway Journal* 38, no. 20 (November 11, 1911): 1045.

McGraw Publishing Company, Inc. "Recent Incorporations." *Electric Railway Journal* 38, no. 20 (November 11, 1911): 1046.

McGraw Publishing Company, Inc. "Recent Incorporations." *Electric Railway Journal* 38, no. 23 (December 2, 1911): 1181.

McGraw Publishing Company, Inc. "Track and Roadway." *Electric Railway Journal* 43, no. 9 (February 28, 1914): 502.

McGraw Publishing Company, Inc. "Track and Roadway." *Electric Railway Journal* 46, no. 15 (October 9, 1915): 787.

Mershon, A. U. *Apples of Gold*. Pueblo, CO: Geo. H. Paul Orchard Company, 1911. Special Collections, Robert Hoag Rawlings Public Library. Pueblo City-County Library District, Pueblo, CO.

Mitchell, Karen. "Hulit, Lilian V." Pueblo County, Colorado, Roselawn Cemetery. n.d. Accessed June 6, 2017. http://www.kmitch.com/Pueblo/roseh.html.

Morrison, R. S. *Morrison's Corporation Law: Colorado*. 4th ed. Denver: W. H. Courtwright Publishing, 1922.

National Archives and Records Administration. "Title 49—Transportation and Railroads, Appendix B." *Federal Register* 11, no. 238 (December 7, 1946): 14168. https://cdn.loc.gov/service/ll/fedreg/fr011/fr011238/fr011238.pdf.

National Cyclopaedia of American Biography, The. Vol. 44. New York: James T. White and Company, 1962.

"New Road, Extensions, and Project." *Railway Age* 11, no. 43 (October 28, 1886): 601.

"Northern Electrical Manufacturing Company." *Madison Past and Present*. Madison: Wisconsin State Journal, 1902.

"Obituary." *Railway Age* 56, no. 13 (March 29, 1912): 290.

Oldham, Lee. "Bridging the Past." Unpublished manuscript. 2004.

Osborne, Brian S. "The Kansas-Colorado Power and Railroad Project: A Multifunctional Plan for the Development of the Arkansas Valley." *Pioneer America* 6, no. 2 (1974): 22–33.

Pearce, James B. *Fourteenth Biennial Report of the Bureau of Labor Statistics of the State of Colorado, 1913–1914*. Denver: Smith-Brooks Printing Company, State Printers, 1914.

Powell, J. W., director. *Twelfth Annual Report of the United State Geological Survey to the Secretary of the Interior: 1890–91, Part II: Irrigation*. Washington, DC: Government Printing Office, 1891.

Pueblo City Directory. Kansas City, MO: R. L. Polk, 1940.

Pueblo City Directory. Kansas City, MO: R. L. Polk, 1941.

Pueblo City Directory. Kansas City, MO: R. L. Polk, 1945.

Pueblo County Recorder. Articles of Incorporation. Pueblo County Recording Department, Pueblo, CO.

Pueblo County Recorder. Land Deeds Reservoirs and Ditches. Pueblo County Recording Department, Pueblo, CO.

Pueblo County Recorder. Miscellaneous Records. Pueblo County Recording Department, Pueblo, CO.

Pueblo County Recorder. Quit Claim Deeds. Pueblo County Recording Department, Pueblo, CO.

Pueblo County Recorder. Warranty Deeds. Pueblo County Recording Department, Pueblo, CO.

Pueblo Gardens. Pueblo, Colo: Teller Reservoir & Irrigation Company, 1910. Special Collections, Robert Hoag Rawlings Public Library. Pueblo City-County Library District, Pueblo, CO.

Pueblo Quarries, Inc. Company records. 1938–1967. Colorado-Kansas Railway Collection, Colorado Railroad Museum, Golden.

Pueblo West Metropolitan District. Pueblo West, Colorado. "History." n.d. Accessed November 21, 2018. https://pueblowestmetro.com/322/History.

Railway Equipment and Publication Company. *Official Railway Equipment Register* 28, no. 5, October 1912. New York: Railway Equipment & Publication Company, 1912.

Railway Equipment and Publication Company. *Official Railway Equipment Register* 28, no. 9, February 1913. New York: Railway Equipment & Publication Company, 1913.

Railway Equipment and Publication Company. *Official Railway Equipment Register* 28, no. 10, March 1913. New York: Railway Equipment & Publication Company, 1913.

Railway Equipment & Publication Company. *The Pocket List of Railroad Officials* 57, no. 8, Third Quarter, 1951. New York: Railway Equipment & Publication Company, 1951.

Rapid Transit Railway: Pueblo and Beulah Valley. N.p., n.d., ca. 1902.

"Reclamation Notes, Colorado," *Irrigation Age* 25, no. 3. (January 1910): 129.

"Reclamation Notes, Colorado," *Irrigation Age* 25, no. 8 (June 1910): 374.

"Reclamation Notes, Colorado," *Irrigation Age* 26, no. 3 (January 1911): 744.

"Reclamation Notes, Colorado," *Irrigation Age* 28, no. 1 (November 1912): 23–24.

Ridgway, Arthur. *The Case of Train Number 3*. Denver: Rocky Mountain Railroad Club, 1956.

R.L. Polk & Co.'s Pueblo City Directory, 1899–1900. Vol. 2. Pueblo, CO: Chieftain Printers, 1900.

R.L. Polk & Co.'s Pueblo City Directory, 1904–1905. Vol. 7. Pueblo, CO: Chieftain Printers, 1905.

Sasser Family Holdings, Inc. *This Is Our Story*. n.d. Accessed May 25, 2018. https://static1.squarespace.com/static/56c9e8217c65e44270c7c0a6/t/5b535fb12b6a280bdeb93f52/1532190669666/Sasser+Book+compressed.pdf.

Scott, Roy V. *Railroad Development Programs in the Twentieth Century*. Ames: Iowa State University Press, 1985.

Sherow, James Earl. *Watering the Valley: Development along the High Plains Arkansas River, 1870–1950*. Lawrence: University Press of Kansas, 1990.

Simmons-Boardman Publishing Corporation. "Alaska Gets Troop Cars." *Railway Age* 121, no. 10 (September 7, 1946): 418.

Simonich, Ed. "Pueblo West, 1917." *Pueblo Lore* (January 1983): 6–7.

Sketches of Colorado in Four Volumes. Vol. 1. Denver: Western Press Bureau Company, 1911.

Smith, Duane. *Henry M. Teller: Colorado's Grand Old Man*. Boulder: University Press of Colorado, 2002.

Sparks, Lyra Haisley. Papers, 1896–1963. Center for American History. University of Texas, Austin.

Spurr, Henry C., ed. *Public Utilities Reports Containing Decisions of the Public Service Commissions, and of State and Federal Courts*. 1924A. Rochester, NY: Public Utilities Reports, 1924.

State of Utah. "Utah State Capitol Planning & Historic Structures Report, vol. 2: Construction History of the State Capitol and Capitol Hill." Accessed April 1, 2021. https://utahstatecapitol.utah.gov/wp-content/uploads/02capitolconstruc tiondesign.pdf.

Stephens, Kent. "The Colorado Railroad." *New Mexico Railroader* 7 (October 1965; issued January 1966): 1–8.

Stone, Tammy. *The Prehistory of Colorado and Adjacent Areas*. Salt Lake City: University of Utah Press, 1999.

Stone, Wilbur Fiske. *History of Colorado*, Vol. 2. Chicago: S. J. Clarke Publishing Co., 1918.

Stone, Wilbur Fiske. *History of Colorado*, Vol. 3. Chicago: S. J. Clarke Publishing Company, 1918.

Stone, Wilbur Fiske. *History of Colorado*, Vol. 4. Chicago: S. J. Clarke Publishing Company, 1919.

Stover, John F. *American Railroads*. 2nd ed. Chicago: University of Chicago Press, 1997.

Street Railway Publishing Company. "Interurban Railroading at Cripple Creek." *Street Railway Journal* 14, no. 11 (November 1898): 701.

Street Railway Publishing Company. "Prospects for New Business." *Street Railway Journal* 14, no. 1 (January 1898): 46.

Street Railway Publishing Company. "Street Railway News." *Street Railway Journal* 7, no. 1 (January 1891): 41.

Sutton, Charles E. Papers. Pueblo County Historical Society, Pueblo, CO.

Taylor, Ralph C. *Pueblo*. Pueblo, CO: Published for the Pueblo Board of Education, 1979.

United States v. Teller. RG 21 US District Court of Wyoming, Entry 9 Criminal Case Files, 1890–1969. Box 10, Case file 284 US v Teller.

United States v. Teller. RG 21 US District Court of Wyoming, Entry 9 Criminal Case Files, 1890–1969. Box 10, Case file 285 US v Teller.

US Army Garrison Fort Carson, Colorado. *Integrated Cultural Resources Management Plan for U.S. Army Garrison, Fort Carson, Colorado Fiscal Years 2017–2021*. US Army Garrison Fort Carson, Colorado: March 2017. Accessed September 21, 2018. https://www.carson.army.mil/assets/docs/dpw/Cultural/2017-2021-icrmp.pdf.

US Bureau of the Census. *Colorado State Census, 1885*. Pitkin County, Aspen, Colorado, Enumeration District 1, 13. National Archives microfilm M158, Roll 7.

Washington, DC: National Archives and Records Administration, Records of the Bureau of the Census, RG 29, 1885. Digital image, *Ancestry*.com. https://www .ancestry.com/interactive/6837/cot158_7-0071.1?pid=153805.

US Bureau of the Census. "Current Population Reports." Series P-60, No. 146. *Money Income of Households, Families, and Persons in the United States, 1983*. Washington, DC: US Government Printing Office, 1985.

US Bureau of the Census. *Ninth Census of the United States, 1870*. Erie County, Buffalo, New York, Buffalo Ward 8, sheet 384A. National Archives microfilm M593, Roll 934. Washington, DC: National Archives and Records Administration, Records of the Bureau of the Census, RG 29, 1870. Digital image, *Ancestry.com*. https://www.ancestry.com/interactive/7163/4274972_00781?pid=29672518.

US Bureau of the Census. "QuickFacts, Pueblo West CDP, Colorado," April 1, 2010. https://www.census.gov/quickfacts/fact/table/pueblowestcdpcolorado/PST 045217#qf-flag-X.

US Bureau of the Census. *Tenth Census of the United States, 1880*. Bay County, Bay City, Michigan, Second Ward, Enumeration District 015, sheet 366A. National Archives microfilm T9, Roll 571. Washington, DC: National Archives and Records Administration, Records of the Bureau of the Census, RG 29, 1880. Digital image, *Ancestry.com*. https://www.ancestry.com/interactive/6742/4241653-00316 ?pid=31419938.

US Bureau of the Census. *Thirteenth Census of the United States, 1910*. Pueblo County, Colorado, Precinct 1, Enumeration District 0142, sheets 1A–4A. National Archives microfilm T624, Roll 124. Washington, DC: National Archives and Records Administration, Records of the Bureau of the Census, RG 29, 1910. Digital image, *Ancestry.com*. https://www.ancestry.com/interactive/7884/31111_4327327-00421.

US Bureau of the Census. *Fourteenth Census of the United States, 1920*. Pueblo County, Colorado, Precinct 1, Enumeration District 190, sheets 1A–2B. National Archives microfilm T625, Roll 169. Washington, DC: National Archives and Records Administration, Records of the Bureau of the Census, RG 29, 1920. Digital image, *Ancestry.com*. https://www.ancestry.com/interactive/6061/4294439-01028.

US Bureau of the Census. *Fifteenth Census of the United States, 1930*. Pueblo County, Colorado, Precinct 101, Enumeration District 51–69, sheets 1A–2A. National Archives microfilm T626, Roll 250. Washington, DC: National Archives and Records Administration, Records of the Bureau of the Census, RG 29, 1930. Digital image, *Ancestry.com*. https://www.ancestry.com/interactive/6224/4532395 _00097.

US Bureau of the Census. *Sixteenth Census of the United States, 1940*. Pueblo County, Colorado, Precinct 101, Enumeration District 51–72, sheets 1A–2B. National Archives microfilm T627, Roll 477. Washington, DC: National Archives and Records Administration, Records of the Bureau of the Census, RG 29, 1940. Digital image, *Ancestry.com*. https://www.ancestry.com/interactive/2442/m-t0627 -00477-00108.

US Department of the Interior, Bureau of Land Management. "General Land Office Records, Land Patents," 1885–1892. Accessed July 23, 2018. https://glorecords.blm.gov/results/default.aspx?searchCriteria=type=patent|st=CO|cty=101|ln=Teller|twp_nr=20|twp_dir=S|rng_nr=66|rng_dir=W|m=06|sp=true|sw=true|sadv=false.

US Geological Survey. *Stone City Quadrangle, Colorado*. Topographic map. 1:24,000, 7.5 minute Series. Reston, VA: Geological Survey, 1963, 1978.

US Selective Service System. World War I Selective Service System Draft Registration Cards, 1917–1918, Washington County, Iowa. National Archives microfilm M1509. Washington, DC: National Archives and Records Administration, RG 163. Ancestry.com. *U.S., World War I Draft Registration Cards, 1917–1918*. https://www.ancestry.com/interactive/6482/005250418_02096?pid=30031498.

Usselman, Steven W. "Running the Machine: The Management of Technological Change on American Railroads, 1850–1910." *Business and Economic History* 17 (1988): 213–218.

Waagé, Karl M. *Refractory Clay Deposits of South Central Colorado*. Geological Survey Bulletin 993. Washington, DC: United States Government Printing Office, 1953.

Waller, Jerry. Hand-drawn map of Stone City. Waller Collection, Folder 93–29, Local History Center, Cañon City Public Library, Cañon City, CO.

Watson, David R., "Bring Shop to the Cars," *Modern Railroads* 3, no. 6 (June 1948): 47.

Ward, Evan R. "Geo-environmental Disconnection and the Colorado River Delta: Technology, Culture, and the Political Ecology of Paradise." *Environment and History* 7, no. 2 (May 2001): 219–246.

Wells, E. T., *Cases Argued and Determined in the Court of Appeals of Colorado at the April and September Terms A. D. 1913*. Vol. 24. Denver: Mills Publishing Co., 1913.

Wells, E. T., Reporter. *Cases Argued and Determined in the Supreme Court of the State of Colorado at the Term of September A.D. 1917, January, April and September, A.D. 1918*. Vol. 65. Chicago: Callaghan and Company, 1920.

White, Richard. *Railroaded: The Transcontinentals and the Making of Modern America*. New York: W. W. Norton and Company, 2011.

Newspapers

Alamosa Journal (Alamosa, CO)

Boyden Reporter (Boyden, IA)

Burlington Weekly Hawk-Eye (Burlington, IA)

Chicago Tribune (Chicago, IL)

Cincinnati Enquirer (Cincinnati, OH)

Colorado Daily Chieftain (Pueblo, CO)

Colorado Springs Sun Silhouette (Colorado Springs, CO)
Colorado Transcript (Golden, CO)
Colorado Weekly Chieftain (Pueblo, CO)
Current Local (Van Buren, MO)
Daily Times (Davenport, IA) .
Democratic Messenger (Eureka, KS)
Denver Post (Denver, CO)
Denver Republic (Denver, CO)
Des Moines Register (Des Moines, IA)
Deseret Evening News (Salt Lake City, UT)
El Paso Herald (El Paso, TX)
Evansville Press (Evansville, IN)
Evening Herald (Ottawa, Kansas)
Evening Kansan-Republican (Newton, KS)
Evening Star (Independence, KS)
Evening Telegram (Garden City, KS)
Evening Times Republican (Marshalltown, IA)
Indian Sentinel (Tahlequah, OK)
Indianapolis Star (Indianapolis, IN)
Inter Ocean (Chicago, IL)
Kansas Farmer (Topeka, KS)
Kingston Daily Freeman (Kingston, NY)
Lawrence Daily Journal-World (Lawrence, KS)
Leavenworth Times (Leavenworth, KS)
Lebo Enterprise (Lebo, KS)
Montrose Daily Press (Montrose, CO)
Omaha Daily Bee (Omaha, NE)
Pueblo Chieftain (Pueblo, CO)
Pueblo Indicator (Pueblo, CO)
Pueblo Leader (Pueblo, CO)
Pueblo Star-Journal (Pueblo, CO)
Pueblo Sun (Pueblo, CO)
Rocky Mountain Sun (Aspen, CO)
Saint Paul Globe (Saint Paul, MN)
Salt Lake Herald (Salt Lake City, UT)
Salt Lake Telegram (Salt Lake City, UT)

Salt Lake Tribune (Salt Lake City, UT)
San Francisco Chronicle (San Francisco, CA)
Silver Cliff Rustler (Silver Cliff, CO)
St. Louis Post-Dispatch (St. Louis, MO)
St. Louis Republic (St. Louis, MO)
Tennessean (Nashville, TN)
Topeka Daily Capital (Topeka, KS)
Topeka State Journal (Topeka, KS)
Weekly Gazette (Colorado Springs, CO)
Wet Mountain Tribune (Westcliffe, CO)
Wichita Beacon (Wichita, KS)

Index